âhkami-nêhiyawêtân
Let's Keep Speaking Cree

SOLOMON RATT

University of Regina Press

COVER AND TEXT DESIGN: Duncan Campbell, University of Regina Press
INTERIOR LAYOUT: John van der Woude, JVDW Designs
PROOFREADER: Donna Grant
COVER ART: *Peggy Bull*, 1993, by George Littlechild

Library and Archives Canada Cataloguing in Publication

Title: Âhkami-nêhiyawêtân = Let's keep speaking Cree / Solomon Ratt.
Other titles: Let's keep speaking Cree
Names: Ratt, Solomon, author.
Description: Text in English and Cree.
Identifiers: Canadiana (print) 20220189919 | Canadiana (ebook) 20220189943 | ISBN 9780889778467 (softcover) | ISBN 9780889778498 (hardcover) | ISBN 9780889778481 (PDF) | ISBN 9780889778474 (EPUB)
Subjects: LCSH: Cree language—Textbooks. | CSH: Cree language—Textbooks for second language learners—English speakers. | LCGFT: Textbooks.
Classification: LCC PM986 .R38 2022 | DDC 497/.3238—dc23

We acknowledge the support of the Canada Council for the Arts for our publishing program. We acknowledge the financial support of the Government of Canada. / Nous reconnaissons l'appui financier du gouvernement du Canada. This publication was made possible through Creative Saskatchewan's Book Publishing Production Grant Program.

nikî-mâmitonêyimâwak nikihci-âniskotâpânak

ta-âpacihtâcik ôma masinahikan.

This is dedicated to my great-great-grandchildren,

who I hope will use this book.

âhkami-nêhiyawêtân

     kipîkiskwêwininâhk astêw kinisitohtamowininaw;

âhkami-nêhiyawêtân

     kipîkiskwêwininâhk astêw kinisitawêyimitowininaw;

âhkami-nêhiyawêtân

     kipîkiskwêwininâhk astêw kipimâtisiwininaw;

âhkami-nêhiyawêtân

     kipîkiskwêwininâhk astêw kinêhiyâwiwininaw.

Let's keep on speaking Cree:

     In our language is our understanding;

Let's keep on speaking Cree:

     In our language is recognition of each other;

Let's keep on speaking Cree:

     In our language is our life;

Let's keep on speaking Cree:

     In our language is our identity.

—Solomon Ratt (1994)

CONTENTS

Acknowledgements..ix

CHAPTER 1: BASIC CONVERSATIONS

1.1. Cree Sound System 1

    1.1.A. Chants for Learning the Sounds
            of the Y-Dialect 1

    1.1.B. Chants Word List...........................2

    1.1.C. Dictation...3

    1.1.D. Translation 4

1.2. Basic Conversations.........................5

    1.2.A. Vocabulary...................................5

    1.2.B. Introducing Yourself 5

    1.2.C. Dialogue.....................................6

CHAPTER 2: KINSHIP

2.1. Kinship Terms 8

    2.1.A. Generations 9

    2.1.B. Forms of Address (Vocative Forms) .11

    2.1.C. Cousins and Siblings 15

    2.1.D. Aunts and Uncles......................15

    2.1.E. Generic Kinship Terms 16

    2.1.F. Discussing Those Kin Who Have
           Passed On to the Spirit World ...17

2.2. Exercises...18

    2.2.A. Kinship Chart Exercise 18

    2.2.B. Vital Statistics Exercise I 19

    2.2.C. Vital Statistics Exercise II 22

    2.2.D. Talking about Yourself and Others....25

    2.2.E. Talking about Travel 28

CHAPTER 3: SEASONAL AND DAILY ACTIVITIES

3.1. Numbers and Dates 31

    3.1.A. Review of Numbers....................31

    3.1.B. Dates 32

3.2. Months and Seasons......................33

    3.2.A. Months....................................33

    3.2.B. Seasons: ispîhtaskîwina (VII) 34

3.3. Days of the Week 34

    3.3.A. Questions 35

    3.3.B. Translation 36

3.4. More on the Days of the Week 37

    3.4.A. Exercises 38

3.5. Time of Day 40

    3.5.A. Translation..............................40

    3.5.B. Temporal Words........................41

CHAPTER 4: TIME AND OTHER TEMPORAL WORDS

4.1. Time...43

    4.1.A. Questions 44

4.2. It's About Time...............................46

    4.2.A. VAIS in 1st Person.....................46

    4.2.B. VAIS in 1st Person in
           Future Conditional.................48

    4.2.C. VAIS in 3rd Person.....................50

    4.2.D. VAIS in 3rd Person in
           Future Conditional.................52

    4.2.E. What Time Do You...? 54

    4.2.F. More Questions about
           the Days of the Week 59

4.3. Compound Sentences................59

    4.3.A. Translation................60

4.4. Speaking about Time
and the Days of the Week................62

    4.4.A. Text Exercises................63

    4.4.B. Exercises with Time
and Times of Day................66

CHAPTER 5: INTRANSITIVE VERBS

5.1. Animate Intransitive Verbs (VAI)................69

    5.1.A. VAI Imperatives................69

5.2. Animate Intransitive Verb Charts................73

    5.2.A. Exercises with VAIS................75

    5.2.B. VAI Conjugations................78

5.3. VAI Paradigms................81

    5.3.A. Some Activities................83

    5.3.B. Self-Test................90

5.4. Indefinite Actor Verb
Forms for VAIS and VTAS................99

5.5. Subordinate Clauses................100

    5.5.A. Subordinate Clause Exercise................102

    5.5.B. Sentence Structures
with VAIS and VIIS................103

    5.5.C. Daily Activity Exercises................106

    5.5.D. Daily Activity Translation
and Questions................108

CHAPTER 6: TRANSITIVE VERBS

6.1. Transitive Inanimate Verbs—
Class 1 (VTI-1)................111

    6.1.A. VTI-1 Imperatives................111

6.2. Transitive Inanimate Verb Charts—
Class 1................113

    6.2.A. Exercises with VTI-1S................115

    6.2.B. VTI-1 Conjugations................117

6.3. VTI-1 Paradigms................120

    6.3.A. Translation................122

    6.3.B. Conversion................123

    6.3.C. Expansion Drills................124

6.4. Values in Cree................127

**CHAPTER 7: POSSESSIVE FORMS,
BODY PARTS, AND SHOPPING**

7.1. Possessive Forms................129

    7.1.A. Asking Where
Something Is Located................132

    7.1.B. Possessive Form Exercises................133

7.2. Body Parts................149

    7.2.A. Body Parts Exercise................150

    7.2.B. A Visit to the Clinic................152

    7.2.C. Text Exercises................157

7.3. Shopping................160

    7.3.A. Possessives................160

    7.3.B. Shopping Trips................162

    7.3.C. Colours and Clothes................168

    7.3.D. Shopping Exercises................172

**CHAPTER 8: TRANSITIVE ANIMATE
VERBS: DIRECT FORMS (VTA-DIRECT)**

8.1. Transitive Animate Verbs................176

    8.1.A. VTA Imperatives................176

8.2. Transitive Animate Verb Charts................178

    8.2.A. Exercises with VTAS................180

    8.2.B. VTA Conjugations................182

8.3. VTA Paradigms................185

    8.3.A. Translation 1................186

    8.3.B. Translation 2................187

    8.3.C. Text Exercises................189

**CHAPTER 9: TRANSITIVE ANIMATE
VERBS: INVERSE AND REFLEXIVE FORMS**

9.1. Inverse VTAS................198

    9.1.A. The You and Me (Local) Set................198

    9.1.B. The Mixed Set................201

    9.1.C. VTA-Inverse 1................202

    9.1.D. VTA-Inverse 2................205

    9.1.E. VTA-Inverse 3................208

9.2. VTA: Reflexives................211

    9.2.A. VTA-Reflexive 1................211

    9.2.B. VTA-Reflexive 2................215

    9.2.C. VTA-Reflexive 3................218

9.3. Text Exercises with vta-Direct,
-Inverse, and -Reflexive Forms..................221

9.4. Indicative and Conjunct Forms of
vta-Direct, -Inverse, and -Reflexive.........223

    9.4.A. Indicative Forms.................................223

    9.4.B. Conjunct Forms.................................224

CHAPTER 10: STORIES

10.1. Stories to Inspire.................................226

    10.1.A. Activities through the Seasons.......226

    10.1.B. Activities through the Day.............229

10.2. Stories with Audio 232

    10.2.A. kistêyihtamowin – Respect 232

    10.2.B. ka-ispitisihk isîhcikêwin –
    Protocol: Age-Appropriate
    Conduct....................................... 235

    10.2.C. tapahtêyimisowin – Humility 237

    10.2.D. nikwatisowin êkwa
    mâtinamâkêwin – Sharing
    and Generosity 241

    10.2.E. tâpokêyihtamowin – Faith 244

    10.2.F. kisêwâtisiwin – Kindness.............246

    10.2.G. âniskô-kiskinwahamâkêwin –
    Passing On Teachings 248

ANSWERS

Chapter 1 Exercises 253

Chapter 2 Exercises....................................254

Chapter 3 Exercises....................................258

Chapter 4 Exercises 260

Chapter 5 Exercises....................................264

Chapter 6 Exercises 273

Chapter 7 Exercises....................................276

Chapter 8 Exercises....................................283

Chapter 9 Exercises 287

Chapter 10 Exercises..................................292

Glossary 297

Bibliography...317

ACKNOWLEDGEMENTS

This book is a direct result of my teaching of intermediate Cree classes at First Nations University of Canada, as many of my students requested a follow-up textbook to *mâci-nêhiyawêwin*/Beginning Cree. *âhkami-nêhiyawêtân*/Let's Keep Speaking Cree contains expanded explanations and exercises for the information first introduced in the earlier text.

Once again, I thank my mentor Jean Okimâsis for her invaluable guidance and support with my work. I also thank my colleagues Arok Wolvengrey and Andrea Custer who proofread drafts of this book. And of course, thanks to my students who used this material in their studies and caught some typos which we all missed in our proofreading, with a special mention to my students Heather Dietz and Shannon Dumba for telling me about many of these typos.

Any misspellings and/or misuse of words are entirely mine.

Solomon Ratt
2021

CHAPTER 1

· · · · · · · · · · ·

BASIC CONVERSATIONS

1.1. Cree Sound System

The following is adapted from **mâci-nêhiyawêwin**, pages 4 to 6, Solomon Ratt (2016).

1.1.A. CHANTS FOR LEARNING THE SOUNDS OF THE Y-DIALECT

In writing Cree using the standard roman orthography (SRO) we will use seven vowel sounds and ten consonants. There are three short vowel sounds and four long vowel sounds. The long vowel sounds are marked with either a bar or a circumflex over the vowel.

Short Vowels

a	a-a-a	aciyaw, aciyaw, aciyaw pê-atoskê.
i	i-i-i	ispimihk, ispimihk, ispimihk ispahtâ.
o	o-o-o	otina, otina, otina omaskisina.

Long Vowels

â	â-â-â	âstam, âstam, âstam pê-âcimo.
ê	ê-ê-ê	êkosi, êkosi, êkosi itwê.
î	î-î-î	yiyîkicihcîs, yiyîkicihcîs, yiyîkicihcîs itwahikâkê.
ô	ô-ô-ô	ôta, ôta, ôta ôtênâhk oskana kâ-asastêki.

Consonants

c	c-c-c	cêskwa, cêskwa, cêskwa capasis nawac.
h	h-h-h	hâw, hâw, hâw mâka âhâsiw hâw.
k	k-k-k	kiyipa, kiyipa, kiyipa kîwê kiya.
m	m-m-m	mahti, mahti, mahti mâmitonêyihta ôma.
n	n-n-n	nikamo, nikamo, nihtâ-nikamow ana nâpêw.
p	p-p-p	pahkwên, pahkwên, pahkwên pahkwêsikan.
s	s-s-s	sîwisiw, sîwisiw, sîwinôs sîwisiw.
t	t-t-t	têpakohp, têpakohp, têpakohp têhtapiwina ôta.
w	w-w-w	wâpan, wâpan, waniskâ wâpan ôma.
y	y-y-y	yôskâw, yôskâw, yôskaskisin yôskâw.

1.1.B. CHANTS WORD LIST

aciyaw	*a bit*
ana	*that*
atoskê	*work* (VAI)*
âcimo	*tell a story* (VAI)
âhâsiw	*a crow*
âstam	*come*
capasis	*lower*
cêskwa	*wait*
êkosi	*there*
hâw	*okay*
hâw mâka	*okay then*
ispahtâ	*run up to* (VAI)
ispimihk	*up*
itwahikâkê	*point with* (VAI)
itwê	*say* (VAI)
kiya	*you*
kiyipa	*hurry*
kîwê	*go home* (VAI)
mahti	*please*
mâmitonêyihta	*think about it* (VTI-1)
nawac	*more*

* The abbreviations used here and throughout the text refer to the following:
  VAI – animate intransitive verb   VII – inanimate intransitive verb
  VTI – transitive inanimate verb   VTA – transitive animate verb
  NA – animate noun   NI – inanimate noun
  PR – pronoun   IPC – indeclinable particle
  IPV – indeclinable preverb
The above abbreviations are from *nêhiyawêwin: itwêwina/Cree: Words*, compiled by Arok Wolvengrey (University of Regina Press, 2001).

nâpêw	*a man*
nihtâ-	*ability to do well* (IPV)
nikamo	*sing* (VAI)
nikamow	*she/he sings*
omaskisina	*her/his shoes*
oskana kâ-asastêki	*Regina*
otina	*take it* (VTI-1)
ôma	*this*
ôta	*here*
ôtênâhk	*in town*
pahkwên	*break off* (VTA)
pahkwêsikan	*bannock*
pê-	*come* (IPV)
sîwinôs	*candy*
sîwisiw	*it is sweet* (VAI)
têhtapiwina	*chairs*
têpakohp	*seven*
waniskâ	*get up* (VAI)
wâpan	*it is dawn* (VII)
yiyîkicihcîs	*a finger*
yôskaskisin	*a rubber overshoe*
yôskâw	*it is soft* (VII)

1.1.C. DICTATION

Write out the words the instructor says in the spaces below:

_____ _____

_____ _____

_____ _____

_____ _____

_____ _____

_____ _____

_____ _____

1.1.D. TRANSLATION

Try translating the chants using the above word list *(answers are on page 253)*:

aciyaw, aciyaw, aciyaw pê-atoskê. _____

ispimihk, ispimihk, ispimihk ispahtâ. _____

otina, otina, otina omaskisina. _____

âstam, âstam, âstam pê-âcimo. _____

êkosi, êkosi, êkosi itwê. _____

yiyîkicihcîs, yiyîkicihcîs, yiyîkicihcîs itwahikâkê. _____

ôta, ôta, ôta ôtênâhk oskana kâ-asastêki. _____

cêskwa, cêskwa, cêskwa capasis nawac. _____

hâw, hâw, hâw mâka âhâsiw hâw. _____

kiyipa, kiyipa, kiyipa kîwê kiya. _____

mahti, mahti, mahti mâmitonêyihta ôma. _____

nikamo, nikamo, nihtâ-nikamow ana nâpêw. _____

pahkwên, pahkwên, pahkwên pahkwêsikan. _____

sîwisiw, sîwisiw, sîwinôs sîwisiw. _____

têpakohp, têpakohp, têpakohp têhtapiwina ôta. _____

wâpan, wâpan, waniskâ wâpan ôma. _____

yôskâw, yôskâw, yôskaskisin yôskâw. _____

1.2. Basic Conversations

Introducing Yourself and Getting to Know Someone

1.2.A. VOCABULARY

isiyihkâsow	*her/his name is* (VAI)	itahtopiponêw	*she/he is that age* (VAI)
ohci	*from* (IPC)	wîkiw	*she/he lives (at)* (VAI)
nihtâwikiw	*she/he is born* (VAI)	tipiskam	*she/he has a birthday* (VTI-1)
akim	*count someone* (VTA)	okiskinwahamâkan	*a student* (NA)
cîhkêyihtam	*she/he likes* (VTI-1)	itôtam	*she/he does it* (VTI-1)
tânisi	*how/what* (IPC)	tânitê	*where* (IPC)
tânitahto	*how many* (IPC)	kîko	*which* (IPC)
tâniyikohk	*how much* (IPC)	kîkwây	*what* (IPC)
pîsim	*month, sun, moon* (NA)	êwako	*that one* (PR)
mâna	*usually* (IPC)	kiya	*you* (PR)
kî-	*past tense indicator* (IPV)	kayâhtê	*originally, formerly* (IPC)
mêkwâc	*now, presently* (IPC)	ispîhtaskîwin	*season* (NI)
cî	*a polarity question indicator* (IPC)		

Note: The question *tânitahtopiponêyan?* "How old are you?" literally means "How many winters are behind you?" It is a combination of *tânitahto* "how many" + *itahtopiponêw* "she/he is that age" in the conjunct form.

1.2.B. INTRODUCING YOURSELF

Using your own personal information, answer the following questions *(sample answers are on page 254).* See Chapter 3 for vocabulary and information on seasons, dates, numbers, and months.

tânisi kitisiyihkâson? – *What is your name?*

_____

tânitahtopiponêyan? – *How old are you?*

_____

tânitê ohci kiya kayâhtê? – *Where are you from originally?*

_____

tânitê mêkwâc kiwîkin? – *Where do you currently reside?*

_____

tânitê kâ-kî-nihtâwikiyan? – *Where were you born?*

_____

kîko ispîhtaskîwin kâ-kî-nihtâwikiyan? – *Which season were you born in?*

_____

kîko pîsim mâna kâ-tipiskaman? – *Which month do you have a birthday?*

_____

tâniyikohk ê-akimiht êwako pîsim mâna kâ-tipiskaman? – *What is the date of that month when you have a birthday?*

_____

okiskinwahamâkan cî kiya? – *Are you a student?*

_____

kîkwây kicîhkêyihtên ta-itôtaman? – *What do you like to do?*

_____

1.2.C. DIALOGUE

Practise the following dialogue with a classmate. Modify the information in **bold type** to suit your situation:

Speaker A: tânitahtwasiyêk kiwîtisânîhitowinihk?
How many of you are in your family?

Speaker B: kayâhtê cî? mâmawi **ayinânêw** kayâhtê nikî-ihtasinân.
*Originally? Altogether there were **eight** of us originally.*

Speaker A: ostêsimâw cî kiya? (Ask only if the other person is male.)
Are you the eldest brother?

Speaker B:	namôya, namôya ostêsimâw niya. (Or "âha, ostêsimâw niya.")
	No, I am not the eldest brother. (Or "Yes, I am the eldest brother.")
Speaker A:	omisimâw cî kiya? (Ask only if the other person is female.)
	Are you the eldest sister?
Speaker B:	âha, omisimâw niya. (Or "namôya, namôya omisimâw niya.")
	Yes, I am the eldest sister. (Or "No, I am not the eldest sister.")
Speaker A:	osîmimâw cî kiya?
	Are you the youngest sibling?
Speaker B:	namôya, namôya osîmimâw niya. (Or "âha, osîmimâw niya.")
	No, I am not the youngest sibling. (Or "Yes, I am the youngest sibling.")
Speaker A:	tânitahto kitostêsin?
	How many older brothers do you have?
Speaker B:	**nîso** kayâhtê nikî-ostêsin. ostêsimâw âsay kayâs nikî-wanihânân.
	*I originally had **two** older brothers. We lost the eldest brother long ago.*
Speaker A:	tânitahto kitomisin?
	How many older sisters do you have?
Speaker B:	**nîso** kayâhtê nikî-omisin. **pêyak** nimisipan nikî-wanihânân anohcihkê.
	*Originally, I had **two** older sisters. We lost **one** of my older sisters just recently.*
Speaker A:	tânitahto kitosîmisin?
	How many younger siblings do you have?
Speaker B:	kayâhtê **nisto** nikî-osîmisin. **pêyak** nisîmisipan nikî-wanihânân kayâsês.
	*Originally, I had **three** younger siblings. We lost **one** younger sibling a while ago.*

CHAPTER 2

· · · · · · · · · · · ·

KINSHIP

2.1. Cree Kinship Terms

In this chapter we will look at Cree kinship terms. The family unit is the most important unit in Cree society, and this is evident in the kinship terms themselves. For example, there is a term for older brother and a term for older sister, but only one term for younger sibling—this teaches respect for those who are older and also teaches that we are to take care of the younger ones.

Making sure that the children are taken care of is central to the kinship system. Cree have extended families. Parallel cousins (father's brother's children and mother's sister's children) are considered as brothers and sisters, and we use the terms for older brother, older sister, and younger sibling with those cousins. This system helped to identify who would take care of the children should they become orphaned.

Non-Cree often wonder how Cree have so many grandparents. At the risk of over-simpification, but to highlight the importance of children in the family unit, all children in your grandchildren's generation are considered as grandchildren. Furthermore, the terms for great-grandparents apply to all those in that generation, as do the terms for great-great-grandparents and great-great-great-grandparents—and these are the same terms used for great-grandchildren, great-great-grandchildren, and great-great-great-grandchildren.

2.1.A. GENERATIONS

Figure 1: Cree Kinship System

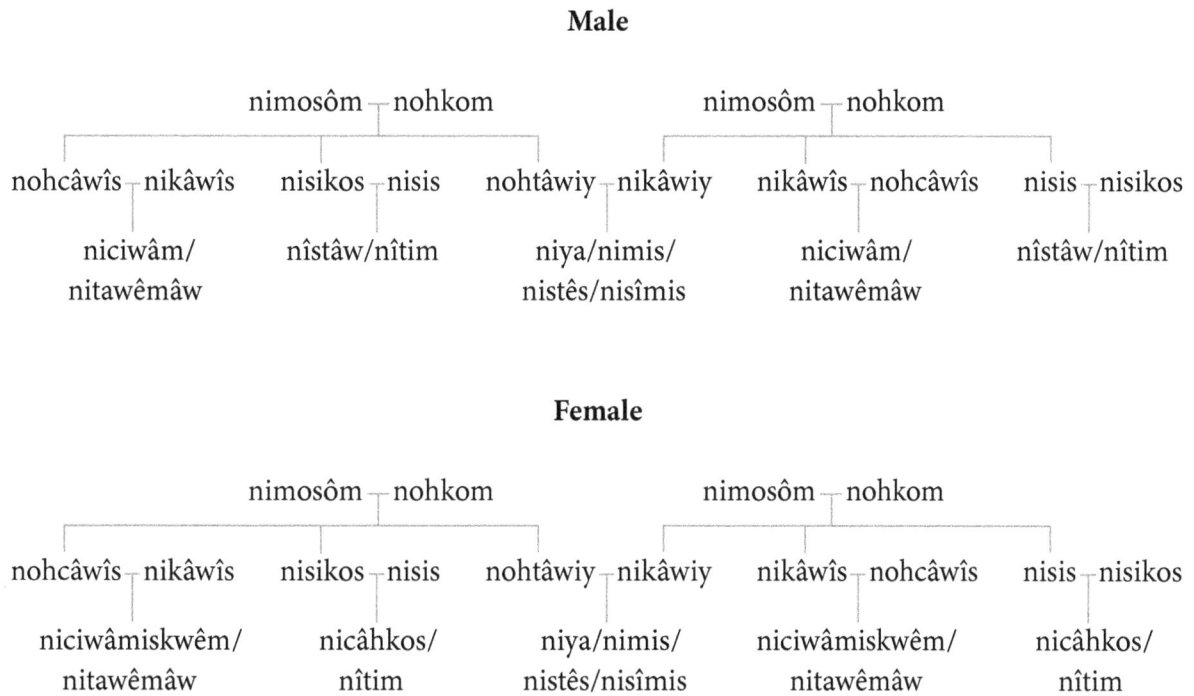

Male

	nimosôm — nohkom						nimosôm — nohkom		

nohcâwîs—nikâwîs   nisikos—nisis   nohtâwiy—nikâwiy   nikâwîs—nohcâwîs   nisis—nisikos

niciwâm/   nîstâw/nîtim   niya/nimis/   niciwâm/   nîstâw/nîtim
nitawêmâw   nistês/nisîmis   nitawêmâw

Female

	nimosôm — nohkom						nimosôm — nohkom		

nohcâwîs—nikâwîs   nisikos—nisis   nohtâwiy—nikâwiy   nikâwîs—nohcâwîs   nisis—nisikos

niciwâmiskwêm/   nicâhkos/   niya/nimis/   niciwâmiskwêm/   nicâhkos/
nitawêmâw   nîtim   nistês/nisîmis   nitawêmâw   nîtim

Kinship Terms

Grandparents / Grandchildren

nikihci-âniskotâpân	*my great-great-great-grandparent, my great-great-great-grandchild*
nitâniskotâpân	*my great-great-grandparent, my great-great-grandchild*
nocâpân	*my great-grandparent, my great-grandchild*
nimosôm	*my grandfather*
nohkom	*my grandmother*
nôsisimak	*my grandchildren*

Parents and Partners

ninîkihikwak	*my parents*
nohtâwiy	*my father*
nikâwiy	*my mother*
niwîkimâkan	*my spouse*
ninâpêm	*my husband*
nitiskwêm	*my wife*

Aunts and Uncles

Father's siblings and their spouses:

nohcâwîs	*my uncle* (father's brother)
nikâwîs	*my aunt* (father's sister-in-law)
nisikos	*my aunt* (father's sister)
nisis	*my uncle* (father's brother-in-law)

Mother's siblings and their spouses:

nisis	*uncle* (mother's brother)
nisikos	*my aunt* (mother's sister-in-law)
nikâwîs	*my aunt* (mother's sister)
nohcâwîs	*my uncle* (mother's brother-in-law)

Siblings

niya	*me*
nîtisânak	*my siblings*
nistês	*my older brother*
nimis	*my older sister*
nisîmis	*my younger sibling*

Cousins

Parallel cousins (father's brother's children or mother's sister's children):

niciwâm	*my cousin* (used by males to one another)
niciwâmiskwêm	*my cousin* (used by females to one another)
nitawêmâw	*my cousin* (used by female to male or male to female)

Cross cousins (Father's sister's children or mother's brother's children):

nicâhkos	*my cousin* (used by females to one another; also used by females for sister-in-law)
nîtim	*my cousin* (used between male and female; also term used between males and females for brother-in-law and sister-in-law)
nîstâw	*my cousin* (used by males; also used by males for brother-in-law)

Children

nitawâsimisak	*my children*
nikosis	*my son*
nitânis	*my daughter*
ninahâhkisîm	*my son-in-law*
ninahâhkaniskwêm	*my daughter-in-law*

Nieces and Nephews

My brother's children (if male) and my sister's children (if female):

nitôsim	*my nephew* (alternate term is nikosim "my nephew")
nitôsimiskwêm	*my niece* (alternate term is nitânis "my daughter")

My brother's children (if female) and my sister's children (if male):

nistim	*my niece*
nitihkwatim	*my nephew*

2.1.B. FORMS OF ADDRESS (VOCATIVE FORMS)

	Kinship – talking *about* them	Vocative – talking *to* them
my grandfather	nimosôm	nimosô
my grandmother	nohkom	nohkô
my father	nohtâwiy	nohtâ
my mother	nikâwiy	nêkâ *and* nikâ
my uncle (father's brother; mother's sister's husband; godfather; stepfather)	nohcâwîs*	
my aunt (father's brother's wife; mother's sister; godmother; stepmother)	nikâwîs	
my uncle (father's sister's husband; mother's brother; father-in-law)	nisis	nisisê
my aunt (father's sister; mother's brother's wife; mother-in-law)	nisikos	nisikosê
my older brother	nistês	nistêsê
my older sister	nimis	nimisê
my younger sibling	nisîmis	nisîmê, *also* nisîm
my cousin (parallel cousin, used by males)	niciwâm	niciwâ *(most will use the brother term)*
my cousin (parallel cousin, used by females)	niciwâmiskwêm	*Most will use the sister term*
my cousin (cross cousin, used by males)	nîstâw	nîstâ *(but the more common term is* nîscâs*)*
my cousin (cross cousin, used by females)	nicâhkos	nicâhkosê
my son	nikosis	nikosê
my daughter	nitânis	nitân
my grandchild	nôsisim	nôsisê

	Kinship – talking *about* them	Vocative – talking *to* them
my nephew (males: brother's son; females: sister's son)	nitôsim	*Often use* nikosim
my niece (males: brother's daughter; females: sister's daughter)	nitôsimiskwêm	*Often use* nitân
my nephew (males: sister's son; females: brother's son); *son-in-law*	nitihkwatim	nitihkwâ
my niece (males: sister's daughter; females: brother's daughter); *daughter-in-law*	nistim	
my son-in-law	ninahâhkisîm	
my daughter-in-law	ninahâhkaniskwêm	
my husband	ninâpêm	*The wife will often use* kisêyiniw *(old man)*
my wife	nitiskwêm	*The husband will often use* nôtokwêsiw *(old lady)*
my spouse	niwîkimâkan	

*Blanks above in the Vocative column use the same terms as those in the kinship column.

Here is a more detailed chart, including plural forms:

Kinship: Forms of Address				
	talking about (sg)	**talking about (pl)**	**talking to (voc – sg)**	**talking to (voc – pl)**
my relative	niwâhkômâkan	niwâhkômâkan**ak**	niwâhkômâkan	niwâhkômâkan**itik**
my friend	nitôtêm	nitôtêm**ak**	nitôtêm	nitôtêm**itik**
my grandfather	nimosôm	nimosôm**ak**	nimosô	nimosôm**itik**
my grandmother	nohkom	nohkom**ak**	nohkô	nohkom**itik**
my father	nohtâwiy	—	nohtâ	—
my mother	nikâwiy	—	nikâ or nêkâ	—
my older sister	nimis	nimis**ak**	nimisê	nimis**itik**
my older brother	nistês	nistês**ak**	nistêsê	nistês**itik**
my younger sibling	nisîmis	nisîmis**ak**	nisîmê	nisîm**itik** nisîmis**itik**

	talking about (sg)	talking about (pl)	talking to (voc – sg)	talking to (voc – pl)
my daughter	nitânis	nitânis**ak**	nitân	nitânis**itik**
my son	nikosis	nikosis**ak**	nikos**ê**	nikosis**itik**
my grandchild	nôsisim	nôsisim**ak**	nôsis**ê**	nôsisim**itik**
my parallel uncle	nohcâwîs	nohcâwîs**ak**	nohcâwîs	nohcâwîs**itik**
my parallel aunt	nikâwîs	nikâwîs**ak**	nikâwîs	nikâwîs**itik**
parallel cousin of opposite sex	nitawêmâw	nitawêmâw**ak**	nitawêm**â**	nitawêmâw**itik**
my parallel cousin (used by males)	niciwâm	niciwâm**ak**	niciw**â**	niciwâm**itik**
my parallel cousin (used my females)	niciwâmiskwêm	niciwâmiskwêm**ak**	niciwâmiskwêm	niciwâmiskwêm**itik**
my cross uncle	nisis	nisis**ak**	nisis**ê**	nisis**itik**
my cross aunt	nisikos	nisikos**ak**	nisikos**ê**	nisikos**itik**
my cross cousin (of the opposite sex)	nîtim	nîtim**wak**	nîtim	nîtim**itik**
my cross cousin (female to female)	nicâhkos	nicâhkos**ak**	nicâhkos**ê**	nicâhkos**itik**
my cross cousin (male to male)	nîstâw	nîstâw**ak**	nîst**â**	nîstâw**itik**
my parallel nephew (male: brother's son; female: sister's son)	nitôsim	nitôsim**ak** nikosim**ak**	nikosim	nitôsim**itik** nikosim**itik**
my parallel niece (male: brother's daughter; female: sister's daughter)	nitôsimiskwêm	nitôsimiskwêm**ak**	nitân	nitôsimiskwêm**itik**

	talking about (sg)	talking about (pl)	talking to (voc – sg)	talking to (voc – pl)
my cross niece (male: sister's daughter; female: brother's daughter)	nistim	nistim**wak**	nistim	nistim**itik**
my cross nephew (male: sister's son; female: brother's son)	nitihkwatim	nitihkwatim**ak**	nitihkwâ nitêhkwâ	nitihkwatim**itik**
my son-in-law	ninahahkisîm	ninahahkisîm**ak**	nitihkwâ	ninahahkisîm**itik**
my daughter-in-law	ninahâhkaniskwêm	ninahâhkaniskwêm**ak**	nistim	ninahâhkaniskwêm**itik**
my husband	ninâpêm	ninâpêm**ak**	*As couples age, wives often address their husbands as* kisêyiniw (*old man*), nikisêyinîm (*my old man*)	—
my wife	nitiskwêm	nitiskwêm**ak**	nîwa *As couples age, husbands often address their wives as* nôtokwêsiw (*old lady*), ninôtokwêm (*my old lady*)	—
my spouse	niwîkimâkan	niwîkimâkan**ak**	niwîkimâkan	—
my companion	niwîcêwâkan	niwîcêwâkan**ak**	niwîcêwâkan nîcêwâkan	niwîcêwâkan**itik** nîcêwâkan**itik**

(This more detailed chart was created with help from Arok Wolvengrey.)

2.1.C. COUSINS AND SIBLINGS

This is how you would talk about your immediate family. Compare the following columns:

Speaker	Children of father's brother or mother's sister	Siblings	Children of father's sister or mother's brother
Female to female	niciwâmiskwêm (nîtisân)	nîtisân	nicâhkos (also *my sister-in-law*)
Female to younger female	nisîmis	nisîmis	nicâhkos (also *my sister-in-law*)
Female to older female	nimis	nimis	nicâhkos (also *my sister-in-law*)
Female to male/ male to female	nitawêmâw (nîtisân)	nîtisân	nîtim (also *my brother-in-law/ sister-in-law*)
Female to older male	nistês	nistês	nîtim (also *my brother-in-law/ sister-in-law*)
Female to younger male	nisîmis	nisîmis	nîtim (also *my brother-in-law/ sister-in-law*)
Male to male	niciwâm (nîtisân)	nîtisân	nîstâw (also *my brother-in-law*)
Male to older male	nistês	nistês	nîstâw (also *my brother-in-law*)
Male to younger male	nisîmis	nisîmis	nîstâw (also *my brother-in-law*)
Male to older female	nimis	nimis	nîtim (also *my brother-in-law/ sister-in-law*)
Male to younger female	nisîmis	nisîmis	nîtim (also *my brother-in-law/ sister-in-law*)

(This chart is adapted from *mâci-nêhiyawêwin / Beginning Cree*, p. 208)

2.1.D. AUNTS AND UNCLES

Who	Maternal	Paternal
Aunt	nikâwîs (Y) / nitôsis (TH)	nisikos (also *my mother-in-law*)
Uncle	nisis (also *my father-in-law*)	nohcâwîs (Y) / nohkomis (TH)

Note: Y = Y-dialect (Plains Cree); TH = TH-dialect (Woodland Cree)

2.1.E. GENERIC KINSHIP TERMS

Kinship terms are almost always used with a possessive pronoun (*my* or *his*, for example), but people always ask for generic terms (*a* or *an*), so here they are:

ohkomimâw	*a grandmother*
omosômimâw	*a grandfather*
onîkihikomâw	*a parent*
ohtâwîmâw	*a father*
okâwîmâw	*a mother*
owîtisânimâw	*a sibling*
ostêsimâw	*an older brother*
omisimâw	*an older sister*
osîmimâw	*a younger sibling*
otânisimâw	*a daughter*
okosisimâw	*a son*
ôsisimimâw	*a grandchild*
ocâpânimâw	*a great-grandchild* or *a great-grandparent*
otâniskotâpânimâw	*a great-great-grandchild* or *a great-great-grandparent*
okihci-âniskotâpânimâw	*a great-great-great-grandchild* or *a great-great-great-grandparent*
ohcâwîsimâw	*an uncle* (father's brother)
okâwîsimâw	*an aunt* (mother's sister)
osikosimâw	*an aunt* (father's sister)
osisimâw	*an uncle* (mother's brother)
ociwâmimâw	*a male cousin* (males: son of father's brother or mother's sister)
ociwâmiskwêmâw	*a female cousin* (females: daughter of father's brother or mother's sister)
otawêmâw	*a cousin* (m-f-m*: child of father's brother or mother's sister)
owîtimimâw	*a cousin* (m-f-m: child of father's sister or mother's brother)
owîstâwimâw	*a cousin* (males: son of father's sister or mother's brother)
ocahkosimâw	*a cousin* (females: daughter of father's sister or mother's brother)
ostimimâw	*a niece* (males: sister's daughter; females: brother's daughter)
otihkwatimâw	*a nephew* (males: sister's son; females: brother's son)
otôsimimâw	*a nephew* (males: brother's son; females: sister's son)
otôsimiskwêmâw	*a niece* (males: brother's daughter; females: sister's daughter)
ocihcâwâw	*a co-parent-in-law*
onahâhkisîmâw	*a son-in-law*
onahâhkaniskwêmâw	*a daughter-in-law*
awâsis	*a child*
nîwa	*my wife* (rarely used but *wîwa* "his wife" is common)
iskwêw	*a woman*
nâpêw	*a man*

---

*   The abbreviation *m-f-m* stands for male to female, as well as female to male.

owîkimâkanimâw	*a spouse*
owîcêwâkanimâw	*a companion*
otôtêmimâw	*a friend*

2.1.F. DISCUSSING THOSE KIN WHO HAVE PASSED ON TO THE SPIRIT WORLD

Cree people are hesitant to talk of the recently departed. If the departed are unavoidably mentioned, they are usually discussed in a voice in a low volume, almost a whisper, in respect for the departed. There are specific vocabulary words and phrases that are used for the departed, such as the following verbs:

kî-itâw	*she/he was named thus*
kâ-kî-itiht	*as she/he was named thus*
kî-nakataskêw	*she/he departed the earth*

The morpheme *-ipan* is used on kinship terms and on names as well.

nohtâwîpan	*my late father*	Williamipan	*the late William*

The *-iy* in the kinship terms changes to a long *î* because of the combination *iy + i = î*.

nikâwiy	*my mother*	nikâwîpan	*my late mother*
nohtâwiy	*my father*	nohtâwîpan	*my late father*

For the rest of the kinship terms simply add the *-ipan* to the original form. Here's how I would talk about my late grandparents and my late parents.

William kî-itâw nohtâwîpan.
nimosômipan, nohtâwîpan
    ohtâwîpana, Patrick kî-itâw.
nohkomipan, nohtâwîpan okâwîpana,
    Elizabeth kî-itâw.

My late father was named William.
My late grandfather, my late father's father,
    was named Patrick.
My late grandmother, my late father's mother,
    was named Elizabeth.

Alice kî-itâw nikâwîpan.
nimosômipan, nikâwîpan ohtâwîpana,
    McKiver kî-itâw.
nohkomipan, nikâwîpan okâwîpana,
    Maggie kî-itâw.

My late mother was named Alice.
My late grandfather, my late mother's father,
    was named McKiver.
My late grandmother, my late mother's mother,
    was named Maggie.

There are no exercises for this, out of respect for the departed. Although this is for information purposes only, it should not be ignored when discussing kinship terms.

2.2. Exercises

2.2.A. KINSHIP CHART EXERCISE

Complete the list of kinship terms *(answers are on page 254)*:

Kinship	1st Person	2nd Person	3rd Person
ohkomimâw – *a grandmother*	nohkom – *my grandmother*		
omosômimâw – *a grandfather*		kimosôm – *your grandfather*	
ohtâwîmâw – *a father*			ohtâwiya – *her/his father*
okâwîmâw – *a mother*			okâwiya – *her/his mother*
ostêsimâw – *an older brother*		kistês – *your older brother*	
omisimâw – *an older sister*	nimis – *my older sister*		
osîmimâw – *a younger sibling*		kisîmis – *your younger sibling*	
otânisimâw – *a daughter*			otânisa – *her/his daughter*
okosisimâw – *a son*		kikosis – *your son*	
ohcâwîsimâw – *an uncle*	nohcâwîs – *my uncle*		
okâwîsimâw – *an aunt*		kikâwîs – *your aunt*	
osikosimâw – *an aunt*			osikosa – *her/his aunt*
osisimâw – *an uncle*		kisis – *your uncle*	
ociwâmimâw – *a male cousin*	niciwâm – *my cousin*		
ociwâmiskwêmâw – *a female cousin*		kiciwâmiskwêm – *your cousin*	

Kinship	1st Person	2nd Person	3rd Person
otawêmâw – a cousin			otawêmâwa – her/his cousin
wîtimowâw – a cousin		kîtim – your cousin	
wîstâwimâw – a male cousin	nîstâw – my cousin		
ocâhkosimâw – a female cousin		kicâhkos – your cousin	
atim – a dog			otêma – her/his dog

2.2.B. VITAL STATISTICS EXERCISE I

Answer the following questions (*answers are on page 255*).

Name (verb stem: *isiyihkâso*)

    Question in 2nd person: *tânisi kitisiyihkâson?*

    Answer in 1st person: _____

    Question in 3rd person: *tânisi isiyihkâsow wiya?*

    Answer in 3rd person: _____

Age (verb stem: *itahtopiponê*)

    Question in 2nd person: *tânitahtopiponêyan?*

    Answer in 1st person: _____

    Question in 3rd person: *tânitahtopiponêt wiya?*

    Answer in 3rd person: _____

Place of Origin

    Question in 2nd person: *tânitê ohci kiya?*

    Answer in 1st person: _____

    Question in 3rd person: *tânitê ohci wiya?*

    Answer in 3rd person: _____

Present Residence (verb stem: *wîki*)

    Question in 2nd person: *tânitê mêkwâc kiwîkin?*

    Answer in 1st person: _____

    Question in 3rd person: *tânitê mêkwâc wîkiw wiya?*

    Answer in 3rd person: _____

Birth Place (verb stem: *nihtâwiki*)

    Question in 2nd person: *tânitê kâ-kî-nihtâwikiyan?*

    Answer in 1st person: _____

    Question in 3rd person: *tânitê kâ-kî-nihtâwikit wiya?*

    Answer in 3rd person: _____

Season of Birth (verb stem: *nihtâwiki*)

    Question in 2nd person: *kîko ispîhtaskîwin kâ-kî-nihtâwikiyan?*

    Answer in 1st person: _____

    Question in 3rd person: *kîko ispîhtaskîwiniyiw kâ-kî-nihtâwikit wiya?*

    Answer in 3rd person: _____

Birth Month (verb stem: *tipiska*)

    Question in 2nd person: *kîko pîsim mâna kâ-tipiskaman?*

    Answer in 1st person: _____

    Question in 3rd person: *kîko pîsimwa mâna kâ-tipiskahk wiya?*

    Answer in 3rd person: _____

Birth Date (verb stem: *tipiska*)

    Question in 2nd person: *tâniyikohk ê-akimiht êwako pîsim mâna kâ-tipiskaman?*

    Answer in 1st person: _____

    Question in 3rd person: *tâniyikohk ê-akimimiht êwakoni pîsimwa mâna kâ-tipiskahk wiya?*

    Answer in 3rd person: _____

Family Size

Question in 2nd person: *tânitahtwasiyêk kiwîtisânîhitowinihk?*

Answer in 1st person: _____

Question in 3rd person: *tânitahtwasicik owîcisânîhitowinihk?*

Answer in 3rd person: _____

Youngest Sibling

Question in 2nd person: *osîmimâw cî kiya?*

Answer in 1st person: _____

Question in 3rd person: *osîmimâw cî wiya?*

Answer in 3rd person: _____

Eldest Sister

Question in 2nd person: *omisimâw cî kiya?*

Answer in 1st person: _____

Question in 3rd person: *omisimâw cî wiya?*

Answer in 3rd person: _____

Eldest Brother

Question in 2nd person: *ostêsimâw cî kiya?*

Answer in 1st person: _____

Question in 3rd person: *ostêsimâw cî wiya?*

Answer in 3rd person: _____

Younger Siblings

Question in 2nd person: *tânitahto kitosîmisin?*

Answer in 1st person: _____

Question in 3rd person: *tânitahto osîmisiw?*

Answer in 3rd person: _____

Older Sisters

    Question in 2nd person: *tânitahto kitomisin?*

    Answer in 1st person: _____

    Question in 3rd person: *tânitahto omisiw?*

    Answer in 3rd person: _____

Older Brothers

    Question in 2nd person: *tânitahto kitostêsin?*

    Answer in 1st person: _____

    Question in 3rd person: *tânitahto ostêsiw?*

    Answer in 3rd person: _____

2.2.C. VITAL STATISTICS EXERCISE II

Answer the following questions. Start off with *kiwâhkômâkan* "your relative," but the answer can refer to any relative you want to talk about by using the particular kinship term for that relative. Continue to talk about that relative for the rest of the exercise using that kinship term. Notice that the first question and answer is in 3rd person, while the second question and answer is in 3rd person obviative (3') *(answers are on page 256)*.

Name

    Question in 3rd person, George to Paul: *tânisi isyihkâsow pêyak kiwâkômâkan?*

    Answer in 3rd person, Paul talking about his relative: _____

    _____

    Question in 3', George to Ringo about Paul's relative: *tânisi isiyihkâsow wiya?*

    Answer in 3', Ringo talking about Paul's relative: _____

    _____

Age

Question in 3rd person, George to Paul: *tânitahtopiponêt kitânis?*

Answer in 3rd person, Paul talking about his relative: _____

_____

Question in 3', George to Ringo about Paul's relative: *tânitahtopiponêyit otânisa wiya?*

Answer in 3' Ringo talking about Paul's relative: _____

_____

Place of Origin

Question in 3rd person, George to Paul: *tânitê ohci kitânis?* (Use VAI *ohcîw* "-she/he is from".)

Answer in 3rd person, Paul talking about his relative: _____

_____

Question in 3', George to Ringo about Paul's relative: *tânitê ohcîyiwa otânisa wiya?*

Answer in 3', Ringo talking about Paul's relative: _____

_____

Present Residence

Question in 3rd person, George to Paul: *tânitê mêkwâc wîkiw kitânis?*

Answer in 3rd person, Paul talking about his relative: _____

_____

Question in 3', George to Ringo about Paul's relative: *tânitê mêkwâc wîkiyiwa otânisa wiya?*

Answer in 3', Ringo talking about Paul's relative: _____

_____

Birth Place (verb stem: *nihtâwiki*)

Question in 3rd person, George to Paul: *tânitê kâ-kî-nihtâwikit kitânis?*

Answer in 3rd person, Paul talking about his relative: _____

_____

Question in 3', George to Ringo about Paul's relative: *tânitê kâ-kî-nihtâwikiyit otânisa wiya?*

Answer in 3', Ringo talking about Paul's relative: _____

_____

Season of Birth

Question in 3rd person, George to Paul: *kîko ispîhtaskîwiniyiw kâ-kî-nihtâwikit kitânis?*

Answer in 3rd person, Paul talking about his relative: _____

_____

Question in 3', George to Ringo about Paul's relative: *kîko ispîhtaskîwiniyiw kâ-kî-nihtâwikiyit otânisa wiya?*

Answer in 3', Ringo talking about Paul's relative: _____

_____

Birth Month

Question in 3rd person, George to Paul: *kîko pîsimwa mâna kâ-tipiskahk kitânis?*

Answer in 3rd person, Paul talking about his relative: _____

_____

Question in 3', George to Ringo about Paul's relative: *kîko pîsimwa mâna kâ-tipiskamiyit otânisa wiya?*

Answer in 3', Ringo talking about Paul's relative: _____

_____

Birth Date

Question in 3rd person, George to Paul: *tâniyikohk ê-akimimiht êwakoni pîsimwa mâna kâ-tipiskahk kitânis?*

Answer in 3rd person, Paul talking about his relative: _____

_____

Question in 3', George to Ringo about Paul's relative: *tâniyikohk ê-akimimiht êwakoni pîsimwa mâna kâ-tipiskamiyit otânisa wiya?*

Answer in 3', Ringo talking about Paul's relative: _____

_____

Student?

    Question in 3rd person, George to Paul: *okiskinwahamâkan cî kitânis?*

    Answer in 3rd person, Paul talking about his relative: _____

    _____

    Question in 3', George to Ringo about Paul's relative: *okiskinwahamâkan cî otânisa wiya?*

    Answer in 3', Ringo talking about Paul's relative: _____

    _____

What do you like to do?

    Question in 3rd person, George to Paul: *kîkwây cîhkêyihtam ta-itôtahk kitânis?*

    Answer in 3rd person, Paul talking about his relative: _____

    _____

    Question in 3', George to Ringo about Paul's relative: *kîkwây cîhkêyihtamiyiwa ta-itôtamiyit otânsa*

    Answer in 3', Ringo talking about Paul's relative: _____

    _____

2.2.D. TALKING ABOUT YOURSELF AND OTHERS

Verbs to use for the assignment:

VERB	1st person – I	2nd person – You	3rd person – She/he
isiyihkâso – *be named* (VAI)	**nit**isiyihkâso**n**	**kit**isiyihkâso**n**	isiyihkâso**w**
wîki – *reside* (VAI)	**ni**wîki**n**	**ki**wîki**n**	wîki**w**
itahtopiponê – *age* (VAI)	**nit**itahtopiponâ**n**	**kit**itahtopiponâ**n**	itahtopiponê**w**
tipiska – *have a birthday* (VTI-1)	**ni**tipiskê**n**	**ki**tipiskê**n**	tipiska**m**
nihtâwiki – *be born* (VAI)	**ni**kî-nihtâwiki**n**	**ki**kî-nihtâwiki**n**	kî-nihtâwiki**w**

Answer the following questions in Cree. Read your answers to the class.

1st person subject: talking about yourself

1. tânisi kitisiyihkâson.

_____

2. tânitê ohci kiya kayâhtê?

_____

3. tânitê mêkwâc kiwîkin?

_____

4. tânitê kikî-nihtâwikin?

_____

5. kîko ispîhtaskîwin kikî-nihtâwikin?

_____

6. tânitahtopiponêyan?

_____

7. kîko pîsim mâna kâ-tipiskaman?

_____

8. tâniyikohk ê-akimiht êwako pîsim mâna kâ-tipiskaman?

_____

9. okiskinwahamâkan cî kiya?

_____

10. kîkwây kicîhkêyihtên ta-itôtaman?

_____

3rd person subject: talking about someone else (in this case, a relative)

1. tânisi isiyihkâsow pêyak kiwâhkômâkan?

   _____

2. tânitê kayâhtê ohci kiwâhkômâkan?

   _____

3. tânitê mêkwâc wîkiw kiwâhkômâkan?

   _____

4. tânitê kî-nihtâwikiw kiwâhkômâkan?

   _____

5. kîko ispîhtaskîwiniyiw kî-nihtâwikiw kiwâhkômâkan?

   _____

6. tânitahtopiponêt kiwâhkômâkan?

   _____

7. kîko pîsimwa mâna kâ-tipiskahk kiwâhkômâkan?

   _____

8. tâniyikohk ê-akimimiht êwako pîsimwa mâna kâ-tipiskahk kiwâhkômâkan?

   _____

9. okiskinwahamâkan cî kiwâhkômâkan?

   _____

10. kîkwây cîhkêyihtam ta-itôtahk kiwâhkômâkan?

   _____

2.2.E. TALKING ABOUT TRAVEL

miyo-pimâcihok!/miyo-pimohtêhok! – *Safe travels!*

Air travel vocabulary

kâ-twêhohk	*arrivals*	kâ-ohpahohk	*departures*
kâ-pimihâhk #	*flight #*	kâ-twêhohk (Place) ohci	*arriving from (Place)*
tipiyawê	*actual*	ita kâ-ayâhk	*status*
itê kâ-itohtêhohk	*destination*	tawâw (Place)	*welcome to (Place)*
pimihâmakan	*airborne*	twêhômakan	*arrived*
kâ-wêpahamihk	*cancelled*	otamipayin	*delayed*
ohpahômakan	*departed*	pîtos itê kâ-isi-ohpahohk	*diverted*
wîpac kâ-twêhohk	*early*	twêhômakan	*landed*
nahîmakan	*on time*	pîtos ispîhk kâ-ohpahohk	*rescheduled*
asawâpiwin	*tower*	kâwi itohtêk pôsiwinihk	*return to ramp*
kanâcihisowikamik	*washroom*	pôsi-masinahikanêkinos	*ticket/boarding pass*
ispîhk kâ-ohpahohk mîna kâ-twêhohk	*schedule*		

Additional vocabulary:

pimihâkan	*airplane*	pimihâkan twêhowinihk	*airport*
ohpaho (VAI)	*fly up*	twêho (VAI)	*land*
ohtâciho (VAI)	*travel from*	ispayi (VAI)	*go/drive*
pimâciho (VAI)	*travel*	môsâhkin (VTA)	*pick up someone*
takopayi (VAI)	*arrive*	pêhowikamikohk	*waiting room*
nîhtaciwêpicikan	*down escalator*	iskwâhtawêpicikan	*up escalator*
kiskinawâcinâpisk	*bulletin board*	apiwinâhpison	*seat belt*
pôsiwat	*suitcase*	mîcisowinâhtikohkân	*tray*
maskimota	*luggage*	pimihâkan pimâcihowi-wîcihiwêw	*airline attendant*
ita kâ-tawâk	*aisle*	kâ-pôsit	*passenger*
opimihâw	*pilot*	papâmi-pimâciho-masinahikanis	*passport*
apiwin	*seat*	ita kâ-takopayiki maskimota	*baggage claim*

Using the vocabulary above, read the following three texts and answer the questions (*answers are on page 257*).

Text 1

pêyakwâw, ê-kî-têpakohpo-kîsikâyik,* pêyak kisêyiniw kî-ispayiw pimihâkan-twêhowinihk isi ê-kî-nitawi-môsâhkinât otânisa. Toronto ohci ê-kî-pê-ohtâcihoyit, pimihâkanihk ê-kî-pimâcihoyit. wîpac kî-takopayiw kisêyiniw pimihâkan-twêhowinihk, nânitaw têpakohp tipahikan ê-kî-ispayiyik.

Questions:

1. kîko kîsikâyiw awa kisêyiniw kâ-kî-ispayit pimihâkan-twêhowinihk?

   _____

2. tânêhki awa kisêyiniw kâ-kî-ispayit pimihâkan-twêhowinihk?

   _____

3. tânitê ôhi otânisa kâ-kî-pê-ohtâcihoyit?

   _____

4. tânitahto tipahikan ê-kî-ispayiyik ispîhk kâ-kî-takopayit pimihâkan-twêhowinihk?

   _____

Text 2

pîhcâyihk pimihâkan-twêhowinihk pa-pêhow kisêyiniw. atâwêstamâsow pihkahtêwâpoy êkwa nitawi-pêhow pêhowikamikohk. mêtoni ati-ayêski-pêhow. nitawi-kanawâpahtam kiskinawâcinâpisk. êkota wâpahtam kâ-pimihâhk 357 Toronto ohci ê-otamipayiyik kanakê pêyak tipahikan.

Questions:

1. tânitê awa kisêyiniw kâ-pêhot?

   _____

....

* *têpakohpo-kîsikâw* – Sunday ("Seventh Day"). (This is in accordance with the rest of the numbered days of the week as an alternate to *ayamihêwi-kîsikâw* – Prayer Day.)

2. kîkwây kâ-atâwêstamâsot?

_____

3. ati-ayêski-pêhow cî awa kisêyiniw?

_____

4. tânitahto tipahikan kâ-otamipayiyik kâ-pimihâhk 357 Toronto ohci?

_____

Text 3

kî-otamipayiyiw pêyak tipahikan kâ-pimihâhk 357 Toronto ohci. piyisk twêhômakaniyiw
mitâtaht tipahikan ê-ispayiyik. pêhêw otânisa awa kisêyiniw nîhc-âyihk nîhtaciwêpicikanihk
(iskwâhtawêpicikanihk) ita kita-pê-nihtâciwêyit. kâ-wâpamât otânisa ê-pê-nîhtaciwêyit,
ê-tahkonâwasoyit! cîhkêyihtam awa kisêyiniw ayisk êkwâni nistam ta-nakiskawât ôsisima!
mêtoni kêkâc ê-sipwêsimot!

Questions:

1. tânitahto tipahikan kâ-otamipayiyik kâ-pimihâhk 357 Toronto ohci?

_____

2. tânitahto tipahikan kâ-twêhômakahk kâ-pimihâhk 357 Toronto ohci?

_____

3. tânitê kâ-pêhât otânisa awa kisêyiniw?

_____

4. tânêhki awa kisêyiniw kâ-cîhkêyihtahk?

_____

CHAPTER 3

• • • • • • • • • •

SEASONAL AND DAILY ACTIVITIES

3.1. Numbers and Dates

3.1.A. REVIEW OF NUMBERS*

Base Numbers	Add *-osâp* or *-sâp* for units 11–19	Add *–omitanaw* for units of ten from 20–100
pêyak – 1	pêyakosâp – 11	mitâtaht – 10
nîso – 2	nîsosâp – 12	nîs(om)itanaw – 20
nisto – 3	nistosâp – 13	nistomitanaw – 30
nêwo – 4	nêwosâp – 14	nê(wo)mitanaw – 40
niyânan – 5	niyânanosâp – 15	niyânanomitanaw – 50
nikotwâsik – 6	nikotwâs(ik)osâp – 16**	nikotwâsikomitanaw – 60
têpakohp – 7	têpakohposâp – 17	têpakohpomitanaw – 70
ayinânêw – 8	ayinânêwosâp – 18	ayinânê(wo)mitanaw – 80
kêkâ-mitâtaht*** – 9	kêkâ-mitâtahtosâp – 19 *or* kêkâ-nîsitanaw	kêkâ-mitâtahtomitanaw – 90
mitâtaht – 10	****	mitâtahtomitanaw – 100

* Section 3.1.A is taken from *mâci-nêhiyawêwin / Beginning Cree*, p. 14.

** The letters in parentheses here and elsewhere on this chart are often left out when speaking.

*** *kêkâ-mitâtaht* literally means "almost ten." The *kêkâ* comes from *kêkâc* – almost, and can be used for other numbers like *kêkâ-nîsitanaw* – 19 ("almost 20"); *kêkâ-nistomitanaw* then is 29 ("almost 30"), and so on down the line.

**** The words for 11–19 can be combined with the words for 20–100 to create numbers from 21–29, 31–39, etc. Alternatively, one can use the numbers above with *ayiwâk* ("more than, plus") and the base numbers for 21–29, etc. For example, 24 can be either *nîsitanaw nêwosâp* or *nîsitanaw ayiwâk nêwo*.

3.1.B. DATES

When saying the dates, the indefinite actor form of akimêw (VTA) is used (*akimâw* – she/he is counted).

Use the following structures for the present tense:

> **Indicative**: __*Number*__ akimâw ____*Month*
> **Conjunct**: __*Number*__ ê-akimiht __*Month*

Time	Indicative	Conjunct
Present: use when other forms are in 1st and 2nd person	nêwo akimâw kisê-pîsim anohc. *It is the 4th of January today.*	nêwo ê-akimiht kisê-pîsim anohc. *It is the 4th of January today.*
Present: use when other forms are in 3rd person (note the *wa* on the month when talking about a 3rd person's birthday.)	nêwo akimimâwa kisê-pîsimwa ispîhk kâ-tipiskahk. *It is the 4th of January when she/he has a birthday.*	nêwo ê-akimimiht kisê-pîsimwa tipiskam. *She/he has a birthday on the 4th of January.*
Future conditional: use when other forms are in 1st and 2nd person	*	nêwo akimihci kisê-pîsim niwî-tipiskên. *I am going to have a birthday on the 4th of January.*
Future conditional: use when other forms are in 3rd person	*	nêwo akimimihci kisê-pîsimwa wî-tipiskam. *She/he is going to have a birthday on the 4th of January.*

* Future conditionals are another form of conjunct forms in Cree so there is nothing under the Indicative column.

Present

> Indicative: nêwo akimâw kisê-pîsim. – *It is the 4th of January.*
> Conjunct: nêwo ê-akimiht kisê-pîsim. – *It is the 4th of January.*

1. nêwo akimâw kisê-pîsim anohc, ê-wî-mâci-kiskinwahamâkosiyan cî?
   Today is January 4th, are you going to be starting classes?

2. nêwo ê-akimimiht kisê-pîsimwa mâna mâci-kiskinwhamâkosiw.
   She/he usually begins classes on January 4th.

Past

> *Indicative*: nêwo kî-akimâw kisê-pîsim. – *It was the 4th of January.*
> *Conjunct*: nêwo ê-kî-akimiht kisê-pîsim – *It was the 4th of January.*

1. nêwo kî-akimâw kisê-pîsim, kâ-kî-mâci-kiskinwahamâkosiyân.
   On January 4th, I started classes.

2. nêwo ê-kî-akimimiht kisê-pîsimwa mâna kâ-kî-mâci-kiskinwahamâkosit.
   She/he usually began classes on January 4th.

Future Conditional

1. nêwo akimihci kisê-pîsim niwî-mâci-kiskinwahamâkosin.
   When/If it is the 4th of January, I am beginning classes.

2. nêwo akimimihci kisê-pîsimwa wî-mâci-kiskinwahamâkosiw.
   When/If it is the 4th of January, she/he is going to begin classes.

3.2. Months and Seasons

3.2.A. MONTHS

Months in Cree vary locally and are usually named after the most common natural event at the time of the current moon phase.

Month in Cree	Common Event during Moon Phase	Month in English
kisê-pîsim	The Great Moon	January
mikisiwi-pîsim	The Eagle Moon	February
niski-pîsim	The Goose Moon	March
ayîki-pîsim	The Frog Moon	April
sâkipakâwi-pîsim	The Leaf-Budding Moon	May
pâskâwihowi-pîsim	The Egg-Hatching Moon	June
paskowi-pîsim	The Moulting Moon	July
ohpahowi-pîsim	The Flying-Up Moon	August
nôcihitowi-pîsim takwâki-pîsim	The Mating Moon The Autumn Moon	September
pinâskowi-pîsim pimihâwi-pîsim	The Leaf-Falling Moon The Migrating Moon	October
ihkopîwi-pîsim	The Frost Moon	November
pawâcakinasîsi-pîsim	The Frost-Exploding Moon	December

3.2.B. SEASONS: *ispîhtaskîwina* (VII)

Last Season

sîkwanohk	*last spring*
miyoskamîhk	*last spring* (refers to ice break-up)
nîpinohk	*last summer*
takwâkohk	*last fall/autumn*
mikiskohk	*last fall/autumn* (ice freeze-up)
piponohk	*last winter*

Present Season (*Indicative and conjunct; tense indicators can be used with these words.*)

sîkwan / ê-sîkwahk	*it is spring*
miyoskamin / ê-miyoskamik	*it is spring* (ice break-up; literally, *good ground*)
nîpin / ê-nîpihk	*it is summer*
takwâkin / ê-takwâkik	*it is fall/autumn*
mikiskon / ê-mikiskohk	*it is fall/autumn*
pipon / ê-pipohk	*it is winter*

Future Season (*Future conditional*)

sîkwahki	*this coming spring* (literally, *if spring comes*)
miyoskamiki	*this coming spring* (literally, *if spring comes*)
nîpihki	*this coming summer* (literally, *if summer comes*)
takwâkiki	*this coming autumn* (literally, *if autumn comes*)
mikiskohki	*this coming fall/autumn* (literally, *if fall/autumn comes*)
pipohki	*this coming winter* (literally, *if winter comes*)

3.3. Days of the Week (VII)

Indicative

ayamihêwi-kîsikâw.	*It is Sunday.*
pêyako-kîsikâw.	*It is Monday.*
nîso-kîsikâw.	*It is Tuesday.*
nisto-kîsikâw.	*It is Wednesday.*
nêwo-kîsikâw.	*It is Thursday.*
niyânano-kîsikâw.	*It is Friday.*
nikotwâso-kîsikâw.	*It is Saturday.*

Conjunct (Use ê- or kâ-, then replace last consonant of the indicative form with k.)

ê-ayamihêwi-kîsikâk.	*It is Sunday.*
ê-pêyako-kîsikâk.	*It is Monday.*
ê-nîso-kîsikâk.	*It is Tuesday.*
ê-nisto-kîsikâk.	*It is Wednesday.*
ê-nêwo-kîsikâk.	*It is Thursday.*
ê-niyânano-kîskâk.	*It is Friday.*
ê-nikotwâso-kîsikâk.	*It is Saturday.*

Future Conditional (Drop ê- from the conjunct form, then add i at the end.)

ayamihêwi-kîsikâki	*this coming Sunday*
pêyako-kîsikâki	*this coming Monday*
nîso-kîsikâki	*this coming Tuesday*
nisto-kîsikâki	*this coming Wednesday*
nêwo-kîsikâki	*this coming Thursday*
niyânano-kîsikâki	*this coming Friday*
nikotwâso-kîsikâki	*this coming Saturday*

3.3.A. QUESTIONS

Answer the following questions (*answers are on page 258*):

Day of the week: tânitahto kîsikâw anohc? *What is the day today?*

_____

Present month: kîko pîsim akimâw mêkwâc? *Which month is it?*

_____

Today's date: tâniyikohk akimâw awa pîsim? *What is the date?*

_____

Weather: tânisi kâ-isiwêpahk? *What's the weather like?*

_____

3.3.B. TRANSLATION

asinîwaciy	*mountain* (NI)	pimipayi	*drive* (VAI)
isi	*toward*	pipon	*it is winter* (VII)
iskonikan	*reserve* (NI)	pwâtisimo	*dance powwow* (VAI)
ispîhk	*when*	sâkahikan	*lake* (NI)
kwâskwêpicikê	*fish* (VAI)	sêsâwohtê	*hike* (VAI)
mâcî	*hunt* (VAI)	sîkwan	*it is spring* (VII)
mâna	*usually*	sôskwaciwê	*slide* (VAI)
nihtâwiki	*be born* (VAI)	takwâkin	*it is fall* (VII)
nîpawi-sôskwaciwê	*ski* (VAI)	tipiska	*have a birthday* (VTI-1)
nîpin	*it is summer* (VII)	yahki-sôskoyâpawi	*ski cross-country* (VAI)
nitawi-	*go and* (IPV)		

Translate the following sentences using the vocabulary above (*answers are on page 258*).

1. piponohk nikî-nitawi-nîpawi-sôskwaciwânân asinî-wacîhk.

_____

2. nîpihki niwî-nitawi-kwâskwêpicikân sâkahikanihk.

_____

3. takwâkohk nikî-nitawi-yahki-sôskoyâpawin asinî-wacîhk.

_____

4. sîkwahki niwî-nitawi-sêsâwohtânân asinî-wacîhk.

_____

5. sîkwanohk nikî-pimipayinân asinî-wacîhk isi.

_____

6. pipohki niwî-sôskwaciwânân asinî-wacîhk.

_____

7. nîpinohk nikî-nitawi-pwâtisimonân iskonikanihk.

_____

8. takwâkiki niwî-nitawi-mâcînân asinîwacîhk.

_____

9. kî-pipon ispîhk kâ-kî-nihtâwikiyân.

_____

10. sîkwan mâna ispîhk kâ-tipiskamân.

_____

3.4. More on the Days of the Week

These are the forms used when talking about the days of the week or when the activities are done by the 1st person or 2nd person:

English	Indicative	Conjunct	Future Conditional
Sunday	ayamihêwi-kîsikâw	ê-ayamihêwi-kîsikâk	ayamihêwi-kîsikâki
Monday	pêyako-kîsikâw	ê-pêyako-kîsikâk	pêyako-kîsikâki
Tuesday	nîso-kîsikâw	ê-nîso-kîsikâk	nîso-kîsikâki
Wednesday	nisto-kîsikâw	ê-nisto-kîsikâk	nisto-kîsikâki
Thursday	nêwo-kîsikâw	ê-nêwo-kîsikâk	nêwo-kîsikâki
Friday	niyânano-kîsikâw	ê-niyânano-kîsikâk	niyânano-kîsikâki
Saturday	nikotwâso-kîsikâw	ê-nikotwâso-kîsikâk	nikotwâso-kîsikâki

Examples:

1. kâ-nîso-kîsikâk mâna nikiskinwahamâkosin nêhiyawêwin.
    On Tuesday I usually have Cree class.

2. kâ-nikotwâso-kîsikâk cî mâna kinitawi-papâmi-atâwân?
    Do you usually go shopping on Saturday?

When talking about a 3rd person, add *yi* to the days of the week:

English	Indicative	Conjunct	Future Conditional
Sunday	ayamihêwi-kîsikâ**yi**w	ê-ayamihêwi-kîsikâ**yi**k	ayamihêwi-kîsikâ**yi**ki
Monday	pêyako-kîsikâ**yi**w	ê-pêyako-kîsikâ**yi**k	pêyako-kîsikâ**yi**ki
Tuesday	nîso-kîsikâ**yi**w	ê-nîso-kîsikâ**yi**k	nîso-kîsikâ**yi**ki
Wednesday	nisto-kîsikâ**yi**w	ê-nisto-kîsikâ**yi**k	nisto-kîsikâ**yi**ki
Thursday	nêwo-kîsikâ**yi**w	ê-nêwo-kîsikâ**yi**k	nêwo-kîsikâ**yi**ki
Friday	niyânano-kîsikâ**yi**w	ê-niyânano-kîsikâ**yi**k	niyânano-kîsikâ**yi**ki
Saturday	nikotwâso-kîsikâ**yi**w	ê-nikotwâso-kîsikâ**yi**k	nikotwâso-kîsikâ**yi**ki

Examples:

1. kâ-nîso-kîsikâyik mâna kiskinwahamâkosiw nêhiyawêwin.
   On Tuesday she/he usually has Cree class.

2. kâ-nikwotwâso-kîsikâyik cî mâna nitawi-papâmi-atâwêw?
   Does she/he usually go shopping on Saturday?

3.4.A. EXERCISES

Complete the following chart with the days of the week in the correct tense *(answers are on page 259)*.

Remember: to go from indicative to conjunct, use *ê-* or (*kâ-*) at the beginning, drop the last consonant, and then add the appropriate ending. If the vowel left after dropping the consonant is long, use *-k*; if the stem ends in a short vowel followed by *n*, use *hk*; otherwise, use a *-k*. To go from conjunct to future conditional (for VII), drop the *ê-* (or *kâ-*) and then add *i* at the end.

Days of the Week

English	Indicative	Conjunct	Future Conditional
Sunday	ayamihêwi-kîsikâw *It is Sunday.*		
Monday	pêyako-kîsikâw *It is Monday.*		
Tuesday	nîso-kîsikâw *It is Tuesday.*		
Wednesday	nisto-kîsikâw *It is Wednesday.*		
Thursday	nêwo-kîsikâw *It is Thursday.*		
Friday	niyânano-kîsikâw *It is Friday.*		
Saturday	nikotwâso-kîsikâw *It is Saturday.*		

The days of the week are inanimate intransitive verbs (VII). As verbs, the above days of the week in both the indicative and subjunctive columns can be placed in the past tense for the indicative and the conjunct. Fill in the following chart in the past tense (*answers are on page 259*):

English	Indicative Past Tense	Conjunct Past Tense
Sunday	kî-ayamihêwi-kîsikâw *It was Sunday.*	ê-kî-ayamihêwi-kîsikâk *As it was Sunday*
Monday		
Tuesday		
Wednesday		
Thursday		
Friday		
Saturday		

3.5. Time of Day

Temporal words deal with times of day, from dawn until midnight. They also include words for last week, yesterday, last night, and next week. Using the term for *morning*, the following examples outline the various forms in the indicative:

Indicative

present tense	kîkisêpâyâw	It **is** morning.
past tense	**kî**-kîkisêpâyâw	It **was** morning.
future intentional	**wî**-kîkisêpâyâw	It's **going to** be morning.
future definite	**ta**-kîkisêpâyâw	It **will be** morning.
present with preverb	**pê**-kîkisêpâyâw	Morning's **coming**.

Conjunct

Add *ê-* at the beginning of the indicative and replace the last consonant with *-k* if the last vowel is long or with *-hk* if the last vowel is short.

present tense	ê-kîkisêpâyâ**k**	It **is** morning.
past tense	ê-kî-kîkisêpâyâ**k**	It **was** morning.
future intentional	ê-wî-kîkisêpâyâ**k**	It's **going to be** morning.
future definite	(not possible in conjunct mood)	
present with preverb	ê-pê-kîkisêpâyâ**k**	Morning's **coming**.
future conditional	kîkisêpâyâk**i**	**If it is** morning

3.5.A. TRANSLATION

itohtê	*go*	sâkahikan	*lake*
takosin	*she/he arrives*	kîsahkamikisi	*be done an activity*
sipwêhtê	*leave*	kotawê	*start the fire*

Translate the following sentences using the vocabulary above (*answers are on page 259*).

1. In the morning we (excl) will go to the lake.

_____

2. It was morning when he arrived here.

_____

3. It will be morning when we (incl) finish.

_____

4. Let's go now, it's morning.

_____

5. Start the fire, it's morning.

_____

3.5.B. TEMPORAL WORDS

Transform the following temporal words into their conjunct and future conditional forms (*answers are on page 259*):

Conjunct: use *ê-* in regular subordinate clauses (usually after *ayisk/osâm* "because") and *kâ-* in relative clauses (usually after *ispîhk* "when")

Future Conditional: these forms can be used in conditional clauses (*kîspin* "if" need not be included) or temporal clauses (*ispîhk* "when" needs to be included)

Temporal Words	Conjunct	Future Conditional
otâkosîhk – *yesterday* (IPC)	n/a	n/a
tipiskohk – *last night* (IPC)	n/a	n/a
kîkisêp – *this past morning* (IPC)	n/a	n/a
anohc – *today/now* (IPC)	n/a	n/a
pêtâpan – *it is dawn (daybreak)* (VII)	ê-pêtâpahk	pêtâpahki – *if/when it is dawn*
sâkâstêw – *it is sunrise* (VII)	ê-sâkâstêk	sâkâstêki – *if/when the sun rises*
wâpan – *it is dawn* (VII)		
kîkisêpâyâw – *it is morning* (VII)		
âpihtâ-kîsikâw – *it is noon* (VII)		

Temporal Words	Conjunct	Future Conditional
pôni-âpihtâ-kîsikâw – *it is afternoon* (VII)		
otâkosin – *it is evening* (VII)		
pahkisimon – *it is sundown* (VII)		
wawâninâkwan – *it is evening (twilight)* (VII)		
tipiskâw – *it is night* (VII)		
âpihtâ-tipiskâw – *it is midnight* (VII)		

Other Temporal Words

wîpac	*soon/early*	pitamâ	*for now*
pâtos	*only later*	anohc kâ-ispayik	*this week*
pâtimâ	*later*	otâhk ispayiw	*last week*
pâtimâ ici	*okay, later*	kotak ispayiki	*next week*
mwêstas	*later*		

CHAPTER 4
· · · · · · · · · · · · · ·
TIME AND OTHER TEMPORAL WORDS

4.1. Time

Talking about time in the 24-hour cycle in Cree is a borrowed concept from the Euro-Canadian culture, so we translate their forms for "on the hour," "minutes past the hour," "half past the hour," and "minutes toward the hour" as follows:

tipahikan	*on the hour*
cipahikanis miyâskam	*minutes past the hour*
mîna âpihtaw	*half past the hour* (literally, *plus half*)
cipahikanis pâmwayês	*minutes toward the hour*

Use *ispayin* (or its conjunct form *ê-ispayik*) when talking about time; otherwise, one is talking about how long an activity takes to do. All the above words fall into a standard formula, as shown here. The underlined numbers can be replaced for whatever time is relevant.

On the hour:	<u>pêyak</u> tipahikan ispayin.	*It is 1:00.*
Past the hour:	<u>nîsitanaw</u> cipahikanis miyâskam <u>pêyak</u> tipahikan ispayin.	*It is 1:20.*
Half past the hour:	<u>pêyak</u> tipahikan mîna âpihtaw ispayin.	*It is 1:30.*
Toward the hour:	<u>nîsitanaw</u> cipahikanis pâmwayês <u>nîso</u> tipahikan ispayin.	*It is 1:40.*

4.1.A. QUESTIONS

Answer the questions below using the following word list. Remember: when we use *mâna* "usually," then the verbs in the sentence are in present tense (*answers are on page 260*).

Preverbs (IPV)		Verbs (VAI)	
ati-	*start*	waniskâ	*get up*
pôni-	*stop*	kîkisêpâ-mîciso	*eat breakfast*
kîsi-	*finish*	kiskinwahamâkosi	*be in class*
nitawi-	*go and*	âpihtâ-kîsikani-mîciso	*eat lunch*
nôhtê-	*want to*	otâkwani-mîciso	*eat supper*
kakwê-	*try*	kîwê	*go home*
papâsi-	*hurriedly*	kawisimo	*lay down*
nisîhkâci	*carefully*	nipâ	*sleep*
pê-	*come*	takosini	*arrive*
mâci-	*begin*	itahkamikisi	*do*

1. tânitahto tipahikan mâna ê-ispayik kâ-waniskâyan ispîhk kâ-kîkisêpâyâk?
   What time do you usually get up in the morning?

   _____

2. tânitahto tipahikan mâna ê-ispayik kâ-kîkisêpâ-mîcisoyan?
   What time do you usually eat breakfast?

   _____

3. tânitahto tipahikan mâna ê-ispayik kâ-nitawi-kiskinwahamâkosiyan?
   What time do you usually go to school?

   _____

4. tânitahto tipahikan mâna ê-ispayik kâ-takosiniyan kiskinwahamâtowikamikohk?
   What time do you usually arrive at school?

   _____

5. tânitahto tipahikan mâna ê-ispayik kâ-mâci-kiskinwahamâkosiyan nêhiyawêwin?
   What time do you usually begin Cree class?

   _____

6. tânitahto tipahikan mâna ê-ispayik kâ-âpihtâ-kîsikani-mîcisoyan?
   What time do you usually eat lunch?

   _____

7. tânitahto tipahikan mâna ê-ispayik kâ-kîsi-kiskinwahamâkosiyan?
What time do you usually finish class?

_____

8. tânitahto tipahikan mâna ê-ispayik kâ-ati-kîwêyan?
What time do you begin to go home?

_____

9. tânitahto tipahikan mâna ê-ispayik kâ-otâkwani-mîcisoyan?
What time do you usually eat supper?

_____

10. tânisi mâna kâ-itahkamikisiyan ispîhk kâ-otâkosik?
What do you usually do in the evening?

_____

11. tânitahto tipahikan mâna ê-ispayik kâ-kawisimoyan?
What time do you usually lie down to sleep?

_____

4.2. It's About Time

4.2.A. VAIs IN 1ST PERSON

Complete the following charts using temporal words, time, and VAIs in the appropriate forms. *Note:* the first three must be in the past tense (*answers are on page 260*).

Temporal Words	Time	Activity
Yesterday	*about 4:00,*	*I went home.*
otâkosîhk	nânitaw nêwo tipahikan ê-**kî**-ispayik,	ni**kî**-kîwân.
Last night	*about 11:30,*	*I went to lie down.*
tipiskohk	nânitaw pêyakosâp tipahikan mîna âpihtaw ê-**kî**-ispayik,	ni**kî**-kawisimon.
This past morning	*about 7:45,*	*I got up.*
kîkisêp		
Today	*about 1:15,*	*I am going to work hard.*
anohc		
When it is dawn (daybreak),	*usually about 5:00,*	*I slowly brew coffee.*
ispîhk kâ-pêtâpahk,		
When it is sunrise,	*usually about 5:30,*	*I begin to cook.*
ispîhk kâ-sâkâstêk,		
When it is dawn,	*usually about 5:50,*	*I finish cooking.*
ispîhk kâ-wâpahk,		

When it is morning,	usually about 6:00,	I eat breakfast.
ispîhk kâ-kîkisêpâyâk,		
When it is noon,	usually at 12:30,	I eat lunch.
ispîhk kâ-âpihtâ-kîsikâk,		
When it is afternoon,	usually about 3:00,	I take a little rest.
ispîhk kâ-pôni-âpihtâ-kîsikâk,		
When it is evening,	usually about 6:30,	I eat supper.
ispîhk kâ-otâkosik,		
When it is sundown,	usually about 7:00,	I walk for exercise.
ispîhk kâ-pahkisimok,		
When it is evening (twilight),	usually about 7:30,	I am at home.
ispîhk kâ-wawâninâkwahk,		
When it is night,	usually about 11:00,	I try to sleep.
ispîhk kâ-tipiskâk,		

4.2.B. VAIs IN 1ST PERSON IN FUTURE CONDITIONAL

The temporal words are in the future conditional form. These are also the forms for the temporal clause preceded by *ispîhk* "when," but the forms don't change. *Note: ispîhk* "when" is obligatory and *kîspin* "if" is optional.

The word *ispayin* "as it happens" in the second column is in the future conditional form. Verbs in the third column are in the future intentional tense *wî-*.

The first two are done; complete the translations for the rest (*answers are on page 261*).

Temporal Words	Time	Activity
If it is dawn (daybreak),	*about 5:00,*	*I am going to slowly brew coffee.*
pêtâpah**ki**,	nânitaw niyânan tipahikan ispayi**ki**,	ni**wî**-nisihkâc-pihkahtêwâpôhkân.
If it is sunrise,	*about 5:30,*	*I am going to begin cooking.*
sâkâstê**ki**,	nânitaw niyânan tipahikan mîna âpihtaw ispayi**ki**,	ni**wî**-ati-piminawason.
If it is dawn,	*about 5:50,*	*I am going to finish cooking.*
wâpah**ki**,		
If it is morning,	*about 6:00,*	*I am going to eat breakfast.*
kîkisêpâyâ**ki**,		
If it is noon,	at 12:30,	I am going to eat lunch.
âpihtâ-kîsikâ**ki**,		
If it is afternoon,	*usually about 3:00,*	*I am going to take a little rest.*
pôni-âpihtâ-kîsikâ**ki**,		

If it is evening,	*about 6:30,*	*I am going to eat supper.*
otâkosiki,		
If it is sundown,	*about 7:00,*	*I am going to walk for exercise.*
pahkisimoki,		
If it is evening (twilight),	*about 7:30,*	*I am going to be at home.*
wawâninâkwahki,		
If it is night,	*about 11:00,*	*I am going to try to sleep.*
tipiskâki,		

4.2.C. VAIs IN 3RD PERSON

The temporal words end in -yik when the subject of the main clause is in 3rd person. *Note*: The first three must be in the past tense.

The first two are done; complete the translations for the rest (*answers are on page 261*).

Temporal Words	Time	Activity
Yesterday	*about 4:00,*	*she/he went home.*
otâkosîhk	nânitaw nêwo tipahikan ê-**kî**-ispayi**yi**k,	**kî**-kîwê**w**.
Last night	*about 11:30,*	*she/he went to lie down.*
tipiskohk	nânitaw pêyakosâp tipahikan mîna âpihtaw ê-**kî**-ispayi**yi**k,	**kî**-kawisimo**w**.
This past morning	*about 7:45,*	*she/he got up.*
kîkisêp		
Today	*about 1:15,*	*she/he is going to work hard.*
anohc		
When it is dawn (daybreak),	*usually about 5:00,*	*she/he slowly brews coffee.*
ispîhk kâ-pêtâpa**niyik**,		
When it is sunrise,	*usually about 5:30,*	*she/he begins to cook.*
ispîhk kâ-sâkâstê**yik**,		
When it is dawn,	*usually about 5:50,*	*she/he finishes cooking.*
ispîhk kâ-wâpa**niyik**,		

When it is morning,	usually about 6:00,	she/he eats breakfast.
ispîhk kâ- kîkisêpâyâ**yik**,		
When it is noon,	usually at 12:30,	she/he eats lunch.
ispîhk kâ-âpihtâ- kîsikâ**yik**,		
When it is afternoon,	usually about 3:00,	she/he takes a little rest.
ispîhk kâ-pôni- âpihtâ-kîsikâ**yik**,		
When it is evening,	usually about 6:30,	she/he eats supper.
ispîhk kâ- otâkosi**niyik**,		
When it is sundown,	usually about 7:00,	she/he walks for exercise.
ispîhk kâ- pahkisimo**yik**,		
When it is evening (twilight),	usually about 7:30,	she/he is at home.
ispîhk kâ- wawâninâkwa**niyik**,		
When it is night,	usually about 11:00,	she/he tries to sleep.
ispîhk kâ-tipiskâ**yik**,		

4.2.D. VAIs IN 3RD PERSON IN FUTURE CONDITIONAL

The temporal words below are in the future conditional form. These are also the forms for the temporal clause preceded by *ispîhk* "when," but the forms don't change. *Note: ispîhk* "when" is obligatory and *kîspin* "if" is optional. The temporal words end in *-yiki* when the subject of the main clause is in 3rd person.

The word *ispayin* "as it happens" in the second column is in the future conditional form and ends in *-yiki* when the subject of the main clause is in 3rd person. Verbs in the third column are in the future intentional tense *wî-*.

The first two are done; complete the translations for the rest (*answers are on page 262*).

Temporal Words	Time	Activity
If it is dawn (daybreak),	*about 5:00,*	*she/he is going to slowly brew coffee.*
pêtâpa**niyiki**,	nânitaw niyânan tipahikan ispayi**yiki**,	**wî**-nisihkâc -pihkahtêwâpohkê**w**.
If it is sunrise,	*about 5:30,*	*she/he is going to begin cooking.*
sâkâstê**yiki**,	nânitaw niyânan tipahikan mîna âpihtaw ispayi**yiki**,	**wî**-ati-piminawaso**w**.
If it is dawn,	*about 5:50,*	*she/he is going to finish cooking.*
wâpa**niyiki**,		
If it is morning,	*about 6:00,*	*she/he is going to eat breakfast.*
kîkisêpâyâ**yiki**,		
If it is noon,	*at 12:30,*	*she/he is going to eat lunch.*
âpihtâ-kîsikâ**yiki**,		

If it is afternoon,	*about 3:00,*	*she/he is going to take a little rest.*
pôni-âpihtâ- kîsikâ**yiki**,		
If it is evening,	*about 6:30,*	*she/he is going to eat supper.*
otâkosi**niyiki**,		
If it is sundown,	*about 7:00,*	*she/he is going to walk for exercise.*
pahkisimo**niyiki**,		
If it is evening (twilight),	*about 7:30,*	*she/he is going to be at home.*
wawâninâkwa**niyiki**,		
If it is night,	*about 11:00,*	*she/he is going to try to sleep.*
tipiskâ**yiki**,		

4.2.E. WHAT TIME DO YOU...?

When it is Monday, what time do you wake up? On the following pages, for each of the days of the week, do these exercises:

1. Say the activities in 1st person singular and the time when each activity is done. Read the columns from left to right to make complete sentences.

2. Answer the question below each day of the week.

3. Practise creating new questions by replacing the underlined verb stem in each question with the other verbs from that day's chart.

Monday

Day of the Week	Activity	Time of Activity
When it is Monday	*I get up/wake up*	*at 7:30.*
ispîhk mâna kâ-pêyako-kîsikâk	niwaniskân	têpakohp tipahikan mîna âpihtaw kâ-ispayik.
	I bathe/shower	*at 7:45.*
	nikisîpêkinastân	niyânanosâp cipahikanis pâmwayês ayinânêw tipahikan kâ-ispayik.
	I comb my hair	*at 8:00.*
	nisîkahon	ayinânêw tipahikan kâ-ispayik.
	I eat breakfast	*at 8:15.*
	nikîkisêpâ-mîcison	niyânanosâp cipahikanis miyâskam ayinânêw tipahikan kâ-ispayik.

kiya mâka, tânitahto tipahikan mâna ê-ispayik kâ-<u>waniskâ</u>yan ispîhk kâ-pêyako-kîsikâk?
How about you, what time do you get up when it is Monday?

_____

_____

Practise creating new questions by replacing the underlined verb stem from the question above with the other verbs in Monday's chart.

Tuesday

Day of the Week	Activity	Time of Activity
When it is Tuesday	*I go to school/class*	*at 8:30.*
ispîhk mâna kâ-nîso-kîsikâk	ninitawi-kiskinwahamâkosin	ayinânêw tipahikan mîna âpihtaw kâ-ispayik.
	I finish school/class	*at 11:15.*
	nikîsi-kiskinwahamâkosin	niyânanosâp cipahikanis miyâskam pêyakosâp tipahikan kâ-ispayik.
	I eat lunch	*at 12:00.*
	nitâpihtâ-kîsikani-mîcison	nîsosâp tipahikan kâ-ispayik.
	I begin to go home	*at 4:40.*
	nitati-kîwân	nîsitanaw cipahikanis pâmwayês niyânan tipahikan kâ-ispayik.

kiya mâka, tânitahto tipahikan mâna ê-ispayik kâ-<u>nitawi-kiskinwahamâkosiyan</u>
   ispîhk kâ-nîso-kîsikâk?
How about you, what time do you go to class on Tuesday?

_____

_____

Practise creating new questions by replacing the underlined verb stem (and IPV) from the question above with the other verbs in Tuesday's chart.

Wednesday

Day of the Week	Activity	Time of Activity
On Wednesday	*I exercise*	*at 5:30.*
ispîhk mâna kâ-nisto-kîsikâk	nisêsâwîn	niyânan tipahikan mîna âpihtaw kâ-ispayik.
	I read	*at 8:45.*
	nitayamihcikân	niyânanosâp cipahikanis pâmwayês kêkâ-mitâtaht tipahikan kâ-ispayik.
	I write	*at 10:00.*
	nimasinahikân	mitâtaht tipahikan kâ-ispayik.
	I begin to lie down to sleep	*at 11:10.*
	nitati-kawisimon	mitâtaht cipahikanis miyâskam pêyakosâp tipahikan kâ-ispayik.

kiya mâka, tânitahto tipahikan mâna ê-ispayik kâ-<u>sêsâwî</u>yan ispîhk kâ-nisto-kîsikâk?
How about you, what time do you exercise when it is Wednesday?

_____

_____

Practise creating new questions by replacing the underlined verb stem from the question above with the other verbs in Wednesday's chart.

Thursday

Day of the Week	Activity	Time of Activity
On Thursday	I go and work	at 7:30.
ispîhk mâna kâ-nisto-kîsikâk	ninitawi-atoskân	têpakohp tipahikan mîna âpihtaw kâ-ispayik.
	I finish work	at 6:00.
	nikîsi-atoskân	nikotwâsik tipahikan kâ-ispayik.
	I begin to drive home	at 6:12.
	nitati-kîwêpayin	nîsosâp cipahikanis miyâskam nikotwâsik tipahikan kâ-ispayik.
	I begin to cook	at 7:40.
	nitati-piminawason	nîsitanaw cipahikanis pâmwayês ayinânêw tipahikan kâ-ispayik.

kiya mâka, tânitahto tipahikan mâna ê-ispayik kâ-<u>nitawi-atoskê</u>yan ispîhk kâ-nêwo-kîsikâk?
How about you, what time do you go to work when it is Thursday?

_____

_____

Practise creating new questions by replacing the underlined verb stem (and IPV) from the question above with the other verbs in Thursday's chart.

Friday

Day of the Week	Activity	Time of Activity
When it is Friday ispîhk mâna kâ-niyânano-kîsikâk	*I jog* nisêsâwipahtân	at 6:30. nikotwâsik tipahikan mîna âpihtaw kâ-ispayik.
	I wash dishes nikisîpêkiyâkanân	at 6:45. niyânanosâp cipahikanis pâmwayês têpakohp tipahikan kâ-ispayik.
	I drink coffee niminihkwân pihkahtêwâpoy	at 3:00. nisto tipahikan kâ-ispayik.
	I eat supper nitotâkwani-mîcison	at 6:15. niyânanosâp cipahikanis miyâskam nikotwâsik tipahikan kâ-ispayik.

kiya mâka, tânitahto tipahikan mâna kâ-<u>sêsâwi</u>pahtâyan ispîhk kâ-niyânano-kîsikâk?
How about you, what time do you jog on Fridays?

_____

_____

Practise creating new questions by replacing the underlined verb stem from the question above with the other verbs in Friday's chart.

Saturday

Day of the Week	Activity	Time of Activity
When it is Saturday ispîhk mâna kâ-nikotwâso-kîsikâk	*I go shopping* ninitawi-papâmi-atâwân	at 9:30. kêkâ-mitâtaht tipahikan mîna âpihtaw kâ-ispayik.
	I ride around nipapâmitâpâson	at 2:15. niyânanosâp cipahikanis miyâskam nîso tipahikan kâ-ispayik.
	I go dancing ninitawi-nîmihiton	at 10:00. mitâtaht tipahikan kâ-ispayik.
	I finish dancing nikîsi-nîmihiton	at 1:40. nîsitanaw cipahikanis pâmwayês nîso tipahikan kâ-ispayik.

kiya mâka, tânitahto tipahikan mâna ê-ispayik kâ-<u>nitawi-papâmi-atâwê</u>yan ispîhk
    kâ-nikotwâso-kîsikâk?
How about you, what time do you go shopping on Saturdays?

_____

_____

Practise creating new questions by replacing the underlined verb stem (and IPVs) from the
question above with the other verbs in Saturday's chart.

Sunday

Day of the Week	Activity	Time of Activity
When it is Sunday	*I try to get up*	*at 7:30.*
ispîhk mâna kâ-ayamihêwi-kîsikâk	nikakwê-waniskân	têpakohop tipahikan mîna âpihtaw kâ-ispayik.
	I go to church	*at 10:45.*
	ninitawi-ayamihân	niyânanosâp cipahikanis pâmwayês pêyakosâp tipahikan kâ-ispayik.
	I go about visiting	*at 4:00.*
	nipapâmi-kiyokân	nêwo tipahikan kâ-ispayik.
	I try to barbecue	*at 6:05.*
	nikakwê-maskatêpwân	niyânan cipahikanis miyâskam nikotwâsik tipahikan kâ-ispayik.

kiya mâka, tânitahto tipahikan mâna ê-ispayik kâ-<u>kakwê-waniskâ</u>yan ispîhk
    kâ-ayamihêwi-kîsikâk?
How about you, what time do you try to get up on Sundays?

_____

_____

Practise creating new questions by replacing the underlined verb stem (and IPV) from the
question above with the other verbs in Sunday's chart.

1. tânitahto kîsikâw anohc?
What day is it today?

Possible answers:

pêyako-kîsikâw anohc.	*It is Monday today.*
nîso-kîsikâw anohc.	*It is Tuesday today.*
nisto-kîsikâw anohc.	*It is Wednesday today.*
nêwo-kîsikâw anohc.	*It is Thursday today.*
niyânano-kîsikâw anohc.	*It is Friday today.*
nikotwâso-kîsikâw anohc.	*It is Saturday today.*
ayamihêwi-kîsikâw anohc.	*It is Sunday today.*

2. tânispîhk mâna kiya kâ-papâmi-atâwêyan?
When do you go shopping?

A: nipapâmi-atawân mâna ispîhk kâ-nikotwâso-kîsikâk.
I usually go shopping on Saturday.

3. kinitawi-ayamihân cî mâna ispîhk kâ-ayamihêwi-kîsikâk?
Do you go to church whenever it is Sunday (or on Sunday)?

Possible answers:

âha, ninitawi-ayamihân mâna ispîhk kâ-ayamihêwi-kîsikâk.
Yes, I go to church on Sunday.

namôya, namôya ninitawi-ayamihân ispîhk kâ-ayamihêwi-kîsikâk.
No, I do not go to church on Sunday.

4. tânisi mâna kâ-itahkamikisiyan ispîhk kâ-nikotwâso-kîsikâk?
What do you do when it is Saturday (replace with any day of the week)?

A: nipapâmi-atâwân mâna ispîhk kâ-nikotwâso-kîsikâk.
I usually go shopping on Saturday.

4.3. Complex Sentences

Independent and Dependent Clauses

In the lessons above we have some complex sentences made up of independent and dependent (or subordinate) clauses. Independent clauses can stand on their own to make complete statements. Dependent or subordinate clauses, however, cannot stand on their own and, instead, depend on another clause to complete the statement. Let's take the answer to question 4 above as an example:

(nipapâmi-atâwân) [mâna ispîhk kâ-nikotwâso-kîsikâk].

(Independent clause): nipapâmi-atâwân. – *I go shopping.*
[Subordinate clause]:   mâna ispîhk kâ-nikotwâso-kîsikâk – *usually when it is Saturday*

Independent clauses are usually in the indicative while the subordinate clauses are usually in one form of the conjunct, or they can also be in the delayed imperative form. Conjunct forms include the *ê-* form, the *kâ-* form, and the future conditionals.

The *ê-* form of the conjunct and the *kâ-* form share endings, but they are used in different situations. At this point, let's keep it simple: use the *kâ-* form after mention of "when" or in *tân-* questions; use the *ê-* form after *ayisk* "because."

Here are some examples of complex sentences:

wî-takosin wâpan**iyiki**. – *He's going to arrive at dawn.*

Independent clause with 3rd person subject: wî-takosin. – *He's going to arrive.*
Subordinate clause in future conditional agrees with subject: wâpan**iyiki**. – *If it is dawn*

niwî-takosinin wâpa**hki**. – *I'm going to arrive at dawn (tomorrow).*

Independent clause with 1st person subject: niwî-takosinin. – *I'm going to arrive.*
Subordinate clause agrees with subject: wâpa**hki**. – *If it is dawn (tomorrow)*

4.3.A. TRANSLATION

Translate the sentences below using the following words (*answers are on page 263*). Be sure the make the subject of the verbs agree with the VIIs.

cikâstêpayihcikan	*movie*	nitawi-	*go and* (IPV)
itohtê	*go* (VAI)	ôtênaw	*town*
kawisimo	*lie down to sleep* (VAI)	pakâsimo	*swim* (VAI)
kîwê	*go home* (VAI)	papâmiskâ	*go canoeing* (VAI)
mâcî	*hunt* (VAI)	pê-	*come* (IPV)
mîciso	*eat* (VAI)	pîcicî	*round-dance* (VAI)
miyo-	*good* (IPV)	yahki-sôskoyâpawi	*cross-country ski* (VAI)
âpihtâ-kîsikâw	*it is noon* (VII)	otâkosin	*it is evening* (VII)
âpihtâ-tipiskâw	*it is midnight* (VII)	pôni-âpihtâ-kîsikâw	*it is afternoon* (VII)
kîkisêpâyâw	*it is morning* (VII)	tipiskâw	*it is night* (VII)
miyo-kîsikâw	*it is a good day* (VII)	wâpan	*it is dawn* (VII)
nîpin	*it is summer* (VII)	wawâninâkwan	*it is twilight* (VII)

1. I'm going cross-country skiing this evening.

    _____

2. She/he is going cross-country skiing this evening.

    _____

3. Are you going hunting at dawn?

    _____

4. Is she/he going hunting at dawn?

    _____

5. We (inclusive) are going to go to town in the morning.

    _____

6. They are going to go to town in the morning.

    _____

7. Are you (plural) going swimming if it is a good day?

    _____

8. Is her/his friend going swimming if it is a good day?

    _____

9. We (exclusive) are going to eat at the restaurant at noon.

    _____

10. She/he is going to go eat at the restaurant at noon.

    _____

11. Are you (plural) going to the movie this afternoon?

    _____

12. Are they going to the movie this afternoon?

    _____

13. I'm going to go round-dancing tonight.

    _____

14. She/he is going round-dancing tonight.

_____

15. I usually lie down to go to sleep at midnight.

_____

16. She/he usually lies down to sleep at midnight.

_____

17. I'll come home before twilight.

_____

18. She/he is going to come home at twilight.

_____

19. Are you going canoeing this summer?

_____

20. Is she/he going canoeing this summer?

_____

4.4. Speaking about Time and the Days of the Week

ê-ispayik – _as it comes about_

This particle is needed to indicate the time on the clock; without it we would be telling about the duration of the activity under discussion. Use _ê-ispayik_ when the verb in the other clause is in the 1st or 2nd person, and use _ê-ispayiyik_ when the verb in the other clause is in the 3rd person.

Examples:

1st person subject in an independent clause in past tense:

nikî-waniskân kîkisêp têpakohp tipahikan ê-kî-ispayik.
I got up this past morning at seven o'clock.

2nd person subject in an independent clause in past tense:

kikî-waniskân cî kîsta kîkisêp têpakohp tipahikan ê-kî-ispayik?
Did you too get up this past morning at seven o'clock?

3rd person subject in an independent clause in past tense:

> kî-waniskâw kîkisêp têpakohp tipahikan ê-kî-ispayiyik.
> *She/he got up this past morning at seven o'clock.*

ê-akimiht – *it is counted*

This particle is used for identifying dates. The same rule as above applies here: use *ê-akimiht* when the verb in the other clause is in the 1st and 2nd person and in talking about the present date; use *ê-akimimiht* when the verb in the other clause is in the 3rd person.

Examples:

1st person subject in an independent clause in present tense:

> nitipiskên mâna nîsitanaw nêwosâp ê-akimiht ihkopîwi-pîsim.*
> *I have a birthday on the 24th of November.*

2nd person subject in an independent clause in present tense:

> kîko pîsim mâna ê-akimiht kitipiskên?
> *In which month do you have a birthday?*

3rd person subject in an independent clause in present tense (the month also needs to end in *wa*):

> tipiskam mâna nisîsim nikotwâsik ê-akimimiht nôcihitowi-pîsimwa.
> *My younger sibling has a birthday on September 6th.*

4.4.A. TEXT EXERCISES

In the following five short texts, the speaker is talking about his or her daily activities in 1st person. The questions following are in the 3rd person and the 2nd person.

Text 1
wîpac kîkisêp nikî-waniskân, nânitaw êtikwê nikotwâsik tipahikan **ê-kî-ispayik.**
I woke up early this morning, perhaps about six o'clock.

1. Question in 3rd person, answer in 3rd person:

> wîpac cî awa kî-waniskâw kîkisêp?
> *Did she/he wake up early this past morning?*

---

* *mâna* – "usually" is used in Cree quite regularly to indicate the Cree view that we only have this one day, that future days are not guaranteed.

Possible answers:
>âha, wîpac kî-waniskâw kîkisêp.
>*Yes, she/he woke up early this past morning.*

>namôya, namôya wîpac kî-waniskâw.*
>*No, she/he did not wake up early.*

2. Question in 2nd person, answer in 1st person:
>kiya mâka, wîpac cî kikî-waniskân kîkisêp?
>*How about you, did you wake up early this past morning?*

Possible answers:
>âha, wîpac nikî-waniskân kîkisêp.
>*Yes, I got up early this past morning.*

>namôya, namôya wîpac nikî-waniskân kîkisêp.
>*No, I did not get up early this past morning.*

3. Question in 3rd person, answer in 3rd person:
>tânitahto tipahikan ê-kî-ispayiyik kâ-kî-waniskât awa?
>*What time did she/he wake up?*

A: kî-waniskâw nânitaw êtikwê nikotwâsik tipahikan ê-kî-ispayiyik.
    She/he woke up about 6:00.

4. Question in 2nd person, answer in 1st person:
>kiya mâka, tânitahto tipahikan ê-kî-ispayik kâ-kî-waniskâyan?
>*How about you, what time did you wake up?*

A: nîsta nikî-waniskân nânitaw êtikwê nikotwâsik tipahikan kâ-kî-ispayik.
    I woke up about 6:00 too.

Text 2
nikî-papâsi-postayiwinisân ayisk êkâ ê-kî-nôhtê-mwêstasisiniyân.**
I got dressed in a hurry because I did not want to be late.

1. tânêhki awa kâ-kî-papâsi-postayiwinisêt?
   Why did she/he dress in a hurry?

A: kî-papâsi-postayiwinisêw ayisk êkâ ê-kî-nôhtê-mwêstasisinit.
    She/he dressed in a hurry because she/he did not want to be late.

---

* *namôya, namôya*: the first is "no"; the second negates the verb "she/he did not wake up early."
** *êkâ* – "not." This is the negative marker for verbs in the conjunct mood.

Text 3

nikî-nitawi-kiskinwahamâkosin nânitaw têpakohp tipahikan ê-kî-ispayik.
I went to school at about seven o'clock.

1. tânitahto tipahikan ê-kî-ispayiyik kâ-kî-nitawi-kiskinwahamâkosit awa?
   What time did she/he go to school?

   A: kî-nitawi-kiskinwahamâkosiw nânitaw têpakohp tipahikan ê-kî-ispayiyik.
        She/he went to school at about 7:00.

2. kiya mâka, tânitahto tipahikan ê-kî-ispayik kâ-kî-nitawi-kiskinwahamâkosiyan?
   How about you, what time did you go to school?

   A: nikî-nitawi-kiskinwahamâkosin nânitaw kêkâ-mitâtaht tipahikan ê-kî-ispayik.
        I went to school at about 9:00.

Text 4

nitakopayin mâna kihci-kiskinwahamâtowikamikohk nânitaw kêkâ-mitâtaht tipahikan mîna
   âpihtaw ê-ispayik.
I usually arrive at the university at about half past nine.

1. tânitahto tipahikan mâna ê-ispayiyik awa kâ-takopayit kihci-kiskinwahamâtowikamikohk?
   What time does she/he usually arrive at the university?

   A: takopayiw mâna kihci-kiskinwahamâtowikamikohk nânitaw kêkâ-mitâtaht tipahikan
        mîna âpihtaw ê-ispayiyik.
        She/he arrives at the university at about 9:30.

2. kiya mâka, tânitahto tipahikan mâna ê-ispayik kâ-takopayiyan kihci-kiskinwahamâtowikamikohk?
   How about you, what time do you usually arrive at the university?

   A: nîsta mâna nitakopayin kihci-kiskinwahamâtowikamikohk nânitaw kêkâ-mitâtaht
        tipahikan mîna âpihtaw ê-ispayik.
        I also usually arrive at the university at about 9:30.

Text 5

iyaw, kî-âpihtakahikâtêw iskwâhtêm. nikî-kanawâpamâw nipîsimohkânis.
Whoa, the door was locked. I looked at my watch.

kî-nikotwâso-kîsikâw êsa. namôya katâc ta-kî-kiskinwahamâkosiyân anohc!*
Apparently, it was Saturday. I didn't have to be in class today!

....

* *ta-kiskinwahamâkosiyân* – "to go to school." The *ta-* unit used here is as close to the English infinitive form we have in Cree.
   The English infinitives are not marked for subject or for tense. The Cree form, however, is marked for subject with the use
   of the verb endings that are used for verbs in the conjunct mood.

4.4.B. EXERCISES WITH TIME AND TIMES OF DAY

Use the space provided to draw figures for these units to help with understanding the text.
Use the following vocabulary to answer the questions (*answers are on page 263*).

Verbs:

wanisikâ	*get up*	postayawinisê	*put on clothes*
mîciso	*eat*	nîmihito	*dance*
sêsâwî	*exercise*	kisîpêkinastê	*bathe/shower*
nipa	*sleep*	nôhtêhkwasi	*be sleepy*

1. 6:00 ispayin kâ-kîkisêpâyâk

nikotwâsik tipahikan mâna ê-ispayiyik waniskâw.

Q: kiya mâka, tânitahto tipahikan mâna ê-ispayik kiwaniskân kâ-kîkisêpâyâk?

A: _____

_____

2. 6:30 ispayin kâ-kîkisêpâyâk

nikotwâsik tipahikan mîna-âpihtaw mâna ê-ispayiyik postayiwinisêw.

Q: kiya mâka, tânitahto tipahikan mâna ê-ispayik kipostayiwinisân kâ-kîkisêpâyâk?

A: _____

_____

3. 7:45 ispayin kâ-kîkisêpâyâk

niyânanosâp cipahikanis miyâskam ayinânêw tipahikan mâna ê-ispayiyik sêsâwîw.

Q: kiya mâka, tânitahto tipahikan mâna ê-ispayik kimîcison kâ-kîkisêpâyâk?

A: _____

_____

4. 8:15 ê-ispayik kâ-kîkisêpâyâk

niyânanosâp cipahikanis pâmwayês ayinânêw tipahikan mâna ê-ispayiyik mîcisow.

Q: kiya mâka, tânitahto tipahikan mâna ê-ispayik kisêsâwîn kâ-kîkisêpâyâk?

A: _____

_____

5. 9:00 ispayin kâ-tipiskâk

kêkâ-mitâtaht tipahikan mâna ê-ispayiyik kisîpêkinastêw.

Q: kiya mâka, tânitahto tipahikan mâna ê-ispayik kikisîpêkinastân?

A: _____

_____

6. 11:30 ispayin kâ-tipiskâk

pêyakosâp tipahikan mîna âpihtaw mâna ê-ispayiyik nitawi-nîmihitow.

Q: kiya mâka, tânitahto tipahikan mâna ê-ispayik kinitawi-nîmihiton kâ-tipiskâk?

A: _____

_____

7. 2:45 ispayin kâ-kîkisêpâyâk

niyânanosâp cipahikanis pâmwayês nisto tipahikan mâna ê-ispayiyik nôhtêhkwasiw.

Q: kiya mâka, tânitahto tipahikan mâna ê-ispayik kitati-nôhtêhkwasin?

A: _____

_____

8. 3:00 ispayin kâ-kîkisêpâyâk

nisto tipahikan kâ-kîkisêpâyâyik mâna ê-ispayiyik ati-nipâw.

Q: kiya mâka, tânitahto tipahikan mâna ê-ispayik kitati-nipân?

A: _____

_____

CHAPTER 5

• • • • • • • • • • • •

INTRANSITIVE VERBS

5.1. Animate Intransitive Verbs (VAI)

Animate intransitive verbs (VAI) are verbs that are common everyday activities and take no object in the sentence structure. The verb stems of VAIs come from the 2nd person singular form of the imperative.

5.1.A. VAI IMPERATIVES

Imperatives are orders or commands to do things; **negative imperatives** are orders or commands not to do things; and **delayed imperatives** are orders given now to be carried out at a later time. To complete the imperative forms of any VAI, the verb stem is placed in the blanks of the chart below.

Imperative		Negative Imperative		Delayed Imperative	
2	_____	2 êkâwiya _____		2	_____hkan
2P	_____k	2P êkâwiya _____k		2P	_____hkêk
21	_____tân	21 êkâwiya _____tân		21	_____hkahk

Complete the following chart with the imperative forms for 2 (2nd person singular *you*)
(*answers are on page 264*):

English	Imperative	Negative Imperative	Delayed Imperative
Wake up/Get up	waniskâ		
Pray		êkâwiya kâkîsimo	
Wash your face			kâsihkwêhkan
Get dressed	postayiwinisê		
Cook		êkâwiya piminawaso	
Be hungry			nôhtêhkatêhkan
Eat	mîciso		
Drink		êkâwiya minihkwê	
Get up/Stand up			pasikôhkan
Sit/Be at home		êkâwiya api	
Read	ayamihcikê		
Write		êkâwiya masinahikê	
Be sleepy			nôhtêhkwasihkan
Lie down		êkâwiya kawisimo	
Sleep	nipâ		

Complete the following chart with the imperative forms for 2P (2nd person plural *you*)
(*answers are on page 264*):

English	Imperative	Negative Imperative	Delayed Imperative
Wake up/Get up	waniskâk		
Pray		êkâwiya kâkîsimok	
Wash your face			kâsihkwêhkêk
Get dressed	postayiwinisêk		
Cook		êkâwiya piminawasok	
Be hungry			nôhtêhkatêhkêk
Eat	mîcisok		
Drink		êkâwiya minihkwêk	
Get up/Stand up			pasikôhkêk
Sit/Be at home		êkâwiya apik	
Read	ayamihcikêk		
Write		êkâwiya masinahikêk	
Be sleepy			nôhtêhkwasihkêk
Lie down		êkâwiya kawisimok	
Sleep	nipâk		

Complete the following chart with the imperative forms for 21 (2nd person inclusive *Let's*) (*answers are on page 265*):

English	Imperative	Negative Imperative	Delayed Imperative
Wake up/Get up	waniskâtân		
Pray		êkâwiya kâkîsimotân	
Wash your face			kâsihkwêhkahk
Get dressed	postayiwinisêtân		
Cook		êkâwiya piminawasotân	
Be hungry			nôhtêhkatêhkahk
Eat	mîcisotân		
Drink		êkâwiya minihkwêtân	
Get up/Stand up			pasikôhkahk
Sit/Be at home		êkâwiya apitân	
Read	ayamihcikêtân		
Write		êkâwiya masinahikêtân	
Be sleepy			nôhtêhkwasihkahk
Lie down		êkâwiya kawisimotân	
Sleep	nipâtân		

5.2. Animate Intransitive Verb Charts

Animate intransitive verbs (VAIS) are verbs of common everyday activities that take no object in their sentence structure. An example of a VAI is the verb *mîciso* "eat." You can say *nimîcison* "I eat" when you are stating that you are eating. If you say what you are eating then we have to use a transitive verb, depending on the animacy of the food. If the food is inanimate, like an egg, then you'd use the VTI-3* *mîci* "eat it." So we have *nimîcin wâwi* "I eat an egg." If the food is animate, then you'd use the transitive animate verb (VTA) *mow* "eat it." So we have *nimowâw kinosêw* "I eat fish."

More on transitive verbs later. Let's review how the VAIS work. Below is the verb *nipa* "sleep."

Verb Stem: *nipâ* "sleep"

Person and Tense	Indicative	Conjunct
1st present (pres)	ninipân	ê-nipâyân
1st past	nikî-nipân	ê-kî-nipâyân
1st future intentional (fut int)	niwî-nipân	ê-wî-nipâyân
1st future definite (fut def)	nika-nipân	
2nd pres	kinipân	ê-nipâyan
2nd past	kikî-nipân	ê-kî-nipâyan
2nd fut int	kiwî-nipân	ê-wî-nipâyan
2nd fut def	kika-nipân	
3rd pres	nipâw	ê-nipât
3rd past	kî-nipâw	ê-kî-nipât
3rd fut int	wî-nipâw	ê-wî-nipât
3rd fut def	ta-nipâw	
3' pres	nipâyiwa	ê-nipâyit
3' past	kî-nipâyiwa	ê-kî-nipâyit
3' fut int	wî-nipâyiwa	ê-wî-nipâyit
3' fut def	ta-nipâyiwa	
1P pres	ninipânân	ê-nipâyâhk
1P past	nikî-nipânân	ê-kî-nipâyâhk
1P fut int	niwî-nipânân	ê-wî-nipâyâhk
1P fut def	nika-nipânân	
21 pres	kinipânaw	ê-nipâyahk
21 past	kikî-nipânaw	ê-kî-nipâyahk
21 fut int	kiwî-nipânaw	ê-wî-nipâyahk
21 fut def	kika-nipânaw	
2P pres	kinipânâwâw	ê-nipâyêk
2P past	kikî-nipânâwâw	ê-kî-nipâyêk

---

* A VTI-3 is a transitive inanimate verb that follows the intransitive verb patterns, and doesn't end in *â*.

Person and Tense	Indicative	Conjunct
2P fut int	kiwî-nipânâwâw	ê-wî-nipâyêk
2P fut def	kika-nipânâwâw	
3P pres	nipâwak	ê-nipâcik
3P past	kî-nipâwak	ê-kî-nipâcik
3P fut int	wî-nipâwak	ê-wî-nipâcik
3P fut def	ta-nipâwak	

Below we have the verb *atoskê* "work." Two rules for VAIs apply here: 1) change every *ê* to *â* for 1st and 2nd persons in the indicative; and 2) use the connective *t* between person indicator and verb stem that begins with a vowel, in the present tense of 1st and 2nd person forms in the indicative.

Verb Stem: *atoskê* "work"

Person and Tense	Indicative	Conjunct
1st pres	nitatoskân	ê-atoskêyân
1st past	nikî-atoskân	ê-kî-atoskêyân
1st fut int	niwî-atoskân	ê-wî-atoskêyân
1st fut def	nika-atoskân	
2nd pres	kitatoskân	ê-atoskêyan
2nd past	kikî-atoskân	ê-kî-atoskêyan
2nd fut int	kiwî-atoskân	ê-wî-atoskêyan
2nd fut def	kika-atoskân	
3rd pres	atoskêw	ê-atoskêt
3rd past	kî-atoskêw	ê-kî-atoskêt
3rd fut int	wî-atoskêw	ê-wî-atoskêt
3rd fut def	ta-atoskêw	
3' pres	atoskêyiwa	ê-atoskêyit
3' past	kî-atoskêyiwa	ê-kî-atoskêyit
3' fut int	wî-atoskêyiwa	ê-wî-atoskêyit
3' fut def	ta-atoskêyiwa	
1P pres	nitatoskânân	ê-atoskêyâhk
1P past	nikî-atoskânân	ê-kî-atoskêyâhk
1P fut int	niwî-atoskânân	ê-wî-atoskêyâhk
1P fut def	nika-atoskânân	
21 pres	kitatoskânaw	ê-atoskêyahk
21 past	kikî-atoskânaw	ê-kî-atoskêyahk
21 fut int	kiwî-atoskânaw	ê-wî-atoskêyahk
21 fut def	kika-atoskânaw	
2P pres	kitatoskânâwâw	ê-atoskêyêk
2P past	kikî-atoskânâwâw	ê-kî-atoskêyêk
2P fut int	kiwî-atoskânâwâw	ê-wî-atoskêyêk

Person and Tense	Indicative	Conjunct
2P fut def	kika-atoskânâwâw	
3P pres	atoskêwak	ê-atoskêcik
3P past	kî-atoskêwak	ê-kî-atoskêcik
3P fut int	wî-atoskêwak	ê-wî-atoskêcik
3P fut def	ta-atoskêwak	

5.2.A. EXERCISES WITH VAIS

Complete the following chart with the indicative and conjunct forms of the verb stems provided (*answers are on page 265*):

Verb Stem (comes from the 2 of the imperative)	Person and Tense	Indicative	Conjunct
2 wâniskâ – *get up*			
	1st pres		
2P waniskâk – *get up*			
	1st past		
21 waniskâtân – *let's get up*			
	1st fut int		
	1st fut def		
2 kîkisêpâ-mîciso – *eat breakfast*	2nd pres		
2P	2nd past		
21	2nd fut int		
	2nd fut def		

Verb Stem (comes from the 2 of the imperative)	Person and Tense	Indicative	Conjunct
2 itohtê – *go*	3rd pres		
2P	3rd past		
21	3rd fut int		
	3rd fut def		
2 kiskinwahamâkosi – *go/be in class*	3' pres		
2P	3' past		
21	3' fut int		
	3' fut def		
2 âpihtâ-kîsikani-mîciso – *eat lunch*	1P pres		
2P	1P past		
21	1P fut int		
	1P fut def		

Verb Stem (comes from the 2 of the imperative)	Person and Tense	Indicative	Conjunct
2 kîwê – *go home*	21 pres		
2P	21 past		
21	21 fut int		
	21 fut def		
2 otâkwani-mîciso – *eat supper*	2P pres		
2P	2P past		
21	2P fut int		
	2P fut def		
2 kawisimo – *lie down (to sleep)*	3P pres		
2P	3P past		
21	3P fut int		
	3P fut def		

5.2.B. VAI CONJUGATIONS

Part 1

Complete the following conjugations by first finding the verb stems in each row and then making the transformations to the imperatives in each column (*answers are on page 266*).

Subject/Actor		Imperative	Negative Imperative	Delayed Imperative
2	you (sg)	nipâ – *sleep*		
2P	you (pl)		êkâwiya pimipâhtâk – *Don't run!*	
21	Let's (you and I)			atoskêhkahk – *let's work (later)*
2	you (sg)		êkâwiya mêtawê – *don't play*	
2P	you (pl)			masinahikêhkêk – *write (later)*
21	Let's (you and I)	ayamihcikêtân – *let's read*		
2	you (sg)			mîcisohkan – *eat (later)*
2P	you (pl)	sêsâwîk – *exercise*		
21	Let's (you and I)		êkâwiya minihkwêtân – *let's not drink*	

Complete the following indicative and conjunct forms in the charts below (*answers are on page 267*).

Singular subject

Subject/Actor		Indicative	Conjunct
		atoskê – "work," present tense	*api* – "sit/be at home," past tense
1	I	nitatoskân	
2	you		ê-kî-apiyan
3	she/he		
3'	her/his (friend)	atoskêyiwa	

Plural subject

Subject/Actor		Indicative	Conjunct
		mêtawê – "play," future definite tense (with preverb *nôhtê-* – "want to")	*waniskâ* – "get up," future intentional tense
1P	we (excl)		ê-wî-waniskâyâhk
21	we (incl)	kika-nôhtê-mêtawânaw	
2P	you (pl)		
3P	they	ta-nôhtê-mêtawêwak	

Part 2

Using the verbs from the conjugations in Part 1, along with the following vocabulary words, translate the sentences below (*answers are on page 267*):

Preverbs

kakwê-	*try to*
miyo-	*good*
nitawi-	*go and*

Kinship

nistês	*my older brother*
nimis	*my older sister*
nisîmis	*my younger sibling*
osîmisa	*her/his younger sibling*
otôtêmiwâwa	*their friends*

Nouns

pihkahtêwâpoy	*coffee*

Temporal Words

wîpac	*early/soon*
kîkisêpâyâki	*in the morning*
tipiskohk	*last night*
otâkosîhk	*yesterday*
otâkosiki	*in the evening*
tipiskâki	*tonight*
wâpahki	*tomorrow*
kîkisêp	*this past morning*
anohc	*today*

1. tipiskohk kî-miyo-nipâw nistês.

   _____

2. wîpac kîkisêpâyâki kakwê-waniskâhkan.

   _____

3. tipiskohk nikî-miyo-ayamihcikân.

   _____

4. otâkosiki kika-nitawi-sêsâwînaw.

   _____

5. tipiskâki ta-miyo-pimipâhtâwak nimis êkwa nisîmis.

   _____

6. nika-nitawi-atoskânân wîpac wâpahki.

   _____

7. kî-miyo-mêtawêyiwa osîmisa tipiskohk.

_____

8. wîpac cî kiwî-mîcison anohc?

_____

9. kikî-minihkwânâwâw cî pihkahtêwâpoy kîkisêp?

_____

10. kakwê-masinahikêyiwa otôtêmiwâwa.

_____

5.3. VAI Paradigms

Along with the imperatives, the VAIs can be conjugated into various forms by building on the verb stem (taken from the 2 imperative form). By placing the verb stem in the blanks in the paradigm below, the indicative, the conjunct, and the future conditional forms for each verb are created.

VAI—Indicative, Conjunct, and Future Conditional Forms

	Indicative	Conjunct	Future Conditional
1	ni_____n	ê-_____yân	_____yâni
2	ki_____n	ê-_____yan	_____yani
3	_____w	ê-_____t	_____ci
3′	_____yiwa	ê-_____yit	_____yici
1P	ni_____nân	ê-_____yâhk	_____yâhki
21	ki_____naw	ê-_____yahk	_____yahki
2P	ki_____nâwâw	ê-_____yêk	_____yêko
3P	_____wak	ê-_____cik	_____twâwi
3′P	_____yiwa	ê-_____yit	_____yici

There are a couple of rules to follow:

1. when the verb stem ends in *ê*, that *ê* must change to *â* in the indicative mood for the 1st and 2nd persons; and

2. when the verb stem (or preverb) begins with a vowel, then a *t* must connect the person indicator to the verb stem (or preverb), but this applies only in the present tense of the indicative mood.

Tense indicators apply to all verbs for the indicative and conjunct forms. The future definite form is not used in the conjunct form.

Past:	*kî-*
Future Intentional:	*wî-*
Future Definite:	*ka-* for 1st and 2nd person actors
	ta- for 3rd person actors

Sentence Structure for All Verb Forms

person indicator + tense indicator + preverb + verb stem + ending

The following examples show some of these common activities in the various tenses:

Present tense: There is no tense indicator for the present tense.

pê-itohtêwak.	*They are coming.*
kawisimow.	*She/he is going to bed.*
niwaniskân.	*I am getting up.*
kititohtân cî sâkahikanihk?	*Do you go to the lake?*
nipapâmi-pîcicînân.	*We (excl) go about round-dancing.*
kikakwê-nihtâ-nêhiyawânaw.	*We (incl) try to speak Cree well.*
kipê-kiyokânâwâw cî?	*Are you (pl) coming to visit?*

Past tense: The past tense indicator for all verbs is *kî-*, indicating that an event has already happened.

kî-pê-itohtêwak otâkosîhk.	*They came yesterday.*
kî-kawisimow wîpac tipiskohk.	*She/he went to bed early last night.*
ni**kî**-waniskân wîpac kîkisêp.	*I got up early this past morning.*
ki**kî**-itohtân cî sâkahikanihk nîpinohk?	*Did you go to the lake last summer?*
ni**kî**-papâmi-pîcicînân piponohk.	*We (excl) went about round-dancing last winter.*
ki**kî**-kakwê-nêhiyawânaw otâhk ispayiw.	*We (incl) tried to speak Cree last week.*
ki**kî**-pê-kiyokânâwâw cî otâhk askîwin?	*Did you (pl) come visit last year?*

Future definite tense: The future definite tense indicators are *ka-* (for 1st and 2nd persons) and *ta-* (for 3rd persons).

ta-pê-itohtêwak wâpahki.	*They will come tomorrow.*
ta-kawisimow wîpac tipiskâki.	*She/he will go to bed early tonight.*
ni**ka**-waniskân wîpac kîkisêpâyâki.	*I will get up early in the morning.*
ki**ka**-itohtân cî sâkahikanihk nîpihki?	*Will you go to the lake this summer?*
ni**ka**-papâmi-pîcicînân pipohki.	*We* (excl) *will go about round-dancing this winter.*
ki**ka**-kakwê-nêhiyawânaw anohc ispayiki.	*We* (incl) *will try to speak Cree this week.*
ki**ka**-pê-kiyokânâwâw cî anohc askîwiki.	*Will you* (pl) *come visit this year?*

Future intentional tense: The future intentional tense marker is *wî-* and refers to events that are going to happen.

wî-pê-itohtêwak wâpahki.	*They are going to be coming tomorrow.*
wî-kawisimow wîpac tipiskâki.	*She/he is going to bed early tonight.*
ni**wî**-waniskân wîpac kîkisêpâyâki.	*I am going to get up early in the morning.*
ki**wî**-itohtân cî sâkahikanihk nîpihki?	*Are you going to the lake this summer?*
ni**wî**-papâmi-pîcicînân pipohki.	*We* (excl) *are going to go about round-dancing this winter.*
ki**wî**-kakwê-nêhiyawânaw anohc ispayiki.	*We* (incl) *are going to try to speak Cree this week.*
ki**wî**-pê-kiyokânâwâw cî anohc askîwiki.	*Are you* (pl) *going to come visit this year?*

5.3.A. SOME ACTIVITIES

Season – ispîhtaskîwina

sîkwan.	*It is spring.*
nîpin.	*It is summer.*
takwâkin.	*It is fall.*
pipon.	*It is winter.*

Rules for going from indicative to conjunct:

1. At the beginning of the indicative forms, use any of the conjunct indicators: *ê-* (for a subordinate clause after *because*); *kâ-* (for a relative clause); *ta-kî-* (for modals *can, could, would, should*); *ta-* (for an infinitive clause); and

2. Drop the final letter, then add *-hk* (*-k* in *takwâkin*).

Questions: Keep the question form when you ask about the other seasons.

tânisi mâna kâ-itahkamikisiyan ispîhk <u>kâ-sîkwahk</u>?
What do you do when it is spring?

_____kâ-nîpihk?
What do you do when it is summer?

_____kâ-takwâkik?
What do you do when it is fall?

_____kâ-pipohk?
What do you do when it is winter?

Possible answers: Begin with the activity in the indicative (usually a VAI), followed by the last part of the question.

nisâh-sêsâwohtân mâna ispîhk kâ-sîkwahk.
I usually go walking for exercise when it is spring.

nikâh-kwâskwêpicikân mâna ispîhk kâ-nîpihk.
I usually go fishing when it is summer.

nimâh-mâcîn mâna ispîhk kâ-takwâkik.
I usually go hunting when it is fall.

niyâh-yahki-sôskoyâpawin mâna ispîhk kâ-pipohk.
I usually go cross-country skiing when it is winter.

Note: There are two types of reduplication in Cree:

1. For recurring, repeated, or intermittent actions, reduplicate the first consonant, followed by a long *â* and an *h*.

    e.g., nimâh-mîcison – *I eat (again and again; here and there).*

    Use *âh-* when the verb starts with a vowel.

    e.g., api – *sit/be at home* → nitâh-apin. – *I am at home (now and then).*

2. For ongoing actions, reduplicate the first consonant followed by a short *a*.

    e.g., nima-mîcison – *I am eating (for some time).*

    Use *ay* when the verb starts with a vowel.

    e.g., api – *sit/be at home* → nitay-apin. – *I sit/am home (currently).*

Days of the Week

ayamihêwi-kîsikâw.	*It is Sunday.*
pêyako-kîsikâw.	*It is Monday.*
nîso-kîsikâw.	*It is Tuesday.*
nisto-kîsikâw.	*It is Wednesday.*
nêwo-kîsikâw.	*It is Thursday.*
niyânano-kîsikâw.	*It is Friday.*
nikotwâso-kîsikâw.	*It is Saturday.*

Rules for going from indicative to conjunct:

1. At the beginning of the indicative forms, use any of the conjunct indicators: *ê-* (for a subordinate clause after *because*); *kâ-* (for a relative clause); *ta-kî-* (for modals *can, could, would, should*); *ta-* (for an infinitive clause);

2. Drop the final letter, then add *-k*.

3. For future conditional forms, drop the conjunct markers of the conjunct forms and add *-i* at the end.

    e.g., ê-nîso-kîsikâk – *as it is Tuesday* → nîso-kîsikâki – *on Tuesday.*

Questions: Keep the question form but change the day of the week.

tânisi mâna kâ-itahkamikisiyan ispîhk <u>kâ-ayamihêwi-kîsikâk</u>?
What do you do when it is Sunday?

_____kâ-pêyako-kîsikâk?
What do you do when it is Monday?

_____kâ-nîso-kîsikâk?
What do you do when it is Tuesday?

_____kâ-nisto-kîsikâk?
What do you do when it is Wednesday?

_____kâ-nêwo-kîsikâk?
What do you do when it is Thursday?

_____kâ-niyânano-kîsikâk?
What do you do when it is Friday?

_____kâ-nikotwâso-kîsikâk?
What do you do when it is Saturday?

Possible answers: Begin with the indicative, followed by the last part of the question.

nisâh-sêsâwohtân mâna ispîhk kâ-ayamihêwi-kîsikâk.
I usually go walking for exercise when it is Sunday.

ninâh-nitawi-kiskinwahamâkosin mâna ispîhk kâ-pêyako-kîsikâk.
I usually go to school when it is Monday.

nikâh-kanawâpahtên mâna cikâstêpayihcikana cikâstêpayihcikêwikamikohk
   ispîhk kâ-nîso-kîsikâk.
I usually go watch movies at the theatre when it is Tuesday.

nitâh-atoskân mâna ispîhk kâ-nisto-kîsikâk.
I usually work when it is Wednesday.

nikâh-kiskinwahamâkosin mâna nêhiyawêwin ispîhk kâ-nêwo-kîsikâk.
I am learning Cree when it is Thursday.

ninâh-nitawi-nikamon mâna minihkwêwikamikohk ispîhk kâ-niyânano-kîsikâk.
I go singing at the bar when it is Friday.

ninâh-nitawi-papâmi-atâwân mâna ispîhk kâ-nikotwâso-kîsikâk.
I go shopping when it is Saturday.

Temporal Units

wawâninâkwan.	*It is dusk.*
wâpan.	*It is dawn.*
kîsikâw.	*It is day.*
wâpahki	*tomorrow*
kîkisêp	*This past morning*
kîkisêpâyâw.	*It is morning.*
âpihtâ-kîsikâw.	*It is noon.*
pôni-âpihtâ-kîsikâw.	*It is afternoon.*
otâkosin.	*It is evening.*
tipiskâw.	*It is night.*
otâkosîhk	*yesterday*
pôni-âpihtâ-tipiskâki	*after midnight*
tipiskohk	*last night*
tipiskâki	*tonight*

Rules for going from indicative to conjunct:

1. At the beginning of the indicative forms, use any of the conjunct indicators.

2. Drop the final letter, then add *-hk* if the remaining vowel is short (except *otâkosin*); add *-k* if the remaining vowel is long.

3. Drop the conjunct indicator, then add *-i* to make future conditionals.

    e.g., wâpan – *It is dawn.* → ê-wâpahk – *as it is dawn* → wâpahki – *tomorrow (if it is dawn)*

    kîkisêpâyâw – *It is morning.* → ê-kîkisêpâyâk – *as it is morning* →
    kîkisêpâyâki – *in the morning (if it is morning).*

4. *kîkisêp, otâkosîhk, tipiskohk* cannot undergo changes.

Questions: Keep the question form but change the time of day.

tânisi mâna kâ-itahkamikisiyan ispîhk <u>kâ-kîkisêpâyâk</u>?
What do you do when it is morning?

_____kâ-âpihtâ-kîsikâk?
What do you do when it is noon?

_____kâ-pôni-âpihtâ-kîsikâk?
What do you do when it is afternoon?

_____kâ-otâkosik?
What do you do when it is evening?

_____kâ-tipiskâk?
What do you do when it is night?

Possible answers: Begin with the indicative, followed by the last part of the question.

nimâh-minihkwân mâna pihkahtêwâpoy ispîhk kâ-kîkisêpâyâk.
I usually drink coffee when it is morning.

nitâh-âpihtâ-kîsikani-mîcison mâna ispîhk kâ-âpihtâ-kîsikâk.
I usually eat lunch when it is noon.

nikâh-kanawâpahtên mâna cikâstêpayihcikanis ispîhk kâ-pôni-âpihtâ-kîsikâk.
I usually watch television when it is afternoon.

nisâh-sêsâwipahtân mâna ispîhk kâ-otâkosik.
I usually jog when it is evening.

ninâh-nitohtên mâna nêhiyaw-âcimowina ispîhk kâ-tipiskâk.
I usually listen to Cree stories when it is night.

Questions about future events: Keep the question form but change the time of day (or you can use seasons).

tânisi kâ-wî-itahkamikisiyan wâpahki?
What are you going to do tomorrow?

_____tipiskâki?
What are you going to do tonight?

_____otâkosiki?
What are you going do this evening?

_____nîpihki?
What are you going to do this coming summer?

Possible answers: Begin with the activity in the indicative (usually a VAI), followed by the last part of the question.

niwî-sa-sêsâwohtân wâpahki.
I am going to go walking for exercise tomorrow.

niwî-ay-ayamihcikân tipiskâki.
I am going to read tonight.

niwî-ma-masinahikân otâkosiki.
I am going to write this evening.

niwî-papâmi-mânokân nîpihki.
I am going to go camping this summer.

Questions about past events: Keep the question form but change the time of day (or you can use a past season).

> **tânisi kâ-kî-itahkamikisiyan** otâkosîhk?
> *What did you do yesterday?*

> _____tipiskohk?
> *What did you do last night?*

> _____kîkisêp?
> *What did you do this past morning?*

> _____piponohk?
> *What did you do last winter?*

Possible answers: Begin with the activity in the indicative (usually a VAI), followed by the last part of the question.

> nikî-sa-sêsâwohtân otâkosîhk.
> *I went walking for exercise yesterday.*

> nikî-ay-ayamihcikân tipiskohk.
> *I read last night.*

> nikî-ma-masinahikân kîkisêp.
> *I wrote this past morning.*

> nikî-sâh-sôniskwâtahikân piponohk.
> *I skated last winter.*

5.3.B. SELF-TEST

A. Fill in the blanks (answers are on page 267):

Numbers

Base Numbers	Add *-osâp* or *-sâp* for units 11–19	Add *–omitanaw* for units of ten from 20–100
pêyak – 1	pêyakosâp – 11	mitâtaht – 10
nîso – 2		nîs(om)itanaw – 20
nisto – 3	nistosâp – 13	
nêwo – 4		nê(wo)mitanaw – 40
niyânan – 5		
nikotwâsik – 6	nikotwâs(ik)osâp – 16	
têpakohp – 7		têpakohpomitanaw – 70
ayinânêw – 8	ayinânêwosâp – 18	
kêkâ-mitâtaht – 9	kêkâ-mitâtahtosâp – 19 *or* kêkâ-nîsitanaw	
mitâtaht – 10		mitâtahtomitanaw – 100

B. Check the best possible answer or fill in the correct blanks to the following questions (answers are on page 268):

1. tânisi?

   a) _____ namôya nânitaw, kiya mâka?

   b) _____ namôya nânitaw, niya mâka?

   c) _____ namoya nanitaw, kiya mâka?

2. Solomon nitisiyihkâson. kiya mâka, tânisi kitisiyihkâson?

   a) _____ kitisiyihkâson.

   b) _____ nitisiyihkason.

   c) _____ nitisiyihkâson.

3. Stanley Mission ohci niya kayahtê. kiya mâka, tânitê ohci kiya kayahtê?

   a) _____ ohci kiya kayahtê.

   b) _____ ohci niya kayahtê.

   c) _____ ochi niya kayahtê.

4. Regina mêkwâc niwîkin. kiya mâka, tânitê mêkwâc kiwîkin?

   a) _____ mêkwâc kiwîkin.

   b) _____ mêkwâc niwîkin.

   c) _____ mêkwâc nîsta Regina niwîkin.

5. nikotwâsikomitanaw têpakohposâp nititahtopiponân. kiya mâka, tânitahtopiponêyan?

   a) _____ wiya itahtopiponêw.

   b) _____ kiya kititahtopiponân.

   c) _____ niya nititahtopiponân.

6. nîsitanaw nistosâp ê-akimiht ihkopîwi-pîsim mâna kâ-tipiskamân. kiya mâka tânispîhk mâna kâ-tipiskaman? (*Put your information on the correct form.*)

   a) _____ ê-akimiht _____ mâna kâ-tipiskaman.

   b) _____ ê-akimiht _____ mâna kâ-tipiskamân.

7. kîko pîsim mêkwâc ê-akimiht?

   a) _____ kisê-pîsim   g) _____ paskowi-pîsim

   b) _____ mikisiwi-pîsim   h) _____ ohpahowi-pîsim

   c) _____ niski-pîsim   i) _____ takwâki-pîsim

   d) _____ ayîki-pîsim   j) _____ pinâskowi-pîsim

   e) _____ sâkipakâwi-pîsim   k) _____ ihkopîwi-pîsim

   f) _____ pâskâwihowi-pîsim   l) _____ pawâcakinasîsi-pîsim

8. tâniyikohk akimâw awa pîsim?

   a) _____ akimâw ana pîsim.

   b) _____ akimâw awa pîsim.

   c) _____ ê-akimiht kisê-pîsim.

C. Put the following seasons into the conjunct and future conditional forms
(answers are on page 267):

Seasons – ispîhtaskîwina

Last Season	Present Season	Future Season
	Done in the indicative; provide the conjunct form	Provide the future conditional form
sîkwanohk – *last spring*	sîkwan – *It is spring.*	
miyoskamîhk – *last spring (ice break-up)*	miyoskamin – *It is spring.*	
nîpinohk – *last summer*	nîpin – *It is summer.*	
takwâkohk – *last fall/autumn*	takwâkin – *It is fall/autumn.*	
mikiskohk – *last fall/ autumn (ice freeze-up)*	mikiskon – *It is fall/autumn.*	
piponohk – *last winter*	pipon – *It is winter.*	

D. Put the days of the week into the conjunct and future conditional forms (answers are on page 268):

Indicative	Conjunct	Future Conditional
	use ê- or kâ-	
ayamihêwi-kîsikâw – *It is Sunday.*		
pêyako-kîsikâw – *It is Monday.*		
nîso-kîsikâw – *It is Tuesday.*		
nisto-kîsikâw – *It is Wednesday.*		
nêwo-kîsikâw – *It is Thursday.*		
niyânano-kîsikâw – *It is Friday.*		
nikotwâso-kîsikâw – *It is Saturday.*		

E. Choose the correct answers for each of these seasons (answers are on page 268):

1. ispîhk mâna kâ-sîkwahk ôki pîsimwak akimâwak
   When it is spring, these are the months:

   a) _____ pâskâwihowi-pîsim, paskowi-pîsim êkwa ohpahowi-pîsim

   b) _____ niski-pîsim, ayîki-pîsim, êkwa sâkipakâwi-pîsim

   c) _____ takwâki-pîsim, pinâskowi-pîsim êkwa ihkopîwi-pîsim

   d) _____ pawâcakinasîsi-pîsim, kisê-pîsim êkwa mikisiwi-pîsim

2. ispîhk mâna kâ-nîpihk ôki pîsimwak akimâwak

When it is summer, these are the months:

a) _____ niski-pîsim, ayîki-pîsim, êkwa sâkipakâwi-pîsim

b) _____ takwâki-pîsim, pinâskowi-pîsim êkwa ihkopîwi-pîsim

c) _____ pawâcakinasîsi-pîsim, kisê-pîsim êkwa mikisiwi-pîsim

d) _____ pâskâwihowi-pîsim, paskowi-pîsim êkwa ohpahowi-pîsim

3. ispîhk mâna kâ-takwâkik ôki pîsimwak akimâwak

When it is fall, these are the months:

a) _____ takwâki-pîsim, pinâskowi-pîsim êkwa ihkopîwi-pîsim

b) _____ niski-pîsim, ayîki-pîsim, êkwa sâkipakâwi-pîsim

c) _____ pâskâwihowi-pîsim, paskowi-pîsim êkwa ohpahowi-pîsim

d) _____ pawâcakinasîsi-pîsim, kisê-pîsim êkwa mikisiwi-pîsim

4. ispîhk mâna kâ-pipohk ôki pîsimwak akimâwak

When it is winter, these are the months:

a) _____ niski-pîsim, ayîki-pîsim, êkwa sâkipakâwi-pîsim.

b) _____ pawâcakinasîsi-pîsim, kisê-pîsim êkwa mikisiwi-pîsim.

c) _____ pâskâwihowi-pîsim, paskowi-pîsim êkwa ohpahowi-pîsim.

d) _____ takwâki-pîsim, pinâskowi-pîsim êkwa ihkopîwi-pîsim.

5. ispîhk mâna kâ-sîkwahk

When it's spring:

a) _____ kâh-kitowak piyêsiwak, kâh-kisâstêw, êkwa kâh-kimiwan.

b) _____ nîpiya pahkihtinwa, ati-tâh-tahkâyâw, wîpac ta-pipon.

c) _____ tâh-tahkâyâw, mâh-mispon êkwa âskaw pâh-pîwan.

d) _____ tâh-tihkitêw, sâh-sâkipakâw, wâpikwaniya ohpikinwa.

6. ispîhk mâna kâ-nîpihk
When it's summer:

a) _____ nîpiya pahkihtinwa, ati-tâh-tahkâyâw, wîpac ta-pipon.

b) _____ tâh-tihkitêw, sâh-sâkipakâw, wâpikwaniya ohpikinwa.

c) _____ kâh-kitowak piyêsiwak, kâh-kisâstêw, êkwa kâh-kimiwan.

d) _____ tâh-tahkâyâw, mâh-mispon êkwa âskaw pâh-pîwan.

7. ispîhk mâna kâ-takwâkik
When it's fall:

a) _____ tâh-tihkitêw, sâh-sâkipakâw, wâpikwaniya ohpikinwa.

b) _____ kâh-kitowak piyêsiwak, kâh-kisâstêw, êkwa kâh-kimiwan.

c) _____ nîpiya pahkihtinwa, ati-tâh-tahkâyâw, wîpac ta-pipon.

d) _____ tâh-tahkâyâw, mâh-mispon êkwa âskaw pâh-pîwan.

8. ispîhk mâna kâ-pipohk
When it's winter:

a) _____ tâh-tihkitêw, sâh-sâkipakâw, wâpikwaniya ohpikinwa.

b) _____ nîpiya pahkihtinwa, ati-tâh-tahkâyâw, wîpac ta-pipon.

c) _____ kâh-kitowak piyêsiwak, kâh-kisâstêw, êkwa kâh-kimiwan.

d) _____ tâh-tahkâyâw, mâh-mispon êkwa âskaw pâh-pîwan.

F. Answer the following questions *(answers are on page 268):*

1. ispîhk mâna kâ-sîkwahk nicîhkêyihtên ta-papâmi-tihtipiskamân cihcipayapisikanis.

Q: kiya mâka?

A: _____

2. ispîhk mâna kâ-sîkwaniyik cîhkêyihtam nistês ta-papâmi-tihtipiskahk cihcipayapisikanis.

Q: cîhkêyihtam cî nistês ta-papâmi-tihtipiskahk cihcipayapisikanis ispîhk kâ-sîkwaniyik?

A: _____

3. ispîhk mâna kâ-nîpihk nicîhkêyihtên ta-papâmiskâyân.

    Q: kiya mâka?

    A: _____

4. ispîhk mâna kâ-nîpiniyik cîhkêyihtam nimis ta-papâmiskât.

    Q: cîhkêyihtam cî nimis ta-papâmiskât ispîhk kâ-nîpiniyik?

    A: _____

5. ispîhk mâna kâ-takwâkik nicîhkêyihtên ta-papâmi-sêsâwohtêyân.

    Q: kiya mâka?

    A: _____

6. ispîhk mâna kâ-takwâkiniyik cîhkêyihtam nimosôm ta-papâmi-sêsâwohtêt.

    Q: cîhkêyihtam cî nimosôm ta-papâmi-sêsâwohtêt ispîhk kâ-takwâkiniyik?

    A: _____

7. ispîhk mâna kâ-pipohk nicîhkêyihtên ta-yahki-sôskoyâpawiyân.

    Q: kiya mâka?

    A: _____

8. ispîhk mâna kâ-piponiyik cîhkêyihtam nisîmis ta-yahki-sôskoyâpawit.

    Q: cîhkêyihtam cî nisîmis ta-yahki-sôskoyâpawit ispîhk kâ-piponiyik?

    A: _____

G. Read the texts carefully for meaning, then answer the questions (answers are on page 269):

ispîhk kâ-kîkisêpâyâk – *when it is morning*

1. waniskâw awa môswa têpakohp tipahikan ê-ispayiyik.
   This moose wakes up at 7:00.

   a) tânitahto tipahikan mâna ê-ispayiyik kâ-waniskât awa môswa?

   _____

   b) kiya mâka, tânitahto tipahikan mâna ê-ispayik kâ-waniskâyan?

   _____

2. ati-kîsitêpow awa môswa têpakohp tipahikan mîna âpihtaw ê-ispayiyik.
   This moose starts to cook at 7:30.

   a) tânitahto tipahikan mâna ê-ispayiyik kâ-ati-kîsitêpot awa môswa?

   _____

   b) kiya mâka, tânitahto tipahikan mâna ê-ispayik kâ-ati-kîsitêpoyan?

   _____

3. kîkisêpâ-mîcisow awa môswa niyânanosâp cipahikanis pâmwayês ayinânêw tipahikan ê-ispayiyik.
   This moose eats breakfast at 7:45.

   a) tânitahto tipahikan mâna ê-ispayiyik kâ-kîkisêpâ-mîcisot awa môswa?

   _____

   b) kiya mâka, tânitahto tipahikan mâna ê-ispayik kâ-kîkisêpâ-mîcisoyan?

   _____

4. kîsi-kiskinwahamâkosiw awa môswa nîsitanaw cipahikanis miyâskam kêkâ-mitâtaht tipahikan ê-ispayiyik.
   This moose finishes class at 9:20.

   a) tânitahto tipahikan mâna ê-ispayiyik kâ-kîsi-kiskinwahamâkosit awa môswa?

   _____

   b) kiya mâka, tânitahto tipahikan mâna ê-ispayik kâ-kîsi-kiskinwahamâkosiyan?

   _____

5. ati-nipâw awa môswa nânitaw pêyakosâp tipahikan ê-ispayiyik.
This moose starts to sleep about 11:00.

a) tânitahto tipahikan mâna ê-ispayiyik kâ-ati-nipât awa môswa?

_____

b) kiya mâka, tânitahto tipahikan mâna ê-ispayik kâ-ati-nipâyan? .

_____

5.4. Indefinite Actor Verb Forms for VAIS and VTAS

Indefinite actor verb forms talk about an activity, but the actor, or actors, is not mentioned.

Indefinite Actor Forms for VAIs

Rules:

Indicative

TH-Cree: verb stem + nâniwin e.g., mîcisonâniwin – *there is eating (happening)*
Y-Cree: verb stem + nâniwiw e.g., mîcisonâniwiw – *there is eating (happening)*

Conjunct

TH-Cree: verb stem + nâniwik e.g., î-mîcisonâniwik – *there is eating (happening)*
Y-Cree: verb stem + hk e.g., ê-mîcisohk – *there is eating (happening)*

Indefinite Actor Forms for VTAs

VTAS use *-ikaw*. This is the inverse form for the indefinite actor subject, who is not named but who is the animate object of the sentence. Add *-ikawi* to VTA stems, and then conjugate them into the verb paradigm, as in the following example:

VTA stem *wâpam* – "see someone"

niwâpamikawin	*I am seen.*	ê-wâpamikawiyân
kiwâpamikawin	*you are seen*	ê-wâpamikawiyan
wâpamikawiw	*she/he is seen*	ê-wâpamikawit
wâpamikawiyiwa	*her/his _____ is seen*	ê-wâpamikawiyit
niwâpamikawinân	*we (excl) are seen*	ê-wâpamikawiyâhk
kiwâpamikawinaw	*we (incl) are seen*	ê-wâpamikawiyahk
kiwâpamikawinâwaw	*you (pl) are seen*	ê-wâpamikawiyêk
wâpamikawiwak	*they are seen*	ê-wâpamikawicik

5.5. Subordinate Clauses

Subordinate clauses in Cree can take on various forms depending on the situation at the time of the utterance. For convenience, we will call these the *ê*-form, the *kâ*-form, the *ta*-form, the *ta-kî*-form, and the future conditional form. However, before we go into each of these in detail, let's look at a sentence in Cree that has an independent clause followed by a subordinate clause.

> (nikî-wâpamâw [nâpêw) ê-pimohtêt mêskanâhk].
> *I saw a man walking along the road.*

The first clause, marked in parentheses ( ), is the independent clause, and as such can stand on its own to form a meaningful sentence: *nikî-wâpamâw nâpêw* "I saw a man." The verb form is in the indicative mood as it offers new information to open the conversation.

The sentence has the transitive animate verb (VTA) *wâpam* with a first person (I) subject *ni-_____âw* and is in the past tense *kî-*, followed by a singular object *nâpêw*. Had we a plural object *nâpêwak* "men," then the verb, being a VTA, would also reflect that plurality by adding *-ak* to the end: *nikî-wâpamâwak nâpêwak* "I saw men."

The plural object affects not only the verb in its indicative form but also the verb in the subordinate clause. Furthermore, the plural object can only happen in the 1st and 2nd person forms of the paradigm (objects of the 3rd person forms are marked for obviation by adding *-a* at the end of the noun).

The second clause, marked in square brackets [ ], is the subordinate clause, shown in the *ê*-form of the animate intransitive verb (VAI): *nâpêw ê-pimohtêt mêskanâhk* "the man walking along the road." The verb form is in the conjunct mood, or *ê*-form, because it provides information that is dependent on the previous utterance to make sense. On its own it leaves the listener with incomplete information. In other words, *nâpêw ê-pimohtêt mêskanâhk* requires more information to be given before it is a complete thought; thus it is a subordinate clause. It depends on the independent clause *nikî-wâpamâw nâpêw* "I saw a man." The *nâpêw* "man" takes on two grammatical roles: it acts as the object in the independent clause and as the subject in the subordinate clause.

Prior information given determines the type of subordinate clause markers used in the subordinate clause. All subordinate clauses are forms of the conjunct mood of verbs. Regardless of which form is used, they all share the conjunct endings, except for the future conditional form, which drops the conjunct marker from the beginning and adds *-i* (for VTAs and for 1, 2, 3, 3', 3P, and 3'P of the VAIs and VTIs) or *-o* (for 1P, 21, and 2P of VAIs and VTIs) at the end.

The *ê*-form: This is the "regular" subordinate clause marker. Use this form in regular subordinate clauses and after "because" (*ayisk* or *osâm*). The examples below marked with an asterisk * are not meaningful combinations:

> Subordinate clause marked by *kâ-*: niwî-kawisimon ayisk kâ-nêstosiyân.*
> Subordinate clause marked by *ta-*: niwî-kawisimon ayisk ta-nêstosiyân.*
> Subordinate clause marked by *ta-kî-*: niwî-kawisimon ayisk ta-kî-nêstosiyân.*
> Independent clause followed by a subordinate clause: niwî-kawisimon ê-nêstosiyân.*
>
> Two independent clauses connected by "because": nikawisimon ayisk ninêstosin.*
> Two independent clauses connected: nikawisimon ninêstosin.*
> An independent clause followed by a subordinate clause without a unifier:
>   niwî-kawisimon ê-nêstosiyân.*

These sentences are possible:

nikawisimon ayisk ê-nêstosiyân.	*I lie down because I am tired.*
nikî-kawisimon ayisk ê-kî-nêstosiyân.	*I lay down because I was tired.*
niwî-kawisimon ayisk ê-nêstosiyân.	*I'm going to lie down because I am tired.*
niwî-kawisimon nêstosiyâni.	*I'm going to lie down if I am tired.*

The *kâ*-form: This is a "relative clause" marker. Use this form in content questions and in clauses that show the action is caused by the verb in the independent clause.

The *ta*-form: This is the infinitive form. Unlike English, which has infinitives that show no subject or number, Cree shows subject by the verb endings.

The *ta-kî*-form: This is the modal form of the verb for *shall*, *must*, *could*, *would*, and *should*.

The future conditional form: These can also be temporal clauses, but when they are, then *ispîhk* is included in the sentence, otherwise they get translated as "if" clauses. They share the conjunct mood endings of verbs, but only the endings, which have an added *-i* to most of the verbs, an *-o* to the 1P, 21, and 2P verb forms (except the VTAs). The only verb forms which stray from this rule are the 3rd person forms: the *t* in 3, 3' verbs in the conjunct change to *c*, then the *i* is added for future conditionals. The 3P ending of the conjunct is not used at all, but instead we use *-twâwi*, which is added to the verb stem.

5.5.A. SUBORDINATE CLAUSE EXERCISE

Mark the correct subordinate clause in each of the follow sentences with a checkmark (*answers are on page 269*):

1. *I'm going to drink coffee before (/if) going to work.*

   niwî-minihkwân pihkahtêwâpoy _____ ê-mwayî-nitawi-atoskêyân.

   _____ mwayî-nitawi-atoskêyâni.

   _____ kâ-mwayî-nitawi-atoskêyân.

2. *My mother called me to go and eat.*

   nikî-natomik nikâwiy _____ ta-nitawi-mîcisoyân.

   _____ ê-nitawi-mîcisoyân.

   _____ nitawi-mîcisoyâni.

3. *I fed my dog fish because she was hungry.*

   nikî-asamâw nitêm kinosêwa ayisk _____ ta-kî-nôhtêhkatêt.

   _____ nôhtêhkatêci.

   _____ ê-nôhtêhkatêt.

4. *I usually help my older brother when he goes to work.*

   niwîcihâw mâna nistês ispîhk _____ kâ-nitawi-atoskêt.

   _____ ê-nitawi-atoskêt.

   _____ nitawi-atoskêci.

5. *If you want to see your older sister, you should come here tomorrow.*

   kîspin kinôhtê-wâpamâw kimis _____ ê-pê-itohtêyan ôta wâpahki.

   _____ ta-pê-itohtêyan ôta wâpahki.

   _____ ta-kî-pê-itohtêyan ôta wâpahki.

   _____ pê-itohtêyani ôta wâpahki.

   _____ kâ-pê-itohtêyan ôta wâpahki.

5.5.B. SENTENCE STRUCTURES WITH VAIS AND VIIS

Write sentences with VAIS and VIIS, using the temporal units as a cue for the tense (*answers are on page 269*):

1. *anohc* – today; verb stem *itohtê* – go (1st person); with noun *sâkahikan* – lake:

_____

2. *otâkosîhk* – yesterday; verb stem *atoskê* – work (2nd person); with IPV *sôhki-* – hard:

_____

3. *awasi-otâkosîhk* – day before yesterday; verb stem *pimohtê* – walk (3rd person); with noun *mêskanaw* – road (needs locative)

_____

4. *wâpan* – It is day; verb stem *papâmohtê* – walk about (3' obviative); with noun *asinîwaciy* – mountain (needs locative):

_____

5. *wâpahki* – tomorrow; verb stem *sêsâwohtê* – hike/walk for exercise (1P); with noun *ispatinaw* – hill (needs locative):

_____

6. *awasi-wâpahki* – day after tomorrow; verb stem *pimipahtâ* – run (21); with IPV *wayawîtimihk* – outside:

_____

7. *kotak ispayiki* – next week; verb stem *sêsâwipahtâ* – jog (2P); with noun *mêskanâs* – path (needs locative):

_____

8. *kîkisêpâyâki* –in the morning; verb stem *kiyokê* – visit (3P); with preverb *nitawi-* – go and, with *iskonikan* – reserve:

_____

9. *otâhk-ispayiw* – last week; verb stem *pimipayi* – drive (3'P); with noun *asinîwaciy* – mountain (needs *-isi* after for "to the mountains"):

_____

10. *otâhk-askîwin* – last year; verb stem *papâmiskâ* – paddle about/go canoeing (1); with noun *sîpiy* – river (needs locative):

_____

11. *kotak askîwiki* – next year; verb stem *yahki-sôskoyâpawi* – go cross-country skiing (2); with IPV *kîwêtinohk* – in the north:

_____

12. *otâkosiki* – in the evening; verb stem *kisîpêkiyâkanê* – wash dishes (3):

_____

13. *sîkwanohk* – last spring; verb stem *kiskinwahamâkosi* – be in class/be in school (3'); use *kihci-kiskinwahamâtowikamik* – university (needs locative):

_____

14. *sîkwahki* – in the spring; verb stem *kiyôtê* – visit afar (1P); with noun *iskonikan* – reserve (needs locative):

_____

15. *nîpinohk* – last summer; verb stem *pakâsimo* – swim (21); with noun *sîpîsis* – creek (needs locative):

_____

16. *takwâkin* – it is fall; verb stem *wâstêpakâw* – leaves turn colour (VII); use IPV *ati-* – begin:

_____

17. *takwâkiki* – in the fall; verb stem *mâcî* – hunt (2P):

_____

18. *pipohki* – in the winter; verb stem *pîcicî* – dance round dance (3P):

_____

19. *âpihtâ-kîsikâki* – at noon; verb stem *âpihtâ-kîsikani-mîciso* – eat lunch (3'P):

_____

20. *âpihtâ-tipiskâw* – at midnight; verb stem *kîsahkamikisi* – finish (activity) (1):

_____

21. *pôni-âpihtâ-tipiskâw* – after midnight; verb stem *nikamo* – sing (2):

_____

22. *tipiskâw* – it is night; verb stem *nîmihito* – dance (3):

_____

23. *tipiskâki* – tonight: verb stem *kîsitêpo* – cook (3'):

_____

24. *tipiskohk* – last night; verb stem *sôniskwâtahikê* – skate (1P):

_____

25. *awasi-tipiskohk* – night before last; verb stem *papâmi-atâwê* – go shopping (21):

_____

5.5.C. DAILY ACTIVITY EXERCISES

Get into groups of three and answer the questions in columns 2 and 3 in the chart below. The first student will ask the questions in column 2; the second student will answer appropriately by using the information found in column 1; and then the first student will ask the third student to answer the questions in column 3 based on the answers that the second student provided. The answers for the first three questions are provided (*answers are on page 270*).

Statement	Question to 2nd person	Question about 3rd person
kîkisêp kî-kisinâw. *This past morning it was very cold.*	tânisi kâ-kî-isiwêpahk kîkisêp?	tânisi kâ-kî-isiwêpaniyik kîkisêp? **Answer:** kî-kisinâyiw kîkisêp.
têpakohp tipahikan mîna âpihtaw ê-ispayik nikî-waniskân. *I got up at seven thirty.*	tânitahto tipahikan ê-ispayik kikî-waniskân?	tânitahto tipahikan ê-ispayiyik kî-waniskâw awa? **Answer:** têpakohp tipahikan mîna âpihtaw ê-ispayiyik kî-waniskâw.
nikî-pihkahtêwâpôhkân. *I made coffee.*	kikî-pihkahtêwâpôhkân cî?	kî-pihkahtêwâpôhkêw cî awa? **Answer:** âha, kî-pihkahtêwâpôhkêw awa.
nikî-minihkwân pihkahtêwâpoy. *I drank coffee.*	kikî-minihkwân cî pihkahtêwâpoy?	kî-minihkwêw cî pihkahtêwâpoy awa?
nikî-piminawason. *I cooked.*	kikî-piminawason cî?	kî-piminawasow cî awa?
nikî-kîkisêpâ-mîcison. *I ate breakfast.*	kikî-kîkisêpâ-mîcison cî?	kî-kîkisêpâ-mîcisow cî awa?
ispîhk kâ-kîsi-mîcisoyân nikî-itohtân kihci-kiskinwahamâtowikamikohk. *When I finished eating, I went to the university.*	tânisi kikî-itôtên ispîhk kâ-kîsi-mîcisoyan?	tânisi kî-itôtam ispîhk kâ-kîsi-mîcisot?
pêyakosâp tipahikan ê-ispayik nikî-itohtân kihci-kiskinwahamâtowikamikohk. *I went to the university at eleven o'clock.*	tânitahto tipahikan ê-ispayik kikî-itohtân kihci-kiskinwahamâtowikamikohk?	tânitahto tipahikan ê-ispayiyik kî-itohtêw kihci-kiskinwahamâtowikamikohk?

In-Class Assignment

Write ten things you do during the day. Don't forget to mention the season, times of day, and days of the week.

_____

_____

_____

_____

_____

_____

_____

_____

_____

_____

_____

_____

_____

_____

5.5.D. DAILY ACTIVITY TRANSLATION AND QUESTIONS

Here is an example of my activity early Saturday morning when it is spring. Translate the paragraphs below using the following word list (*the translated paragraphs are on page 272*).

acimosihkânisak	*pussy willows* (NA)	maskotêw	*prairie* (NI)
aciyaw	*for a short while*	mêtoni	*very*
âhâsiw	*crow*	mîna	*also*
âskaw mâna	*sometimes, as is usual*	mistahi	*a lot*
askiy	*earth*	miyonâkwan	*it looks beautiful* (VII)
ati-sâkipakâw	*leaves begin to bud*	namôya	*no*
ayinânêwosâp	*eighteen*	nanâtohk	*all kinds*
cahcahkâyos	*blackbird*	nêwosâp	*fourteen*
cahcahkiw	*pelican*	nikotwâso-kîsikâw	*it is Saturday* (VII)
cihcipayapisikanis	*bicycle* (NI)	nîsitanaw	*twenty*
cîhkêyihta	*like something* (VTI-1)	niska	*goose*
cipahaskânis	*kilometre*	ôta	*here*
êkâ	*negator for conjunct*	papâmi-	*out and about*
êkwa	*and*	papâmipayi	*go out and about* (VAI)
isi	*toward a direction*	piyêsîs	*bird* (NA)
isi-têhtapi	*ride in a way* (VAI)	sâkahikanis	*small lake*
ispîhk	*when*	sîkwan	*it is spring*
kakwê-	*try to* (IPV)	sîsîp	*duck*
kâwi	*back*	sôhkiyowêw	*it is very windy* (VII)
kîkisêpâyâw	*it is morning* (VII)	têpiyahk	*at least*
kîspin	*if*	tihtipiska	*ride something with wheels* (VTI-1)
kîwêpayi	*ride home* (VAI)	wâhyaw	*far away*
mâmawi	*all together*	wâpam	*see someone* (VTA)
mâna	*usually*	wîpac	*soon, early*

ispîhk mâna kâ-sîkwahk, wîpac ê-kîkisêpâyâk, kâ-nikotwâso-kîsikâk, nipapâmi-tihtipiskên cihcipayapisikanis. wâhyaw mâna nikakwê-papâmi-tihtipiskên cihcipayapisikanis. kîspin êkâ mistahi sôhkiyowêki nêwosâp cipahaskânisa mâna nitihtipiskên cihcipayapisikanis, sâkahikanisihk isi, êkwa kâwi ta-kîwêpayiyân, mâmawi nîsitanaw ayinânêwosâp cipahaskânisa ê-papâmi-tihtipiskamân cihcipayapisikanis. ispîhk sôhkiyowêki namôya mâna wâhyaw nitisi-têhtapin. têpiyahk aciyaw mâna nipapâmi-tihtipiskên cihcipayapisikanis ispîhk kâ-sôhkiyowêk. âskaw mâna mistahi sôhkiyowêw ôta maskotêhk.

nicîhkêyihtên ta-papâmi-tihtipiskamân cihcipayapisikanis ispîhk kâ-sîkwahk. ispîhk mâna kâ-papâmipayiyân niwâpamâwak nanâtohk piyêsîsak: cahcahkâyosak, cahcahkiwak, niskak, âhâsiwak, êkwa nanâtohk sîsîpak. acimosihkânisak mîna niwâpamâwak ispîhk kâ-ati-sâkipakâk. mêtoni miyonâkwan askiy ispîhk kâ-sîkwahk.

Answer the following questions about Solomon's daily activities (*answers are on page 272*):

1. tânispîhk mâna awa kâ-papâmi-tihtipiskahk cihcipayapisikanis?

   _____

2. wâhyaw cî mâna kakwê-papâmi-tihtipiskam cihcipayapisikanis?

   _____

3. tânitahto cipahaskânisa mâna tihtipiskam cihcipayapisikanis kîspin êkâ mistahi sôhkiyowêyiki?

   _____

4. tânitê mâna kâ-isi-tihtipiskahk cihcipayapisikanis?

   _____

5. wâhyaw cî mâna papâmi-tihtipiskam cihcipayapisikanis ispîhk ê-sôhkiyowêyik?

   _____

6. têpiyâhk cî mâna aciyaw tihtipiskam cihcipayapisikanis ispîhk sôhkiyowêyiki?

   _____

7. âskaw cî mâna mistahi sôhkiyowêw ôta maskotêhk?

   _____

8. cîhkêyihtam cî ta-papâmi-tihtipiskahk cihcipayapisikanis ispîhk kâ-sîkwaniyik?

   _____

9. kiya mâka, kicîhkêyihtên cî ta-papâmi-tihtipiskaman cihcipayapisikanis ispîhk kâ-sîkwahk?

   _____

10. kîko piyêsîsa mâna wâpamêw ispîhk kâ-papâmi-tihtipiskahk cihcipayapisikanis?

   _____

CHAPTER 6

· · · · · · · · · · · · ·

TRANSITIVE VERBS

As we saw in Chapter 5, intransitive verbs need no objects, but transitive verbs do need objects. There are two types of transitive verbs in Cree: *transitive animate verbs* that need **animate** objects and *transitive inanimate verbs* that need **inanimate** objects. In the following chapters, we will look more closely at these two types of transitive verbs.

6.1. Transitive Inanimate Verbs—Class 1 (VTI-1)

Transitive inanimate verbs (VTI-1) are verbs that are common everyday activities and take an inanimate object in the sentence structure. The verb stems of VTIs come from the 2nd person singular form of the imperative.

6.1.A. VTI-1 IMPERATIVES

Imperatives are orders or commands to do things; **negative imperatives** are orders or commands not to do things; and **delayed imperatives** are orders given now to be carried out at a later time. To complete the imperative forms for any VTI-1, the verb stem is placed in the blanks of the chart below.

	Imperative	Negative Imperative	Delayed Imperative
2	_____	êkâwiya _____	_____mohkan
2P	_____mok	êkâwiya _____mok	_____mohkêk
21	_____êtân	êkâwiya _____êtân	_____mohkahk

Complete the following chart following the imperative paradigm above (*answers are on page 273*).

English	2nd Person Singular	2nd Person Plural	2nd Person Inclusive
Imperative: *Look at it.*	kanawâpahta		
Negative Imperative: *Don't look at it.*		êkâwiya kanawâpahtamok	
Delayed Imperative: *Look at it later.*			kanawâpahtamohkahk
Imperative: *See it.*		wâpahtamok	
Negative Imperative: *Don't see it.*	êkâwiya wâpahta		
Delayed Imperative: *See it later.*		wâpahtamohkêk	
Imperative: *Look for it.*			natonêtân
Negative Imperative: *Don't look for it.*		êkâwiya natonamok	
Delayed Imperative: *Look for it later.*	natonamohkan		
Imperative: *Find it.*		miskamok	
Negative Imperative: *Don't find it.*			êkâwiya miskêtân
Delayed Imperative: *Find it later.*		miskamohkêk	
Imperative: *Do it.*	itôta		
Negative Imperative: *Don't do it.*		êkâwiya itôtamok	
Delayed Imperative: *Do it later.*			itôtamohkahk

6.2. Transitive Inanimate Verb Charts—Class 1

An example of a VTI-1 is the verb *kanawâpahta* "look at it." The "it" refers to an inanimate object, as in *nikanawâpahtên waskow* "I look at the cloud."

Let's look at *kanawâpahta* as it is in the conjugation paradigm. Note that the last *a* changes to ê for the 1st and 2nd persons in the indicative mode:

Verb Stem: *kanawâpahta* "look at it"

Person and Tense	Indicative	Conjunct
1st present (pres)	nikanawâpahtên	ê-kanawâpahtamân
1st past	nikî-kanawâpahtên	ê-kî-kanawâpahtamân
1st future intentional (fut int)	niwî-kanawâpahtên	ê-wî-kanawâpahtamân
1st future definite (fut def)	nika-kanawâpahtên	
2nd pres	kikanawâpahtên	ê-kanawâpahtman
2nd past	kikî-kanawâpahtên	ê-kî-kanawâpahtaman
2nd fut int	kiwî-kanawâpahtên	ê-wî-kanawâpahtaman
2nd fut def	kika-kanawâpahtên	
3rd pres	kanawâpahtam	ê-kanawâpahtahk
3rd past	kî-kanawâpahtam	ê-kî-kanawâpahtahk
3rd fut int	wî-kanawâpahtam	ê-wî-kanawâpahtahk
3rd fut def	ta-kanawâpahtam	
3' pres	kanawâpahtamiyiwa	ê-kanawâpahtamiyit
3' past	kî-kanawâpahtamiyiwa	ê-kî-kanawâpahtamiyit
3' fut int	wî-kanawâpahtamiyiwa	ê-wî-kanawâpahtamiyit
3' fut def	ta-kanawâpahtamiyiwa	
1P pres	nikanawâpahtênân	ê-kanawâpahtamâhk
1P past	nikî-kanawâpahtênân	ê-kî-kanawâpahtamâhk
1P fut int	niwî-kanawâpahtênân	ê-wî-kanawâpahtamâhk
1P fut def	nika-kanawâpahtênân	
21 pres	kikanawâpahtênaw	ê-kanawâpahtamahk
21 past	kikî-kanawâpahtênaw	ê-kî-kanawâpahtamahk
21 fut int	kiwî-kanawâpahtênaw	ê-wî-kanawâpahtamahk
21 fut def	kika-kanawâpahtênaw	
2P pres	kikanawâpahtênâwâw	ê-kanawâpahtamêk
2P past	kikî-kanawâpahtênâwâw	ê-kî-kanawâpahtamêk
2P fut int	kiwî-kanawâpahtênâwâw	ê-wî-kanawâpahtamêk
2P fut def	kika-kanawâpahtênâwâw	
3P pres	kanawâpahtamwak	ê-kanawâpahtahkik
3P past	kî-kanawâpahtamwak	ê-kî-kanawâpahtahkik
3P fut int	wî-kanawâpahtamwak	ê-wî-kanawâpahtahkik
3P fut def	ta-kanawâpahtamwak	

There are a couple of rules to keep in mind in conjugating VTI-1s: 1) if the verb stem begins with a vowel, then the *-t* is used to connect the person indicator to the verb stem in the present tense of the indicative for 1st and 2nd persons; 2) the *a* that ends the verb stem of all VTI-1s changes to *ê* for the 21 of the imperative and for the 1st and 2nd persons of the indicative.

Let's look at the VTI-1 *atoskâta* "work at it." It comes from the 2 of the imperative:

2	atoskâta	*work at it*
2P	atoskâtamok	*work at it*
21	atoskâtêtân	*let's work at it*

Verb Stem: *atoskâta* "work at it"

Person and Tense	Indicative	Conjunct
1st pres	nitatoskâtên	ê-atoskâtamân
1st past	nikî-atoskâtên	ê-kî-atoskâtamân
1st fut int	niwî-atoskâtên	ê-wî-atoskâtamân
1st fut def	nika-atoskâtên	
2nd pres	kitatoskâtên	ê-atoskâtaman
2nd past	kikî-atoskâtên	ê-kî-atoskâtaman
2nd fut int	kiwî-atoskâtên	ê-wî-atoskâtaman
2nd fut def	kika-atoskâtên	
3rd pres	atoskâtam	ê-atoskâtahk
3rd past	kî-atoskâtam	ê-kî-atoskâtahk
3rd fut int	wî-atoskâtam	ê-wî-atoskâtahk
3rd fut def	ta-atoskâtam	
3' pres	atoskâtamiyiwa	ê-atoskâtamiyit
3' past	kî-atoskâtamiyiwa	ê-kî-atoskâtamiyit
3' fut int	wî-atoskâtamiyiwa	ê-wî-atoskâtamiyit
3' fut def	ta-atoskâtamiyiwa	
1P pres	nitatoskâtênân	ê-atoskâtamâhk
1P past	nikî-atoskâtênân	ê-kî-atoskâtamâhk
1P fut int	niwîatoskâtênân	ê-wî-atoskâtamâhk
1P fut def	nika-atoskâtênân	
21 pres	kitatoskâtênaw	ê-atoskâtamahk
21 past	kikî-atoskâtênaw	ê-kî-atoskâtamahk
21 fut int	kiwî-atoskâtênaw	ê-wî-atoskâtamahk
21 fut def	kika-atoskâtênaw	
2P pres	kitatoskâtênâwâw	ê-atoskâtamêk
2P past	kikî-atoskâtênâwâw	ê-kî-atoskâtamêk
2P fut int	kiwî-atoskâtênâwâw	ê-wî-atoskâtamêk
2P fut def	kika-atoskâtênâwâw	

3P pres	atoskâtamwak	ê-atoskâtahkik	
3P past	kî-atoskâtamwak	ê-kî-atoskâtahkik	
3P fut int	wî-atoskâtamwak	ê-wî-atoskâtahkik	
3P fut def	ta-atoskâtamwak		

6.2.A. EXERCISES WITH VTI-1S

Complete the following chart with the indicative and conjunct forms of the common VTI verb stems provided. Remember that the *a* changes to *ê* for 21 of the imperative and 1st and 2nd persons of the indicative (*answers are on page 273*).

Verb Stem *(comes from the 2 of the imperative)*	Person and Tense	Indicative	Conjunct
2 otina – *take it*	1st pres		
2P otinamok	1st past		
21 otinêtân	1st fut int		
	1st fut def		
2 nâta – *get it*	2nd pres		
2P nâtamok	2nd past		
21 nâtêtân	2nd fut int		
	2nd fut def		
2 natona – *look for it*	3rd pres		
2P natonamok	3rd past		
21 natonêtân	3rd fut int		
	3rd fut def		

Verb Stem (comes from the 2 of the imperative)		Person and Tense	Indicative	Conjunct
2	miska – *find it*	3' pres		
2P	miskamok	3' past		
21	miskêtân	3' fut int		
		3' fut def		
2	natohta – *listen to it*	1P pres		
2P	natohtamok	1P past		
21	natohtêtân	1P fut int		
		1P fut def		
2	pêhta – *hear it*	21 pres		
2P	pêhtamok	21 past		
21	pêhtêtân	21 fut int		
		21 fut def		
2	nisitohta – *understand it*	2P pres		
2P	nisitohtamok	2P past		
21	nisitohtêtân	2P fut int		
		2P fut def		

Verb Stem (comes from the 2 of the imperative)		Person and Tense	Indicative	Conjunct
2	wâpahta – *see it*	3P pres		
2P	wâpahtamok	3P past		
21	wâpaht**ê**tân	3P fut int		
		3P fut def		

6.2.B. VTI-1 CONJUGATIONS

Part 1

Complete the following conjugations by first finding the verb stems in each row and then making the transformations to the imperatives in each column (*answers are on page 274*).

Subject/Actor		Imperative	Negative Imperative	Delayed Imperative
2	you (sg)	wâpahta – *See it.*		
2P	you (pl)		êkâwiya natonamok – *Don't look for it!*	
21	Let's (you and I)			natohtamohkahk – *Let's listen to it (later).*
2	you (sg)		êkâwiya mêtawâkâta – *Don't disrespect it.*	
2P	you (pl)			atoskâtamohkêk – *Work at it (later).*
21	Let's (you and I)	kanawâpahtêtân – *Let's look at it.*		
2	you (sg)			kîsisamohkan – *Cook it (later).*
2P	you (pl)	kocispitamok – *Taste it.*		
21	Let's (you and I)		êkâwiya nâtêtân – *Let's not fetch it.*	

Complete the following indicative and conjunct forms in the charts below (*answers are on page 274*).

Singular subject

Subject/Actor		Indicative	Conjunct
		atoskâta – "work at it," present tense	*wâpahta* – "look at it," past tense
1	I		ê-kî-wâpahtamân
2	you	kitatoskâtên	
3	she/he		
3'	her/his (friend)		ê-kî-wâpahtamiyit

Plural subject

Subject/Actor		Indicative	Conjunct
		natohta – "listen to it," future definite tense	*natona* – "look for it," future intentional tense
1P	we (excl)	nika-natohtênân	
21	we (incl)		ê-wî-natonamahk
2P	you (pl)		
3P	they	ta-natohtamwak	

Part 2

Using the verbs from the conjugations in Part 1, along with the following vocabulary words, translate the sentences below (*answers are on page 275*):

Preverbs

kakwê-	*try to*
nitawi-	*go and*

Kinship

osîmisiwâwa	*their younger siblings*
nitôtêm	*my friend*

Temporal Words

wîpac	*early/soon*
kîkisêpâyâki	*in the morning*
tipiskohk	*last night*
otâkosiki	*in the evening*
tipiskâki	*tonight*
wâpahki	*tomorrow*
anohc	*today*

Nouns

nikamowina	*songs*
maskisina	*shoes*
kimasinahikana	*your books*
wâwa	*eggs*
wiyâs	*meat*
mînisa	*berries*
cikâstêpayihcikanis	*television*
cikâstêpayihcikan	*a movie*
âtayôhkêwina	*sacred stories*
nêhiyawêwin	*Cree language*

1. tipiskohk nikî-natohtênân nikamowina.

   _____

2. kîsisamohkêk wâwa kîkisêpâyâki.

   _____

3. tipiskohk kî-kanawâpahtamwak cikâstêpayihcikanis.

   _____

4. otâkosiki kika-nitawi-natonênaw kimaskisina.

   _____

5. tipiskâki niwî-kocispitên mînisa.

   _____

6. kika-nitawi-nâtên kimasinahikana wâpahki.

_____

7. kî-wâpahtamiyiwa cikâstêpayihcikan osîmisiwâwa tipiskohk.

_____

8. wîpac cî kiwî-atoskâtênâwâw nêhiyawêwin anohc?

_____

9. natohtamohkahk âtayôhkêwina tipiskâki.

_____

10. kî-kakwê-kîsisam wiyâs nitôtêm otâkosîhk.

_____

6.3. VTI-1 Paradigms

Along with the imperatives, the VTIs can be conjugated into various forms by building on the verb stem (taken from the 2 imperative form). By placing the verb stem in the blanks in the paradigm below, the indicative, the conjunct, and the future conditional forms for each verb are created.

VTI-1: Indicative, Conjunct, and Future Conditional Forms

	Indicative	Conjunct	Future Conditional
1	ni_____n	ê-_____mân	_____mâni
2	ki_____n	ê-_____man	_____mani
3	_____m	ê-_____hk	_____hki
3'	_____miyiw	ê-_____miyit	_____miyici
1P	ni_____nân	ê-_____mâhk	_____mâhki
21	ki_____naw	ê-_____mahk	_____mahki
2P	ki_____nâwâw	ê-_____mêk	_____mêko
3P	_____mwak	ê-_____hkik	_____hkwâwi
3'P	_____miyiwa	ê-_____miyit	_____miyici

There is one rule for VTI-1s to follow:

1. change the last *a* of the verb stem to *ê* for 21 of the imperative and 1, 2, 1P, 21, and 2P of the indicative.

Tense indicators apply to all verbs for the indicative and conjunct forms. The future definite form is not used in the conjunct form.

Past	*kî-*
Future Intentional:	*wî-*
Future Definite:	*ka-* for 1st and 2nd person actors
	ta- for 3rd person actors

Sentence Structure for All Verb Forms:

person indicator   +   tense indicator   +   preverb   +   verb stem   +   ending

The following list shows some of these common VTI-1 verb stems:

atoskâta	*work at it*	natohta	*listen to it*
itôta	*do it*	natona	*look for it*
kanawâpahta	*look at it*	nisitawêyihta	*recognize it*
kêcikoska	*take it off*	nisitohta	*understand it*
kipaha	*close it*	nitawêyihta	*want it*
kisîpêkina	*wash it*	ocipita	*pull it*
kîsisa	*cook it*	ohpina	*lift it up*
kiskêyihta	*know it*	otina	*take it*
kocispita	*taste it*	paswâta	*sniff it*
masinaha	*write it*	pêhta	*hear it*
mêtawâkâta	*disrespect it*	postiska	*put it on*
miska	*find it*	sâmina	*touch it*
mîskona	*feel it*	wâpahta	*see it*
miyahta	*smell it*	yahkiwêpina	*push it*
nâkatawêyihta	*take care of it*	yôhtêna	*open it*
nâta	*fetch it*		

6.3.A. TRANSLATION

Translate the following sentences using the list of verb stems above (*answers are on page 275*).

1. kîkisêp nikî-otinên nimasinahikana mîcisowinâhtikohk ohci.

   _____

2. kîkisêpâyâki niwî-nâtênân mihta.

   _____

3. pêyako-kîsikâki ati-atoskâtamohkêk kimasinahikaniwâwa.

   _____

4. nîso-kîsikâki niwî-natonên niskotâkay.

   _____

5. kotak ispayiki nika-nitawi-kanawâpahtên cikâstêpayihcikan.

   _____

6. otâhk-ispayiw nikî-pêhtên êwako nikamowin.

   _____

7. otâhk-askîwin cî kikî-natohtên nêhiyaw-âtayôhkêwina.

   _____

8. wî-kêcikoskam omaskisina iskwâhtêmihk.

   _____

9. kakwê-nisitohtam nêhiyawêwin.

   _____

10. tahkâyâyiki wî-postiskam opipon-asâkay.

   _____

6.3.B. CONVERSION

In each of the following sentences, convert the first verb from the imperative into the delayed imperative; then convert the second verb from the conjunct into the future conditional *(answers are on page 275)*:

1. nâta kimaskisina ê-nôhtê-atoskâtaman nêhiyawêwin.

   _____

   Fetch your shoes when/if you want to work at your Cree.

2. otinamok kimasinahikaniwâwa ê-pôni-masinahamêk âcimowina.

   _____

   Take your books when/if you stop writing stories.

3. kêcikoskêtân astotina ê-kipahamahk iskwâhtêm.

   _____

   Let's take off the hats if/when we close the door.

4. postiska kiskotâkay ê-nâtaman mihta.

   _____

   Put on your jacket when/if you go fetch firewood.

5. nitawi-kanawâpahtamok cikâstêpayihcikana ê-kîsi-kisîpêkinamêk oyâkana.

   _____

   Go to the movies when/if you finish washing the dishes.

6. postiska astotin ê-tahkâyâk.

   _____

   Put on a hat if it is cold.

7. kipaha iskwâhtêm ê-tahkâyâk.

   _____

   Close the door if it is cold.

8. natohtêtân anima nêhiyawêwin ispîhk ana iskwêw ê-kocihtât.

_____

Let's listen to that Cree when that woman tries it.

9. otinamok anima wiyâs ê-kîsi-manisahk.

_____

Take that meat if she/he finishes cutting it up.

10. kanawâpahta anima masinahikêwin ê-pôni-ayamihtât.

_____

Look at that writing if he stops reading it.

6.3.c. EXPANSION DRILLS

In these next three exercises, follow the instructions to expand your understanding and gain practice with the concepts of this chapter.

Get into groups of three and read aloud what appears in the chart below. One student reads the left-hand column of the first row, the next student reads the middle column, and a third student reads the right-hand column. Continue to read each row of the chart.

ispîhk kâ-sîkwahk *When it's spring*	nimiywêyihtên *I like*	ta-papâmi-têhtapiyân. *to ride a horse.*
ispîhk kâ-sîkwaniyik *When it's spring*	miywêyihtam nistês *my older brother likes*	ta-papâmi-têhtapit. *to ride a horse.*
ispîhk kâ-nîpihk *When it's summer*	nimiywêyihtênân *we like*	ta-papâohtêyâhk sakâhk *to walk about in the bush.*
ispîhk kâ-nîpiniyik *When it's summer*	miywêyihtamiyiwa omosôma *her/his grandfather likes*	ta-papâmohtêyit sakâhk. *to walk about in the bush.*
ispîhk kâ-takwâkik *When it's fall*	nimiywêyihtên *I like*	ta-tihtipiskamân cihcipayapisikanis. *to ride a bike.*
ispîhk kâ-takwâkiniyik *When it's fall*	miywêyihtamwak nîtisânak *my siblings like*	ta-tihtipiskahkik cihcipayapisikanisa. *to ride bikes.*

| ispîhk kâ-pipohk | nimiywêyihtên | ta-yahki-sôskoyâpawiyân. |
| *When it's winter* | *I like* | *to cross-country ski.* |

| ispîhk kâ-piponiyik | miywêyihtamiyiwa omisa | ta-yahki-sôskoyâpawiyit. |
| *When it's winter* | *her/his older sister likes* | *to cross-country ski.* |

Answer the following questions.

1. kimiywêyihtên cî ta-papâmi-têhtapiyan ispîhk kâ-sîkwahk?

Do you like to ride horses when it's spring?

2. miywêyihtam cî nistês ta-papâmi-têhtapit ispîhk kâ-sîkwaniyik.

Does my older brother like to ride a horse when it's spring?

3. kimiywêyihtênâwâw cî ta-papâmohtêyêk sakâhk ispîhk kâ-nîpihk.

Do you (plural) like to walk about in the bush when it's summer?

4. miywêyihtamiyiwa cî omosôma ta-papâmohtêyit sakâhk ispîhk kâ-nîpiniyik?

Does her/his grandfather like to walk about in the bush when it's summer?

5. kimiywêyihtên cî ta-tihtipiskaman cihcipayapisikanis ispîhk kâ-takwâkik?

Do you like to ride a bike when it's fall?

6. miywêyihtamwak cî kîtisânak ta-tihtipiskahkik cihcipayapisikanisa ispîhk kâ-takwâkiniyik?

Do your siblings like to ride bikes when it's fall?

7. kimiywêyihtên cî ta-yahki-sôskoyâpawiyan ispîhk kâ-pipohk?

Do you like to cross-country ski when it's winter?

8. miywêyihtamiyiwa cî omisa ta-yahki-sôskoyâpawiyit ispîhk kâ-piponiyik?

Does his older sister like to cross-country ski when it is winter?

In-Class Assignment

Write a paragraph about things you and a relative like to do during the seasons. Follow the format above. Prepare a text along with questions.

_____

_____

_____

_____

_____

_____

_____

_____

_____

_____

_____

_____

_____

_____

_____

_____

6.4. Values in Cree

Some VTIs are used to express qualities that Cree people value. The VTIs and VTAs in the first two columns help to express those values represented by the nouns listed in the third column.

VTI	VTA	Noun: values
kiskêyihtam *she/he knows something*	kiskêyimêw *she/he knows someone*	kiskêyihtamowin *knowledge*
nisitohtam *she/he understands something*	nisitohtawêw *she/he understands someone*	nisitohtamowin *understanding*
nisitawêyihtam *she/he recognizes something*	nisitawêyimêw *she/he recognizes someone*	nisitawêyihtamowin *recognition*
kistêyihtam *she/he respects something*	kistêyimêw *she/he respects someone*	kistêyihtamowin *respect*
kihcêyihtam *she/he honours something*	kihcêyimêw *she/he honours someone*	kihcêyihtamowin *honour*
tâpôkêyihtam *she/he believes in something*	tâpôkêyimêw *she/he believes in someone*	tâpôkêyihtamowin *faith*
tâpwêhtam *she/he believes something*	tâpwêhtawêw *she/he believes someone*	tâpwêhtamowin *belief*
sîpêyihtam *she/he is patient with something*	sîpêyimêw *she/he is patient with someone*	sîpêyihtamowin *patience*
tapahtêyihtam *she/he thinks lowly of something*	tapahtêyimêw *she/he thinks lowly of someone*	tapahtêyimisowin *humility*
miywêyihtam *she/he is happy with something*	miywêyimêw *she/he is happy with someone*	miywêyihtamowin *happiness*
cîhkêyihtam *she/he likes something*	cîhkêyimêw *she/he likes someone*	cîhkêyihtamowin *pleasure*
kiskinawâpahtam *she/he knows it from watching something*	kiskinawâpamêw *she/he learns from watching someone*	kiskinawâpahtamowin *knowledge from watching*
nanahihtam *she/he obeys something*	nanahihtawêw *she/he obeys someone*	nanahihtamowin *obedience*

Other values that do not have a v TI-1 base:

pakosêyihtâkosiwin	*hope*	sôhkitêhêwin	*courage*
manâcihitowin	*ultimate protection*	iyinîsiwin	*wisdom*
sôhkisiwin	*strength*	sâkihitowin	*love*
nanâskomowin	*thankfulness*	kwayask-itâtisiwin	*honesty*
mâtinamâtowin	*sharing*	miyo-pimâtisiwin	*good life*
wâhkôhtowin	*kinship*	miyo-pimohtêhowin	*good journey*
kanâcihowin	*cleanliness*	tâpwêwin	*truth*
âniskêhtowin	*interconnectedness*	sîpiyawêsiwin	*tolerance*
miyo-ohpikihâwasowin	*good child-rearing*		

CHAPTER 7

• • • • • • • • • • • • •

POSSESSIVE FORMS, BODY PARTS, AND SHOPPING

7.1. Possessive Forms

Making possessive forms in Cree is quite simple. They are formed in a similar way to verbs in the verb paradigms. Consider the VAI paradigm below, where you place the verb stem in the blank spaces:

VAI Paradigm

Person		Verb form
1	I	ni_____n
1P	we (excl)	ni_____nân
21	we (incl)	ki_____naw
2	you	ki_____n
2P	you (pl)	ki_____nâwâw
3	she/he	_____w
3P	they	_____wak
3'	her/his (friend)	_____yiwa
3'P	their (friend)	_____yiwa

The same paradigm can be used for the possessive forms, with a few differences. Compare the verb paradigm above with the possessive forms paradigm below:

Possessive Forms

Person		Possessive form
1	my	**ni**_____
1P	our	**ni**_____inân
21	our	**ki**_____inaw
2	your	**ki**_____
2P	your	**ki**_____iwâw
3	her/his	**o**_____
3P	their	**o**_____iwâw
3'	her/his (friend's)	**o**_____iyiwa
3'P	their (friend's)	**o**_____iyiwa

We will only be concerned with the first three singular possessive forms for this unit (my, your, her/his).

Noun	Possessive Form	Translation
sêhkêpayîs – *car* (NA)	nisêhkêpayîs	*my car*
	kisêhkêpayîs	*your car*
	osêhkêpayîsa*	*her/his car*
âpâpiskahikanis – *key* (NI)	nitâpâpiskahikanisa**	*my keys*
	kitâpâpiskahikanisa	*your keys*
	otâpâpiskahikanisa	*her/his keys*

The Cree language distinguishes between two kinds of nouns—alienable and inalienable.

- **alienable nouns** are items that can be given away (e.g., *nitâs* – my pants)
- **inalienable nouns** are those that cannot be given away (e.g., kin and body parts)

There are specific rules, depending on whether a noun is alienable or inalienable.

---

* The animate noun in its third person possessive form has a final *a*. This is a mark for obviation used by all animate nouns in third person possessive forms.

** Any noun beginning with a vowel must have a *t* to connect the person indicators *ni*, *ki*, and *o* in the possessive forms. The noun here is inanimate, and because we normally talk about keys in the plural, the plural form is used here marked by the *a* as indicating the plural form.

Rules

For most **alienable nouns**, use the following pattern:

my _____	ni_____*
your _____	ki_____
her/his _____	o_____

e.g., *masinahikan* – book (NI)

nimasinahikan	*my book*
kimasinahikan	*your book*
omasinahikan	*her/his book*

For **inalienable nouns starting with *mi***, replace the *mi* with the possessive indicators:

my _____	ni_____
your _____	ki_____
her/his _____	o_____a**

e.g., *misit* – foot (NI)

nisit	*my foot*
kisit	*your foot*
osit	*her/his foot*

For other **inalienable nouns**, replace the first consonant*** with the following:

my _____	n_____
your _____	k_____
her/his _____	w_____

e.g., *maskasiy* – a fingernail (NA)

naskasiy	*my fingernail*
kaskasiy	*your fingernail*
waskasiya	*her/his fingernail*

---

* Add the appropriate plural endings: use *a* for NI and *ak* for NA.

** For NA, the 3rd person forms will be marked with the obviative marker *a*.

*** If a noun begins with a vowel, then the *t* is used to connect the possessive marker to the noun because we can't have two vowels together.

7.1.A. ASKING WHERE SOMETHING IS LOCATED

When asking about the whereabouts of items in possessive forms, you must pay attention to the animacy of the noun. A way of determining the animacy of a new Cree noun is to ask a speaker how they would ask for the items. Would they use *tâniwê* in asking for one's blanket, as in: *tâniwê nitakohp?* "Where is my blanket?" Or would they use *tâniwâ*, as in: *tâniwâ nitakohp?* "Where is my blanket?"

Asking for Animate Nouns

Singular animate nouns use *tâniwâ* "where."

tâniwâ nipôsinâpâsk?	*Where is my bus?*
tâniwâ kipôsinâpâsk?	*Where is your bus?*
tâniwâ opôsinâpâsk**wa**?*	*Where is her/his bus?*

Plural animate nouns use *tâniwêhkâk* "where."

tâniwêhkâk nipôsinâpâsk**wak**?	*Where are my buses?*
tâniwêhkâk kipôsinâpâsk**wak**?	*Where are your buses?*
tâniwêhkâk opôsinâpâsk**wa**?	*Where are her/his buses?*

Asking for Inanimate Nouns

Singular inanimate nouns use *tâniwê* "where."

tâniwê nimaskisin?	*Where is my shoe?*
tâniwê kimaskisin?	*Where is your shoe?*
tâniwê omaskisin?	*Where is her/his shoe?*

Plural inanimate nouns use *tâniwêhâ* "where."

tâniwêhâ nimaskisin**a**?	*Where are my shoes?*
tâniwêhâ kimaskisin**a**?	*Where are your shoes?*
tâniwêhâ omaskisin**a**?	*Where are her/his shoes?*

In Cree we must pay attention to animacy and number agreement with nouns and interrogative pronouns, as well as other grammatical units like demonstrative pronouns and transitive verbs.

---

* The animate noun possessed by a third person is always marked by an *a* to indicate obviation. This could either be singular or plural, depending on the context.

Transitive Animate Verb*		Transitive Inanimate Verb	
natonaw(**ik**)	*look for it/them* (NA)	natona	*look for it* (NI)
miskaw(**ik**)	*find it/them* (NA)	miska	*find it* (NI)
pêsiw(**ik**)	*bring it/them* (NA)	pêtâ	*bring it* (NI)**

7.1.B. POSSESSIVE FORM EXERCISES

Fill in the blanks with the possessive forms for the following nouns (*answers are on page 276*).

Common Items

pôsinâpâsk – bus (NA)

a) my bus _____

b) your bus _____

c) her/his bus _____

âwatawâsiswâkan – school bus (NA)

a) my school bus _____

b) your school bus _____

c) her/his school bus _____

otinikêwi-têhamân – debit card (NA)

a) my debit card _____

b) your debit card _____

c) her/his debit card _____

---

* Transitive animate verbs need number agreement: when the noun is plural then the verb shows the plural: e.g., *natonaw kitêm* "Look for your dog"; *natonawik kitêmak* "Look for your dogs."

** *pêtâ* is a VTI-2, a VTI that follows the VAI paradigm but takes an inanimate object.

masinahikêwi-têhamân – credit card (NA)

a) my credit card   _____

b) your credit card   _____

c) her/his credit card   _____

âhkosîwasinahikan – hospitalization card (NI)

a) my hospitalization card   _____

b) your hospitalization card   _____

c) her/his hospitalization card   _____

otinikêwi-âwacikan – shopping cart (NI)

a) my shopping cart   _____

b) your shopping cart   _____

c) her/his shopping cart   _____

miskîsikohkâna – glasses (NDI)

a) my glasses   _____

b) your glasses   _____

c) her/his glasses   _____

pimihâkan – plane (NI)

a) my plane   _____

b) your plane   _____

c) her/his plane   _____

iskotêwitâpân – train (NA)

a) my train   _____

b) your train   _____

c) her/his train   _____

sîhci-pakwahtêhon – seat belt (NI)

a) my seat belt   _____

b) your seat belt   _____

c) her/his seat belt   _____

sôskopayîs (*skî-tô*) – snow-mobile (NA)

a) my snow-mobile   _____

b) your snow-mobile   _____

c) her/his snow-mobile   _____

cihcipayapisikanis – bicycle (NI)

a) my bicycle   _____

b) your bicycle   _____

c) her/his bicycle   _____

sôniskwâtahikan – skate (NI)

a) my skate   _____

b) your skate   _____

c) her/his skate   _____

sôniskwâtahikanâhtik – hockey stick (NI)

a) my hockey stick _____

b) your hockey stick _____

c) her/his hockey stick _____

pâkahatowân – ball (NA)

a) my ball _____

b) your ball _____

c) her/his ball _____

On the Land: Out and About

pâskisikan – gun (NI)

a) my gun _____

b) your gun _____

c) her/his gun _____

môswasiniy – bullet (NI)

a) my bullet _____

b) your bullet _____

c) her/his bullet _____

cîkahikan – axe (NI)

a) my axe _____

b) your axe _____

c) her/his axe _____

kîskipocikan – saw (NI)

a) my saw _____

b) your saw _____

c) her/his saw _____

ayapiy – gill net (NA)

a) my gill net _____

b) your gill net _____

c) her/his gill net _____

pîminahkwân – rope (NI)

a) my rope _____

b) your rope _____

c) her/his rope _____

tâpakwân – snare (NI)

a) my snare _____

b) your snare _____

c) her/his snare _____

tâpakwânêyâpiy – snare wire (NI)

a) my snare wire _____

b) your snare wire _____

c) her/his snare wire _____

asâm – snowshoe (NA)

a) my snowshoe _____

b) your snowshoe _____

c) her/his snowshoe _____

mâtahikan – hide scraper (NI)

a) my hide scraper _____

b) your hide scraper _____

c) her/his hide scraper _____

mihkihkwan – hide scraper (NI)

a) my hide scraper _____

b) your hide scraper _____

c) her/his hide scraper _____

mânihtoyâsk – hide scraper (NI) (made of bone)

a) my hide scraper _____

b) your hide scraper _____

c) her/his hide scraper _____

mîkiwâhp – tipi (NI)

a) my tipi _____

b) your tipi _____

c) her/his tipi _____

pakwânikamik – tent (NI)

a) my tent   _____

b) your tent   _____

c) her/his tent   _____

kotawân – campfire (NI)

a) my campfire   _____

b) your campfire   _____

c) her/his campfire   _____

akwâwân – drying rack (NI)

a) my drying rack   _____

b) your drying rack   _____

c) her/his drying rack   _____

cîmân – canoe (NI)

a) my canoe   _____

b) your canoe   _____

c) her/his canoe   _____

apoy – paddle (NA)

a) my paddle   _____

b) your paddle   _____

c) her/his paddle   _____

waskitipêsimon – life jacket (NI)

a) my life jacket   _____

b) your life jacket   _____

c) her/his life jacket   _____

In the Classroom

maskimot – bag (NI)

a) my bag   _____

b) your bag   _____

c) her/his bag   _____

masinahikan – book (NI)

a) my book   _____

b) your book   _____

c) her/his book   _____

masinahikanêkin– paper (NI)

a) my paper   _____

b) your paper   _____

c) her/his paper   _____

masinahikanâhtik – pen (NA/NI)

a) my pen   _____

b) your pen   _____

c) her/his pen   _____

masinahikanâhcikos – pencil (NA/NI)

a) my pencil   _____

b) your pencil   _____

c) her/his pencil   _____

masinahikêwinâhtik – desk (NI)

a) my desk   _____

b) your desk   _____

c) her/his desk   _____

ayamâkanis – cell phone (NI)

a) my cell phone   _____

b) your cell phone   _____

c) her/his cell phone _____

mâhtâw-âpacihcikan – computer (NI)

a) my computer   _____

b) your computer   _____

c) her/his computer   _____

cikâstêpayihcikanis – television (NI)

a) my television   _____

b) your television   _____

c) her/his television   _____

In the House

wâskahikan – house (NI)

a) my house   _____

b) your house   _____

c) her/his house   _____

mîkiwâm – home (NI)

a) my home   _____

b) your home   _____

c) her/his home   _____

mîcisowinâhtik – table (NI)

a) my table   _____

b) your table   _____

c) her/his table   _____

têhtapiwin – chair (NI)

a) my chair   _____

b) your chair   _____

c) her/his chair   _____

yôski-têhtapiwin – armchair (NI)

a) my armchair   _____

b) your armchair   _____

c) her/his armchair   _____

kihci-yôski-têhtapiwin – couch (NI)

a) my couch   _____

b) your couch   _____

c) her/his couch   _____

âkôpicikan – curtain (NI)

a) my curtain   _____

b) your curtain   _____

c) her/his curtain   _____

nipêwin – bed (NI)

a) my bed   _____

b) your bed   _____

c) her/his bed   _____

akohp – blanket (NA/NI)

a) my blanket   _____

b) your blanket   _____

c) her/his blanket   _____

aspiskwêsimon – pillow (NI)

a) my pillow   _____

b) your pillow   _____

c) her/his pillow   _____

wâsaskotênikan – lamp (NI)

a) my lamp   _____

b) your lamp   _____

c) her/his lamp   _____

In the Kitchen

tahkascikan – fridge (NI)

a) my fridge   _____

b) your fridge   _____

c) her/his fridge   _____

âhkwatihcikan – freezer (NI)

a) my freezer   _____

b) your freezer   _____

c) her/his freezer _____

kotawânâpisk – stove (NI)

a) my stove   _____

b) your stove   _____

c) her/his stove   _____

sêkowêpinâpisk – oven (NI)

a) my oven   _____

b) your oven   _____

c) her/his oven   _____

kêsiskawihkasikan – microwave oven (NI)

a) my microwave oven   _____

b) your microwave oven   _____

c) her/his microwave oven _____

sâsâpiskisikan – frying pan (NA)

a) my frying pan   _____

b) your frying pan   _____

c) her/his frying pan _____

askihk – pot (NA)

a) my pot   _____

b) your pot   _____

c) her/his pot _____

oyâkan – plate (NI)

a) my plate   _____

b) your plate   _____

c) her/his plate _____

môhkomân – knife (NI)

a) my knife   _____

b) your knife   _____

c) her/his knife _____

êmihkwân – spoon (NA)

a) my spoon _____

b) your spoon _____

c) her/his spoon _____

cîstahâsêpon – fork (NI)

a) my fork _____

b) your fork _____

c) her/his fork _____

minihkwâkan – cup (NI)

a) my cup _____

b) your cup _____

c) her/his cup _____

mîciwin – food (NI)

a) my food _____

b) your food _____

c) her/his food _____

Sewing

kaskikwâswâkan – sewing machine (NI)

a) my sewing machine _____

b) your sewing machine _____

c) her/his sewing machine _____

asapâp – thread (NA)

a) my thread   _____

b) your thread   _____

c) her/his thread   _____

kawiyak – porcupine quills (NA)

a) my porcupine quills   _____

b) your porcupine quills   _____

c) her/his porcupine quills _____

kaskikwâsowinâpisk – thimble (NA)

a) my thimble   _____

b) your thimble   _____

c) her/his thimble   _____

paskwahamâtowin – scissors (NI)

a) my scissors   _____

b) your scissors   _____

c) her/his scissors   _____

mîkis – bead (NA)

a) my bead   _____

b) your bead   _____

c) her/his bead   _____

sâponikan – needle (NI)

a) my needle   _____

b) your needle   _____

c) her/his needle   _____

pahkêkin – leather (NI)

a) my leather   _____

b) your leather   _____

c) her/his leather   _____

ayânis – piece of cloth (NI)

a) my cloth   _____

b) your cloth   _____

c) her/his cloth   _____

sênipân – ribbon (NA)

a) my ribbon   _____

b) your ribbon   _____

c) her/his ribbon   _____

sênipânêkin – satin/silk cloth (NI)

a) my satin cloth   _____

b) your satin cloth   _____

c) her/his satin cloth   _____

sênipânisapâp – silk thread (NA)

a) my silk thread   _____

b) your silk thread   _____

c) her/his silk thread   _____

7.2. Body Parts

Vocabulary

asiskitân	*calf*	misit	*foot*
mahkwan	*heel*	miskâhtik	*forehead*
manaway	*cheek*	miskât	*leg*
masakay	*skin*	miskîsik	*eye*
maskasiy	*fingernail*	miskon	*liver*
maskatay	*abdomen*	misôkan	*backside*
mâskikan	*chest*	mispayowak	*ovaries*
mâskitoy	*buttocks*	mispikay	*rib*
matay	*belly*	mispiskwan	*back*
mêstakay	*hair*	mispiton	*arm*
micihcîwi-âniskôkanân	*wrist*	mistikwân	*head*
micihciy	*hand*	mitâpiskan	*jaw*
mihcikwan	*knee*	mitêh	*heart*
mihkwâkan	*face*	mitêyikom	*nostril*
mihtawakay	*ear*	mitihtiman	*shoulder*
mikohtaskway	*throat*	mitohtôsim	*breast*
mikot	*nose*	mitokan	*hip*
mikwâskoniy	*chin*	mitôn	*mouth*
mikwayaw	*neck*	mitôskwan	*elbow*
mipwâm	*thigh*	miyaw	*body*
miyêsâpiwinân	*eyebrow*	yiyîkicihcân	*finger*
misicihcân	*thumb*	yiyîkisitân	*toe*
misisitân	*big toe*		

Possessive Forms for Parts of the Body

Most parts of the body are dependent nouns and follow these rules for making the possessive form:

1. for nouns beginning with *ma/mâ/mê/mî*, replace the *m* with *n* for the 1st person, with *k* for 2nd person, and with *w* for 3rd person;

2. for nouns beginning with *mi*, replace the *mi* with *ni* for 1st person, with *ki* for 2nd person, and with *o* for 3rd person.

Some body parts (fingers and toes) are not dependent nouns. They take the prefixes (*ni*, *ki*, and *o*) without changes to the stem.

7.2.A. BODY PARTS EXERCISE

Complete the following chart with the correct possessive forms (*answers are on page 279*).

Note that the abbreviations NDI (dependent inanimate noun) and NDA (dependent animate noun) indicate which are dependent nouns.

Noun	My	Your	Her/His
mahkwan – *heel* (NDI)	nahkwan		
manaway – *cheek* (NDI)		kanaway	
masakay – *skin* (NDA)			wasakaya
maskasiy – *fingernail* (NDA)	naskasiy		
mâskikan – *chest* (NDI)		kâskikan	
matay – *belly* (NDI)			watay
mêstakay – *hair* (NDI)			wêstakay
micihcîwi-ânisawikanân – *wrist* (NDI)	nicihcîwi-ânisawikanân		
micihciy – *hand* (NDI)		kicihciy	
mihcikwan – *knee* (NDI)			ohcikwan
mihkwâkan – *face* (NDI)	nihkwâkan		
mihtawakay – *ear* (NDI)		kihtawakay	
mikohtaskway – *throat* (NDI)			okohtaskway

mikot – *nose* (NDI)	nikot	
mikwâskoniy – *chin* (NDI)		kikwâskoniy
mikwayaw – *neck* (NDI)			okwayaw
mipwâm – *thigh* (NDI)	nipwâm	
miyêsâpiwinân – *eyebrow* (NDI)		kiyêsâpiwinân
misit – *foot* (NDI)			osit
miskâhtik – *forehead* (NDI)	niskâhtik	
miskât – *leg* (NDI)		kiskât
misicihcân – *thumb* (NI)			omisicihcân
misisitân – *big toe* (NI)		kimisisitân
miskîsik – *eye* (NDI)			oskîsik
misôkan – *buttocks* (NDI)	nisôkan	
mispiskwan – *back* (NDI)		kispiskwan
mispiton – *arm* (NDI)			ospiton
mistikwân – *head* (NDI)		kistikwân
mitâpiskan – *jaw* (NDI)			otâpiskan
mitihtiman – *shoulder* (NDI)	nitihtiman	
mitêyikom – *nostril* (NDI)		kitêyikom
mitohtôsim – *breast* (NDA)			otohtôsima
mitokan – *hip* (NDI)	nitokan	
mitôn – *mouth* (NDI)		kitôn
mitôskwan – *elbow* (NDI)			otôskwan
miyaw – *body* (NDI)	niyaw	
yiyîkicihcân – *finger* (NI)		kiyiyîkicihcân
yiyîkisitân – *toe* (NI)			oyiyîkisitân

7.2.B. A VISIT TO THE CLINIC

Vocabulary

âhkosi	*be sick* (VAI)	maskihkiya	*medicine*
âhkosîskâkow	*be made ill by something* (VTA)	mâwaci mistahi	*most*
âhkosiwin	*illness*	mêkwâc	*now*
akihtâsowina	*number*	mîci	*eat something* (VTI-3)
anohc	*today*	mîciso	*eat* (VAI)
âpacihtâ	*use* (VTI-2)	mihko	*blood*
apisîs	*a little*	mihkwêyâpiy	*vein*
âsay	*already*	mitâtaht	*10*
aspin	*since*	miyopayiw	*it runs good* (VII)
cahcahkatâmopayi	*have shortness of breath* (VAI)	môsihtâ	*feel something* (VTI-2)
cî	question indicator	nama kîkway	*0 (zero)*
êkosi	*that way*	namôya	*no*
êkwa	*and*	nitawâpênikê	*check something* (VAI)
isi-	*way*	nitawi-	*go and* (IPV)
isko	*up to*	nôhtê-	*want to* (IPV)
itamahciho	*feel thus* (VAI)	ohci	*from*
kakwêcim	*ask someone* (VTA)	ôma	*this*
kapê	*always*	omaskihkîma	*his medicines*
kîko	*which*	ôta	*here*
kîkway	*something*	otina	*take something* (VTI-1)
kîkwây	*what*	pê-	*come* (IPV)
kimihkom	*your blood*	pêtâ	*bring something* (VTI-2)
kinwêsk	*a long time*	pahkahokowin	*pulse*
kisikiwin	*your urine*	sâkaskinahtâ	*fill something* (VTI-2)
kisiso	*have a fever* (VAI)	tânêhki	*why*
kisiwaskatê	*have an upset stomach* (VAI)	tânisi	*how, what, hello*
kîspin	*if*	tânispîhk	*when*
kiyêhyêwin	*your breathing*	tânita	*whereabouts*
mâci-	*begin* (IPV)	tâniyikohk	*how much*
mâyiskâkow	*be made ill by something* (VTA)	wâpam	*see someone* (VTA)
mahti	*let's see, please*	wîsakêyihta	*have/feel pain* (VTI-1)
mâkwahikow	*something/someone causes difficulty for someone* (VTA)		
mâna	*usually*	wîsakisimiso	*hurt oneself* (VAI)
maskihkîwiyiniw	*doctor*	wîsakisini	*hurt oneself* (VAI)

nistam nâtawihiwêwin	*first aid*	maskihkîwiyiniw	*doctor* (NA)
maskihkîwacis	*first-aid kit* (NI)	nâkatohkêwiyiniw	*nurse* (NA) (new word)
ka-yêhyêwêpahokêhk	CPR	maskihkîwiskwêw	*nurse* (NA) (former word)
otâhkosiwa kâ-nânâkacihât	*paramedic*	maskihkîwikamikos	*clinic* (NI)
âhkosîwikamik	*hospital* (NI)	âhkosîwasinahikan	*hospitalization card* (NI)

Questions

Here are some common questions you might hear during a visit to the medical clinic. For those in 2nd person, how might you answer? For those in 3rd person, how might you ask the question to a patient?

1. tânisi kâ-itamahcihoyan anohc?
   How are you feeling today?

2. tânêhki ôma kâ-nôhtê-wâpamat maskihkîwiyiniw?
   What is your concern to see the doctor today?

3. kîko maskihkiya mêkwâc kâ-âpacihtâyan?
   What medications are you currently on?

4. kakwêcim kîspin omaskihkîma kî-pêtâw.
   Ask if the patient brought the medications in with them.

5. tânisi ôma mâna kâ-isi-mîcisoyan? kîkwây mâna kâ-mîciyan?
   How is their diet and what does it consist of?

6. kîkway cî mâna kitâhkosîskâkon (kimâyiskâkon)?
   Do you have any allergies?

7. kicahcahkatâmopayin cî mâna?
   Do you have any problems breathing?

8. tânispîhk kâ-kî-mâci-môsihtâyan?
   When did the pain start?

9. tânisi kâ-isi-wîsakisimisoyan?
   How did you hurt yourself?

10. tânita kâ-wîsakisiniyan. / tânita kâ-wîsakêyihtaman.
    Ask the patient to show where the pain is.

11. âsay cî êkosi kî-isi-môsihtâw? / âsay cî êkosi kî-isi-wâh-wîsakêyihtam?
    Have they had that problem (issue) before?

12. kinwêsk cî êkosi kâ-isi-wîsakêyihtaman? / tânispîhk aspin ohci ôma kâ-itamahcihoyan?
    How long have you had your symptoms?

13. kikî-kisison cî.
    Ask if the patient has had a fever.

14. kikî-kisiwaskatân cî.
    Ask if the patient has had any stomach pain.

15. mahti niwî-nitawâpênikân kîspin ê-kisisoyan.
Ask to check their temperature.

16. mahti niwî-nitawâpênikân kîspin ê-miyopayik kimihkom.
Ask to check their blood pressure.

pahkahokowin: *pulse*
mihkwêyâpiya: *vein*

17. mahti niwî-nitawâpênikân kiyêhyêwin.
Ask to check their oxygen levels.

18. mahti niwî-nitawâpênikân:
Ask to look inside of:

kihtawakâhk – *ears*
kikohtaskwâhk – *throat*
kikotihk – *nose*
kiskîsikohk – *eyes*

19. mahti niwî-otinên apisîs mihko.
Ask for blood samples.

20. mahti kisikiwin nitawi-sâkaskinahtâ ôta.
Ask for urine samples.

21. tânisi kâ-pê-isi-âh-âhkosiyan?
What is your medical history?

22. kîkwây cî âhkosiwin kapê kimâh-mâkwahikon?
Do you have any chronic illnesses or diseases?

23. tâniyikohk kâ-wîsakêyihtaman akihtâsowina ta-âpacihtâyan
nama kîkway isko mitâtaht: nama kîkway namôya kiwîsakêyihtên êkwa mitâtaht
mâwaci mistahi kiwîsakêyihtên.
*What number would you rate your pain on a scale from 0 to 10, with zero being no pain and 10
being the worst pain you ever felt? (Add the number from 1 to 10.)*

Common Ailments

askitipayiwin	*ulcer* (NI)
katôhpinêw	*she/he has tuberculosis* (VAI)
kisiwaskatêw	*she/he has an upset stomach* (VAI)
manicôsâspinêwin	*cancer* (NI)
manicôs oskanâspinêwin	*bone cancer* (NI)
manicôs tohtôsimâspinêwin	*breast cancer* (NI)
misi-omikîwin	*smallpox* (NI)

mitihtihkosâspinêwin	*kidney disease* (NI)
ohpanâspinêwin	*lung disease* (NI)
oskonahpinêwin	*liver disease* (NI)
otakikomiwin	*a cold* (NI)
otêhâspinêwin	*heart disease* (NI)
sîwinikanâspinêwin	*diabetes* (NI)
sôkâwâspinîwin	*diabetes* (wC) (NI)
têwihtawakêw	*she/he has an earache* (VAI)
têwikanêw	*she/he has aching bones* (VAI)
têwikotêw	*she/he has an aching nose* (VAI)
têwipitonêw	*she/he has an aching arm* (VAI)
têwisitêw	*she/he has aching feet* (VAI)
têwistikwânêw	*she/he has a headache* (VAI)
têwistikwânêsiniw	*she/he has a headache from a fall* (VAI)
têyâpitêw	*she/he has a toothache* (VAI)
têyâskikanêw	*she/he has an aching chest* (VAI)
têyi-	*pain* (IPV)
têyicihcêw	*she/he has aching hands* (VAI)
têyihtawakêw	*she/he has pain in the ears* (VAI)
têyikanêw	*she/he has aching bones* (VAI)
têyikâtêw	*she/he has aching legs* (VAI)
têyistikwânêw	*she/he has a headache* (VAI)
têyisiw	*she/he has aches and pains* (VAI)
wâposwâspinêwin	*tumor disease* (NI)

In-Class Assignment

Write a short story about a visit to the clinic using the vocabulary words above. Try to write at least 10 sentences.

_____

_____

_____

_____

_____

_____

7.2.C. TEXT EXERCISES

Read each text and then answer the corresponding questions (*answers are on page 280*).

maskihkîwiyiniw ka-nitawi-wâpamiht
A Visit to the Doctor

> pêyakwâw ê-kîkisêpâyâk nikî-nisîhkâci-waniskân. mêtoni misiwê ê-kî-tâh-têyisiyân.
> *One morning I woke up slowly. I had aches and pains all over.*

1. kî-papâsi-waniskâw cî awa? *Did he get up in a hurry?*

_____

2. kî-têyisiw cî awa? *Did he have aches and pains?*

_____

> kanâcihowikamikohk nikî-itohtân, ê-nitawi-kanâcihisoyân. wâpamonihk nikî-kanawâpamison.
> *I went to the washroom, to clean myself up. I looked at myself in the mirror.*

3. tânitê awa kâ-itohtêt? *Where did he go?*

_____

4. tânisi kâ-itôtahk? *What did he do?*

_____

> wahwâ! nikî-koskwâpisinin! misiwê nihkwâkanihk êkwa niyawihk ê-kî-miyawêsiyân!
> *Wah! I was surprised by what I saw. I was hairy all over my face and all over my body!*

5. kî-koskwâpisin cî awa? *Was he surprised by what he saw?*

_____

6. kîkwây kâ-kî-wâpahtahk? *What did he see?*

_____

nikî-kakwê-kâskipâson mâka kâwi nikî-ati-miyawêsin! wahwâ! ohcitaw piko maskihkîwiyiniw
   ta-nitawi-wâpamak.
I tried to shave but I went back to being hairy. I will have to go see the doctor.

7. kî-kakwê-kâskipâsow cî awa? *Did he try to shave?*

   _____

8. kêyâpic cî kî-miyawêsiw? *Was he still hairy?*

   _____

maskihkîwiyiniw nikî-nitawi-wâpamâw. mêtoni kinwêsk nikî-pêhon mâka piyisk nikî-wâpamâw.
I went to see the doctor. I had to wait for a long time but eventually I was able to see him.

9. kî-nitawi-wâpamêw cî maskihkîwiyiniwa? *Did he go see the doctor?*

   _____

10. kinwêsk cî kî-pêhow? *Did he wait for a long time?*

   _____

maskihkîwiyiniw nikî-wîhtamâk ê-kî-miyawêyâspinêyân. namôya nânitaw ta-kî-isi-nanâtawihit.
   sôskwâc nôhcimihk nikî-itohtân ta-wîcâyâmak mistâpêw.
*The doctor told me I had the hairy disease. There was no way he can cure me. So I went into the
   forest to live with Sasquatch.*

11. tânisi awa kâ-itâspinêt? *What disease did he have?*

   _____

12. tânêhki awa nôhcimihk kâ-itohtêt? *Why did he go into the forest?*

   _____

Read the full text and then answer the questions below (*answers are on page 280*).

ayîkisis nitawi-wâpamêw maskihkîwiyiniwa
Tadpole's Visit to the Doctor

pêyakwâw êsa, ê-kî-kîkisêpâyâyik kî-koskopayiw ayîkisis. misiwê wiyawihk kî-wîsakêyihtam.
Once, in the morning a tadpole woke up. He was aching all over his body.

"âwiyâ, niyaw niwîsakêyihtên," itwêw. "piko maskihkîwiyiniw kita-nitawi-wâpamak."
nitawi-wâpamêw maskihkîwiyiniwa.
"Ouch, my body aches," he says. "I am going to have to go see the doctor." He goes to see the doctor.

"tânita kâ-wîsahkêyihtaman?" isi-kakwêcimik maskihkîwiyiniwa.
"Where does it hurt?" the doctor asks him.

"misiwê niyawihk," itwêw ayîkisis. "nitêhistikwânân, nitêyispitonân, nitêyisitân, nitêyiskâtân,
natay mîna niwîsakêyihtên," itwêw.
*"All over my body," says the tadpole. "My head aches, my arms ache, my feet ache, my legs ache, my
stomach also aches," he says.*

"namôya anima nânitaw ê-itâspinêyan," itwêw maskihkîwiyiniw. "ê-ati-kîsi-ohpikiyan anima.
ê-ohpikiyâspinêyan anima. nipâwi-maskihkiy kika-miyitin êkwa ispîhk waniskâyani wâpahki
kika-kîsi-ohpikin."
*"There is nothing wrong with you," says the doctor. "You are getting to be all grown up. You have
growing pains. I will give you some sleeping pills and when you get up tomorrow you will
finish growing."*

mîciw maskihkiy ayîkisis êkwa ati-nipâw. ispîhk kâ-kîkisêpâyâyik waniskâw. onipêwinihk ohci
kwâskohtiw.
*The tadpole eats his medicine and begins to sleep. When morning comes, he gets up. He jumps off
his bed.*

"wahwâ," itwêw. "tânêhki ôma kâ-kwâskohtiyân?"
"Whoa," he says. "Why am I jumping?"

kanawâpamisow. wahwâ! namôya awasimê ayîkisisiwiw, ayîkisiwiw êkwa! ê-kî-kîsi-ohpikit êsa
ispîhk kâ-kî-nipât.
*He looks at himself. Whoa! He is no longer a tadpole, he is a frog now! Apparently, he had finished
growing while he slept.*

Questions

1. tânita awa kâ-wîsakêyihtahk? *Where is he feeling pain?*

   _____

2. tânêhki awa kâ-wî-nitawi-wâpamât maskihkîwiyiniwa? *Why is he going to see the doctor?*

   _____

3. tânisi kâ-isi-kakwêcimikot maskihkîwiyiniwa? *What does the doctor ask him?*

   _____

4. wiyaw cî wîsakêyihtam ayîkisis? *Does the tadpole have a sore body?*

_____

5. tânisi kâ-itikot maskihkîwiyiniwa? *What does the doctor say to him?*

_____

6. kîkwây kâ-miyikot maskihkîwiyiniwa? *What does the doctor give him?*

_____

7. mîciw cî nipâwi-maskihkiy ayîkisis? *Does he eat the sleeping pill?*

_____

8. onipêwinihk cî ohci-kwâskohtiw? *Does he jump from his bed?*

_____

9. kanawâpamisow cî? *Does he look at himself?*

_____

10. ayîkisiwiw cî êkwa? *Is he now a frog?*

_____

7.3. Shopping

7.3.A. POSSESSIVES

Complete the following chart with the correct form of the possessive (*answers are on page 281*). Remember to follow the rules:

1. for nouns beginning with *mi*, replace the *mi* with *ni* for 1st person, with *ki* for 2nd person, and with *o* for 3rd person;

2. for nouns beginning with other consonants, add *ni* for 1st person, *ki* for 2nd person, and *o* for 3rd person; and

3. for nouns beginning with a vowel, use the *t* between the possessives *ni* and *ki* and *o*.

Refer back to page 150 for the rules for nouns with dependent stems.

Noun	My	Yours	Her/His
asikan – *sock* (NA)	nitasikan		
astotin – *hat* (NI)		kitastotin	
cîpwastotin – *toque* (NI)			ocîpwastotin
iskwêwasâkay – *dress* (NI)		kitiskwêwasâkay	
iskwêwitâs – *women's pants* (NA)	nitiskwêwitâs		
kîskasâkay – *skirt* (NI)		kikîskasâkay	
kîskinakwêwayân – *vest* (NI)			okîskinakwêwayân
maskisin – *shoe* (NI)		kimaskisin	
miskotâkay – *coat* (NDI)	niskotâkay		
mitâs – *pair of pants* (NDA)		kitâs	
pahkêkinwêsâkay – *leather coat* (NI)			opahkêkinwêsâkay
pahkêkinwêskisin – *leather moccasin* (NI)		kipahkêkinwêskisin	
pakwahtêhon – *belt* (NI)	nipakwahtêhon		
papakiwayân – *shirt* (NI)		kipapakiwayân	
piponasâkay – *parka* (NI)			opiponasâkay
pîhconês – *vest* (NI)		kipîhconês	
sênipânasâkay – *ribbon dress* (NI)	nisênipânasâkay		
sênipânipapakiwayân – *ribbon shirt* (NI)		kisênipânipapakiwayân	
sîpêkiskâwasâkay – *sweater* (NA)			osîpêkiskâwasâkay
tâpiskâkan – *scarf* (NA)		kitâpiskâkan	

7.3.B. SHOPPING TRIPS

Read the following two stories about everyday shopping experiences using the vocabulary provided for each story. Answer the corresponding questions to test your understanding.

ka-papâmi-atâwêhk ayawinisa êkwa mîciwin
Shopping for Clothes and Groceries

Words for the Story

âhci piko	*and still*	nakata	*leave it* (VTI-1)
askipwâwi	*potato*	namôya katâc	*not necessary*
asiwatâ	*put it in a container* (VAI-2)	nanâtohk	*any kind*
atâwêwikamik	*store*	nâta	*get it* (VTI-1)
atâwêwikamik-		nawasôna	*choose* (VTI-1)
simâkanis	*store detective*	nikotwâso-kîsikâw	*It is Saturday* (VII)
ati-	*begin* (IPV)	nîpâmâyâtan	*it is purple* (VII)
awîna	*who*	nîpiya	*lettuce*
âtiht	*some*	ohci	*from*
ayiwinisa	*clothes*	otin	*take someone* (VTA)
êkosi	*then*	otina	*take something* (VTI-1)
êkota ohci	*from there*	otinikêwi-âwacikan	*shopping cart* (NI)
êkwa	*and*	pakitina	*let it go* (VTI-1)
isi-	*toward that direction* (IPV)	pamihcikê	*drive* (VAI)
itasinâso	*be coloured so* (VAI)	papakiwayân	*shirt*
itasinâstêw	*it is coloured thus* (VII)	papâmi-	*go about* (IPV)
kapâ	*get out of a vehicle* (VAI)	papêyâhtak	*carefully*
kapê	*always*	picikwâs	*apple*
kaskitêsiw	*it is black* (VAI)	pîhtokwê	*enter* (VAI)
kîko	*which*	piko kîkway	*all things*
kîmôtâpam	*peek at someone* (VTA)	pimitisah	*follow someone* (VTA)
kohkôsiwiyin	*bacon*	piyisk	*eventually*
kotakihk	*at another place*	pîswêhkasikan	*bread*
mêtoni	*very*	sâkaskinahtâ	*fill up* (VTI-2)
mîciwin	*food, groceries*	sêhkêpayîs	*car*
mihcêtinwa	*there are many* (VII)	sîpihkosiw	*it is blue* (VAI)
mihkwâw	*it is red* (VII)	sôskwâc	*regardless*
mînis	*berry*	tânitê	*where*
misiwâc	*in any case*	wâpam	*see someone* (VTA)
miskotâkay	*coat*	wâpiskisiw	*it is white* (VAI)
mistahi	*lots*	wayawî	*exit, go out* (VAI)
mitâs	*a pair of pants*	yahkowêpina	*push it* (VTI-1)
mwêhci	*exactly when, exact*		

Read the full text and then answer the questions below.

ispîhk kâ-kî-nikotwâso-kîsikâk nikî-nitawi-papâmi-atâwân.
When it was Saturday, I went shopping.

ayiwinisa nikî-nôhtê-atâwân.
I wanted to buy clothes.

atâwêwikamikohk nikî-isi-pamihcikân.
I drove to the store.

nikî-kapân sêhkêpayîsihk ohci êkwa nikî-pîhtokwân atâwêwikamikohk.
I got out of the car and entered the store.

otinikêwi-âwacikan nikî-nawasônên êkwa nikî-ati-papâmi-atâwân ayiwinisa.
I selected a shopping cart and went shopping for clothes.

papêyâhtak nikî-yahkowêpinên nitotinikêwi-âwacikan.
I carefully pushed my shopping cart.

ayiwinisa nikî-nâtên.
I went to get clothes.

nikî-otinâw ê-sîpihkosit mitâs.
I bought a pair of blue pants.

nikî-otinâwak ê-kaskitêsicik asikanak êkwa mîna âtiht ê-sîpihkosicik.
I bought black socks and some that were blue.

nikî-otinên ê-mihkwâk papakiwayân êkwa miskotâkay ê-nîpâmâyâtahk.
I bought a red shirt and a coat that was purple.

mwêhci ê-wî-otinakik tâpiskâkanak ê-wâpiskisicik kâ-wâpamak atâwêwikamik-simâkanis
ê-kâh-kîmôtâpamit.
Just when I was going to buy white scarves, I saw a store detective sneaking a look at me.

nipakitinâwak tâpiskâkanak, namôya katâc niwî-otinâwak.
I put down the scarves, not bothering to buy them.

mîciwina nikî-ati-nâtên.
I headed for the food.

êkotê nikî-isi-pimitisahok ana atâwêwikamik-simâkanis.
The store detective followed me that way.

kapê nikî-pimitisahok awa atâwêwikamik-simâkanis.
This store detective was always following me.

mistahi mîciwin nikî-asiwatân nitotinikêwi-âwacikanihk.
I loaded a lot of food into my shopping cart.

âhci-piko nikî-pimitisahok awa atâwêwikamik-simâkanis.
Still, the store detective followed me.

nikî-otinên wâwa, askipwâwa, nanâtohk mînisa, êkwa nîpiya.
I bought eggs, potatoes, all sorts of berries, and lettuce.

nikî-otinâwak pîswêhkasikanak, picikwâsak, mîna kohkôsiwiyin.
I bought bread, apples, and bacon.

âhci-piko nikî-pimitisahok awa atâwêwikamik-simâkanis.
Still the store detective followed me.

nikî-kisiwâhik!
He made me angry!

sôskwâc piko-kîkway nikî-ati-asiwatân nitonikêwi-âwacikanihk.
So I started to put all sorts of stuff into my shopping cart.

piyisk ê-kî-ati-sâkaskinahtâyân nitonikêwi-âwacikan.
Eventually I filled up my shopping cart.

êkosi nikî-nakatên êkota.
In that way I left it there.

namôya katâc kîkway nikî-atâwân êkota ohci.
I didn't bother buying anything from there.

nikî-wayawîn êkwa nikî-pamihcikân kotakihk atâwêwikamikohk isi.
I walked out of there and drove to another store.

misiwâc mihcêtinwa atâwêwikamikwa.
Anyway, there are a lot of stores.

Note: The following questions are in the 1st person, so answer in the 2nd person. The first one is done for you *(answers are on page 281).*

1. tânispîhk kâ-kî-nitawi-papâmi-atâwêyân?

   kâ-kî-nikotwâso-kîsikâk anima ispîhk kâ-kî-nitawi-atâwêyan.

2. tânitê kâ-kî-nitawi-papâmi-atâwêyân?

   _____

3. tânisi kâ-itasinâsot mitâs kâ-kî-otinak?

   _____

4. tânisi kâ-itasinâsocik asikanak kâ-kî-otinakik?

   _____

5. tânisi kâ-itasinâstêk papakiwayân kâ-kî-otinamân?

   _____

6. tânisi kâ-itasinâstêk miskotâkay kâ-kî-otinamân?

   _____

7. kîko mîciwin kâ-kî-otinamân?

   _____

8. awîna kâ-kî-pimitisahot?

   _____

9. tânisi kâ-kî-itôtamân?

   _____

10. nikî-atâwân cî kîkway êkota ohci?

   _____

ka-papâmi-atâwêhk mîciwin
Shopping for Groceries

Words for the Story

âhkwakihtêw	*it is expensive* (VII)	pâhkahâhkwâniwiyâs	*chicken meat*
êwakoni	*those ones*	palôniy	*bologna*
isi-	*toward that direction*	pamihcikê	*drive* (VAI)
ita	*where there is*	papâmi-	*go about* (IPV)
itakihtêw	*it costs* (VII)	sisikopicikaniwiyâs	*ground meat*
itohtê	*go* (VAI)	pêyak sôniyâs	*quarter (25 cents)*
kanawâpahta	*look at something* (VTI-1)	sôniyâs	*little bit of money*
kohkôsiwiyâs	*pork*	sôpirstôrihk	*at Superstore*
kosikwanis	*kilogram*	sôskwâc	*may as well*
mitâtahtwâpisk	*ten dollars*	spâm	*Spam*
mostosowiyâs	*beef*	-tahtwâpisk	*dollars*
nawasôna	*choose something* (VTI-1)	tânitahtwakihtêk	*how much is it?*
osâm	*because, too*	wahwâ!	*whoa!*
osâm âhkwakihtêw	*it is too expensive*	wêhtakihtêw	*it is inexpensive* (VII)
otakisîhkâna	*sausage*	wiyâs	*meat*
otinikêwi-âwacikan	*shopping cart*		

Read the full text and then answer the questions below.

ispîhk kâ-kî-ayamihêwi-kîsikâk nikî-nitawi-papâmi-atâwân.
When it was Sunday, I went shopping.

mîciwina nikî-nôhtê-atâwân.
I wanted to buy groceries.

sôpirstôrihk nikî-isi-pamihcikân.
I drove to Superstore.

otinikêwi-âwacikan nikî-nawasônên êkwa nikî-ati-papâmi-atâwân mîciwina.
I selected a shopping cart and went shopping for groceries.

nikî-itohtân ita wiyâsa kâ-atâwêhk.
I went to the meat section.

nikî-kanawâpahtên mostosowiyâs.
I looked at the beef.

wahwâ! nîstosâp tahtwâpisk mîna nîso sôniyâs pêyak kosikwanis ê-itakihtêk mostosowiyâs.
Whoa!! Beef costs $13.50 for one kg!

osâm âhkwakihtêw!
It is too expensive!

nikî-kanawâpahtên kohkôsiwiyâs.
I looked at the pork.

wahwâ! mitâtahtwâpisk mîna nisto sôniyâs pêyak kosikwanis ê-itakihtêk kohkôsiwiyâs.
Whoa!! Pork costs $10.75 for one kg!

osâm âhkwakihtêw!
It is too expensive!

nikî-kanawâpahtên pâhkahâhkwâniwiyâs.
I looked at the chicken (meat).

wahwâ! kêkâ-mitâtaht-tahtwâpisk pêyak kosikwanis ê-itakihtêk pâhkahâhkwâniwiyâs.
Whoa!! Chicken meat costs $9.00 for one kg!

osâm âhkwakihtêw!
It is too expensive!

sôskwâc nikî-otinên sisikopicikaniwiyâs, otakisîhkâna, spâm êkwa palôniy…êwakoni kî-wêhtakihtêwa.
So I bought ground beef, sausages, Spam, and bologna…those were inexpensive.

The text above is in the 1st person but the questions are in the 3rd person, so answer in the 3rd person. The first one is done for you (*answers are on page 281*).

1. tânispîhk awa kâ-kî-nitawi-papâmi-atâwêt?

   kî-nitawi-papâmi-atâwêw awa ispîhk kâ-kî-ayamihêwi-kîsikâyik.

2. kîkwây awa kâ-kî-nôhtê-atâwêt?

   _____

3. tânitê kâ-kî-nitawi-papâmi-atâwêt?

   _____

4. kîkwây kâ-kakwê-otinahk?

_____

5. tânitahtwakihtêk pêyak kosikwanis mostosowiyâs?

_____

6. osâm cî âhkwakihtêw mostosowiyâs?

_____

7. tânitahtwakihtêk pêyak kosikwanis kohkôsiwiyâs?

_____

8. osâm cî âhkwakihtêw kohkôsiwiyâs?

_____

9. tânitahtwakihtêk pêyak kosikwanis pâhkahâhkwâniwiyâs?

_____

10. kîkwâya wêhtakihtêyiwa kâ-otinahk?

_____

7.3.C. COLOURS AND CLOTHES

Vocabulary

askihtakosiw	_it is green_ (VAI)	askihtako-astis	_green mitt_
askihtakwâw	_it is green_ (VII)	askihtak-asâkay	_green coat/skirt_
kaskitêsiw	_it is black_ (VAI)	kaskitêwi-iskwêwasâkay	_black dress/skirt_
kaskitêwâw	_it is black_ (VII)	kaskitêw-askisin	_black shoe_
mihkosiw	_it is red_ (VAI)	mihkw-asikan	_red sock_
mihkwâw	_it is red_ (VAI)	mihkw-astotin	_red hat_
nîpâmâyâtan	_it is purple_ (VII)	nîpâmâyât-astis	_purple mitt_
nîpâmâyâtisiw	_it is purple_ (VAI)	nîpâmâyât-asâkay	_purple coat/skirt_
osâwâw	_it is orange_ (VII)	osâwi-nâpêwasâkay	_man's orange coat_
osâwisiw	_it is orange_ (VAI)	osâwi-papakiwayân	_orange shirt_
sîpihkosiw	_it is blue_ (VAI)	sîpihko-nîpinasâkay	_blue summer coat_
sîpihkwâw	_it is blue_ (VII)	sîpihko-tâs	_blue pants_

wâpiskâw	*it is white* (VII)	wâpiskâwi-papakiwayân	*white shirt*	
wâpiskisiw	*it is white* (VAI)	wâpiskâwi-kîskitâs	*white shorts*	
wâposâwâw	*it is yellow* (VII)	wâposâwi-tâpiskâkan	*yellow scarf*	
wâposâwisiw	*it is yellow* (VII)	wâposâwi-papakiwayânis	*yellow t-shirt*	

More words used when shopping for clothes:

atâwê	*buy* (VAI-*t*)	papâmi-atâwê	*go shopping* (VAI)
otinikê	*make a purchase* (VAI)	otina	*take/buy something* (VTI)
otinikêwin	*a purchase*	otin	*take/buy something* (VTA)
wêhtakihtêw	*it is cheap* (VII)	wêhtakisow	*it is cheap* (VAI)
âhkwakihtêw	*it is expensive* (VII)	âhkwakisow	*it is expensive* (VAI)

Colour terms are formed by attaching the colour root word to the forms in the other columns, depending on the animacy, number, and colour of the noun.

Root	Item Itself; Item Belongs to 1st and 2nd	Item Belongs to 3rd Person	Item Itself; Item Belongs to 1st and 2nd "It Looks"	Item Belongs to 3rd Person "It Looks"
mihk – *red* sîpihk – *blue* askihtak – *green* cîpêhtak – *grey*	wâw(a) NI (pl) osiw(ak) NA (P1)	wâyiw(a) osiyiwa	onâkwan(wa) onâkosiw(ak)	onâkwaniyiw(a) onâkosiyiwa
osâw – *orange* kaskitê-osâw – *brown* wâposâw – *yellow* wâpisk – *white*	âw(a) NI (pl) isiw(ak) NA (P1)	âyiw(a) isiyiwa	inâkwan(wa) inâkosiw(ak)	inâkwaniyiw(a) inâkosiyiwa
kaskitê – *black*	wâw(a) NI (pl) siw(ak) NA (P1)	wâyiw(a) siyiwa	winâkwan(wa) winâkosiw(ak)	winâkwaniyiw(a) winâkosiyiwa
nîpâmâyât – *purple*	an(wa) NI (pl) isiw(ak) NA (P1)	aniyiw(a) isiyiwa	inâkwan(wa) inâkosiw(ak)	inâkwaniyiw(a) inâkosiyiwa

Based on the patterns above, complete the following two charts for inanimate and animate nouns (*answers are on page 282*).

Colour Prenoun (IPN)	Inanimate Nouns: Colour Root + -wâw	Animate Nouns: Colour Root + -siw
mihko- – *red*		
wâposâwi- – *yellow*		
sîpihko- – *blue*		
osâwi- – *orange*		
askihtako- – *green*		
nîpâmâyâci- – *violet (purple)*		
wâpiski- – *white*		
kaskitêwi- – *black*		
kaskitêwi-osâwi- – *brown*		
cîpêhtako- – *grey*		
mihkosâwi- – *red-orange*		
wâposâwisâwi- – *yellow-orange*		
wâposâwi-askihtako- – *yellow-green*		
osâwasko- – *blue-green*		
mihko-sîpihko- – *blue-violet*		

Colour Prenoun (IPN)	It Looks Like (A Certain Colour) for Inanimate Nouns: Colour Root + -inâkwan	It Looks Like (A Certain Colour) for Animate Nouns: Colour Root + -inâkosiw
mihko- – *red*		
wâposâwi- – *yellow*		
sîpihko- – *blue*		
osâwi- – *orange*		
askihtako- – *green*		
nîpâmâyâci- – *violet (purple)*		
wâpiski- – *white*		
kaskitêwi- – *black*		
kaskitêwi-osâwi- – *brown*		
cîpêhtako- – *grey*		
mihkosâwi- – *red-orange*		
wâposâwisâwi- – *yellow-orange*		
wâposâwi-askihtako- – *yellow-green*		
osâwasko- – *blue-green*		
mihko-sîpihko- – *blue-violet*		

7.3.D. SHOPPING EXERCISES

Part 1: Dialogues

Read the following dialogues with a partner.

Dialogue 1 (imagine you have a picture of a dozen eggs):

A: kîkwây kikî-atâwânâwâw?
What did you (pl) *buy?*

B: wâwa nikî-atâwânân. kiyawâw mâka, kîkwây kiwî-atâwânâwâw?
We bought eggs. How about you (pl), *what are you* (pl) *going to buy?*

A: maskisina niwî-atâwânân.
We are going to buy shoes.

Dialogue 2 (imagine you have a picture of a red dress):

A: kîkwây kikî-atâwân?
What did you (sg) *buy?*

B: iskwêwasâkay nikî-atâwân.
I bought a dress.

Dialogue 3 (imagine you have a picture of a man's jacket):

A: kîkwây wî-atâwêw?
What is she/he going to buy?

B: nâpêwasâkay wî-atâwêw.
She/he is going to buy a man's jacket.

Dialogue 4 (imagine you have a picture of a summer jacket):

A: kîkwây wî-atâwêwak?
What are they going to buy?

B: nîpinasâkay wî-atâwêwak.
They are going to buy a summer jacket.

Part 2: Help!

Help the shopper choose the right colour item on the shopping list. The following exercise shows the colour and clothing item as separate words as well as in their compound forms: the colours are in both conjunct and indicative forms.

Note how the colour terms and the interrogative pronouns change to agree in animacy of the noun: all animate colours end in *siw* or *sit* (singular) or *siwak* or *sicik* (plural); all inanimate colours end in *(w)âw* or *(w)âk* (singular) and *(w)âwa* or *(w)âki* (plural). Also, the interrogative pronouns for *which* need animacy agreement: *tâna* for animate nouns and *tânima* for inanimate nouns. Use *ôma* "this" for inanimate nouns and *awa* for animate nouns in your answers.

In the exercises below, read the dialogue with each other and then describe the colour of the clothing item in the space provided.

A: ninôhtê-atâwân ê-mihkwâk papakiwayân.
I want to buy a shirt that is red.

B: mihko-papakiwayân cî?
A red shirt?

A: âha, tânima mihkwâw papakiwayân?
Yes, which shirt is red?

blue shirt   _____

red shirt   _____

A: ninôhtê-atâwân ê-sîhpihkosit mitâs.
I want to buy a (pair of) pants that is blue.

B: sîpihko-tâs cî?
A blue (pair of) pants?

A: âha, tâna sîpihkosiw mitâs?
Yes, which (pair of) pants is blue?

blue pants   _____

brown pants   _____

A: ninôhtê-atâwân ê-askihtakwâk miskotâkay.
I want to buy a coat that is green.

B: askihtakwa-sâkay cî?
A green coat?

A: âha, tânima askihtakwâw miskotâkay?
Yes, which coat is green?

blue jacket _____

green jacket _____

A: ninôhtê-atâwân ê-osâwâk astotin.
I want to buy a hat that is orange.

B: osâw-astotin cî?
An orange hat?

A: âha, tânima osâwâw astotin?
Yes, which hat is orange?

orange hat _____

black hat _____

A: ninôhtê-atâwân ê-wâposâwisit tâpiskâkan.
I want to buy a scarf that is yellow.

B: wâposâwi-tâpiskâkan cî?
A yellow scarf?

A: âha, tâna wâposâwisiw tâpiskâkan?
Yes, which scarf is yellow?

orange scarf _____

yellow scarf _____

A: ninôhtê-atâwân ê-wâpiskisit asikan.
I want to buy a (pair of) sock(s) that is white.

B: wâpisk-asikan cî?
A white (pair of) sock(s)?

A: âha, tâna wâpiskisiw asikan?
Yes, which (pair of) sock(s) is white?

white sock(s) _____

green sock(s) _____

A: ninôhtê-atâwân ê-kaskitêwâk maskisin.
I want to buy a (pair of) shoe(s) that is black.

B: kaskitêw-askisin cî?
A black (pair of) shoe(s)?

A: âha, tânima kaskitêwâw maskisin?
Yes, which (pair of) shoe(s) is black?

red shoe(s) _____

black shoe(s) _____

A: ninôhtê-atâwân ê-nîpâmâyâtisit astis.
I want to buy a (pair of) mitt(s) that is purple.

B: nîpâmâyât-astis cî?
A purple (pair of) mitt(s)?

A: âha, tâna nîpâmâyâtisiw astis?
Yes, which (pair of) mitt(s) is purple?

purple mitt(s) _____

green mitt(s) _____

CHAPTER 8

. . . .

TRANSITIVE ANIMATE VERBS
DIRECT FORMS (VTA-DIRECT)

8.1. Transitive Animate Verbs

The transitive animate verbs (VTA) take objects that are animate. VTAs need number agreement with their objects in the 1st and 2nd person forms and obviation of the object in the 3rd person forms. The following chart shows the VTA paradigms.

8.1.A. VTA IMPERATIVES

Note: the brackets show number agreement if the third person (3) object is plural.

	Imperative	Negative Imperative	Delayed Imperative
2	_____(ik)	êkâwiya _____(ik)	_____âhkan(ik)
2P	_____ihk(ok)	êkâwiya _____ihk(ok)	_____âhkêk(ok)
21	_____âtân(ik)	êkâwiya _____âtân(ik)	_____âhkahk(ik)

Complete the following chart following the imperative paradigm above (*answers are on page 283*).

English	2nd Person Singular	2nd Person Plural	2nd Person Inclusive
Imperative: *Look at someone.**	kanawâpam(ik)		
Negative Imperative: *Don't look at someone.*		êkâwiya kanawâpamihk(ok)	
Delayed Imperative: *Look at someone later.*			kanawâpamâhkahk(ik)
Imperative: *See someone.*		wâpamihk(ok)	
Negative Imperative: *Don't see someone.*	êkâwiya wâpam(ik)		
Delayed Imperative: *See someone later.*		wâpamâhkêk(ok)	
Imperative: *Look for someone.*			natonawâtân(ik)
Negative Imperative: *Don't look for someone.*		êkâwiya natonawihk(ok)	
Delayed Imperative: *Look for someone later.*	natonawâhkan(ik)		
Imperative: *Find someone.*		miskawihk(ok)	
Negative Imperative: *Don't find someone.*			êkâwiya miskawâtân(ik)
Delayed Imperative: *Find someone later.*		miskawâhkêk(ok)	

* Note that the animate objects of VTAs in English are translated using different words. When the animate noun refers to a person, it is translated as singular "someone" and plural "them," but when the object is not a person, English uses singular "something" or "it" and plural "them," as in the example *kisis* "cook it/them." In this chapter, we use "someone" for most examples, or "it" when necessary.

8.2. Transitive Animate Verb Charts

Verb Stem: kanawâpam(ik) *"look at someone (them)"*

Person and Tense	Indicative	Conjunct
1st present (pres)	nikanawâpamâw(ak)	ê-kanawâpamak(ik)
1st past	nikî-kanawâpamâw(ak)	ê-kî-kanawâpamak(ik)
1st future intentional (fut int)	niwî-kanawâpamâw(ak)	ê-wî-kanawâpamak(ik)
1st future definite (fut def)	nika-kanawâpamâw(ak)	
2nd pres	kikanawâpamâw(ak)	ê-kanawâpamat(cik)
2nd past	kikî-kanawâpamâw(ak)	ê-kî-kanawâpamat(cik)
2nd fut int	kiwî-kanawâpamâw(ak)	ê-wî-kanawâpamat(cik)
2nd fut def	kika-kanawâpamâw(ak)	
3rd pres	kanawâpamêw	ê-kanawâpamât
3rd past	kî-kanawâpamêw	ê-kî-kanawâpamât
3rd fut int	wî-kanawâpamêw	ê-wî-kanawâpamât
3rd fut def	ta-kanawâpamêw	
3' pres	kanawâpamêyiwa	ê-kanawâpamâyit
3' past	kî-kanawâpamêyiwa	ê-kî-kanawâpamâyit
3' fut int	wî-kanawâpamêyiwa	ê-wî-kanawâpamâyit
3' fut def	ta-kanawâpamêyiwa	
1P pres	nikanawâpamânân(ak)	ê-kanawâpamâyâhk(ik)
1P past	nikî-kanawâpamânân(ak)	ê-kî-kanawâpamâyâhk(ik)
1P fut int	niwî-kanawâpamânân(ak)	ê-wî-kanawâpamâyâhk(ik)
1P fut def	nika-kanawâpamânân(ak)	
21 pres	kikanawâpamânaw(ak)	ê-kanawâpamâyahk(ik)
21 past	kikî-kanawâpamânaw(ak)	ê-kî-kanawâpamâyahk(ik)
21 fut int	kiwî-kanawâpamânaw(ak)	ê-wî-kanawâpamâyahk(ik)
21 fut def	kika-kanawâpamânaw(ak)	
2P pres	kikanawâpamâwâw(ak)	ê-kanawâpamâyêk(ok)
2P past	kikî-kanawâpamâwâw(ak)	ê-kî-kanawâpamâyêk(ok)
2P fut int	kiwî- kanawâpamâwâw(ak)	ê-wî-kanawâpamâyêk(ok)
2P fut def	kika- kanawâpamâwâw(ak)	
3P pres	kanawâpamêwak	ê-kanawâpamâcik
3P past	kî-kanawâpamêwak	ê-kî-kanawâpamâcik
3P fut int	wî-kanawâpamêwak	ê-wî-kanawâpamâcik
3P fut def	ta-kanawâpamêwak	

There are a few rules to keep in mind in conjugating VTAs: 1) if the verb stem begins with a vowel, then the *t* is used to connect the person indicator to the verb stem in the present tense of the indicative for 1st and 2nd persons; 2) if the object is plural, then the verb also has to be in the plural form for the 1st and 2nd persons of the indicative; and 3) the object of a 3rd person verb is marked for obviation with a final *a*.

Let's look at the VTA *asam* "feed someone." It comes from the 2 of the imperative:

2	asam(ik)	*feed someone*
2P	asamihk(ok)	*feed someone*
21	asamâtân(ik)	*let's feed someone*

Verb Stem: asam *"feed someone"*

Person and Tense	Indicative	Conjunct
1st present (pres)	nitasamâw(ak)	ê-asamak(ik)
1st past	nikî-asamâw(ak)	ê-kî-asamak(ik)
1st future intentional (fut int)	niwî-asamâw(ak)	ê-wî-asamak(ik)
1st future definite (fut def)	nika-asamâw(ak)	
2nd pres	kitasamâw(ak)	ê-asamat(cik)
2nd past	kikî-asamâw(ak)	ê-kî-asamat(cik)
2nd fut int	kiwî-asamâw(ak)	ê-wî-asamat(cik)
2nd fut def	kika-asamâw(ak)	
3rd pres	asamêw	ê-asamât
3rd past	kî-asamêw	ê-kî-asamât
3rd fut int	wî-asamêw	ê-wî-asamât
3rd fut def	ta-asamêw	
3' pres	asamêyiwa	ê-asamâyit
3' past	kî-asamêyiwa	ê-kî-asamâyit
3' fut int	wî-asamêyiwa	ê-wî-asamâyit
3' fut def	ta-asamêyiwa	
1P pres	nitasamânân(ak)	ê-asamâyâhk(ik)
1P past	nikî-asamânân(ak)	ê-kî-asamâyâhk(ik)
1P fut int	niwî-asamânân(ak)	ê-wî-asamâyâhk(ik)
1P fut def	nika-asamânân(ak)	
21 pres	kitasamânaw(ak)	ê-asamâyahk(ik)
21 past	kikî-asamânaw(ak)	ê-kî-asamâyahk(ik)
21 fut int	kiwî-asamânaw(ak)	ê-wî-asamâyahk(ik)
21 fut def	kika-asamânaw(ak)	
2P pres	kitasamâwâw(ak)	ê-asamâyêk(ok)
2P past	kikî-asamâwâw(ak)	ê-kî-asamâyêk(ok)
2P fut int	kiwî-asamâwâw(ak)	ê-wî-asamâyêk(ok)
2P fut def	kika-asamâwâw(ak)	
3P pres	asamêwak	ê-asamâcik
3P past	kî-asamêwak	ê-kî-asamâcik
3P fut int	wî-asamêwak	ê-wî-asamâcik
3P fut def	ta- asamêwak	

8.2.A. EXERCISES WITH VTAS

Complete the following chart with the indicative and conjunct forms of the common VTA verb stems provided (*answers are on page 283*).

Verb Stem *(comes from the 2 of the imperative)*	Person and Tense	Indicative	Conjunct
2 otin(ik) – *take someone*	1st pres		
2P otinihk(ok)	1st past		
21 otinâtân(ik)	1st fut int		
	1st fut def		
2 nâs(ik) – *get someone*	2nd pres		
2P nâtihk(ok)	2nd past		
21 nâtâtân(ik)	2nd fut int		
	2nd fut def		
2 natonaw(ik) – *look for someone*	3rd pres		
2P natonawihk(ok)	3rd past		
21 natonawâtân(ik)	3rd fut int		
	3rd fut def		
2 miskaw(ik) – *find someone*	3' pres		
2P miskawihk(ok)	3' past		
21 miskawâtân(ik)	3' fut int		
	3' fut def		

Verb Stem (comes from the 2 of the imperative)	Person and Tense	Indicative	Conjunct
2 natohtaw(ik) – *listen to someone*	1P pres		
2P natohtawihk(ok)	1P past		
21 natohtawâtân(ik)	1P fut int		
	1P fut def		
2 pêhtaw(ik) – *hear someone*	21 pres		
2P pêhtawihk(ok)	21 past		
21 pêhtawâtân(ik)	21 fut int		
	21 fut def		
2 nisitohtaw(ik) – *understand someone*	2P pres		
2P nisitohtawihk(ok)	2P past		
21 nisitohtawâtân(ik)	2P fut int		
	2P fut def		
2 wâpam(ik) – *see someone*	3P pres		
2P wâpamihk(ok)	3P past		
21 wâpamâtân(ik)	3P fut int		
	3P fut def		

8.2.B. VTA CONJUGATIONS

Part 1

Complete the following conjugations by first finding the verb stems in each row and then making the transformations to the imperatives in each column (*answers are on page 284*).

Subject/Actor		Imperative	Negative Imperative	Delayed Imperative
2	you (sg)	wâpam – *see someone*		
2P	you (pl)		êkâwiya natonawi**hk** – *Don't look for someone!*	
21	let's (you and I)			natohtaw**âhkahk** – *let's listen to someone (later)*
2	you (sg)		êkâwiya mêtawâkâ**s** – *don't disrespect someone*	
2P	you (pl)			atoskaw**âhkêk** – *work for someone (later)*
21	let's (you and I)	kanawâpam**âtân** – *let's look at someone*		
2	you (sg)			kîsis**wâhkan** – *cook it* (later)*
2P	you (pl)	kocispisi**hk** – *taste it**		
21	let's (you and I)		êkâwiya nât**âtân** – *let's not fetch someone*	

---

* *it* refers to an animate noun

Complete the following indicative and conjunct forms in the charts below (*answers are on page 284*).

Singular subject

Subject/Actor	Indicative	Conjunct
	atoskaw "work for someone" in the present tense	*kanawâpam* "look at someone" in the past tense
1 I	**nit**atoskaw**âw**	
2 you		ê-**kî**-kanawâpam**at**
3 she/he		
3' her/his (friend)	atoskaw**êyiwa**	

Plural subject

Subject/Actor	Indicative	Conjunct
	mow "eat it*" in the future definite tense with preverb *nôhtê-* "want to"	*natonaw* "look for someone" in the future intentional tense
1P we (excl)		ê-**wî**-natonaw**âyâhk**
21 we (incl)	**kika**-nôhtê-mow**ânaw**	
2P you (pl)		
3P they		ê-**wî**-natonaw**âcik**

....

*   *it* refers to an animate noun

Part 2

Using the verbs from the conjugations in Part 1, along with the following vocabulary words, translate the sentences below (*answers are on page 285*).

Preverbs

kakwê-	*try to*
nitawi-	*go and*

Kinship

nistês	*my older brother*
kimosôminawak	*our* (incl) *grandfathers*
kimisinaw	*our* (incl) *older sister*
nimosôminân	*our* (excl) *grandfather*
ohkoma	*her/his grandmother*

Temporal Words

tipiskohk	*last night*
otâkosiki	*in the evening*
tipiskâki	*tonight*
wâpahki	*tomorrow*
anohc	*today*
otâkosîhk	*yesterday*

Nouns

kinosêw	*fish*
onîmihitowa	*dancers* (obviative)
wâpos	*rabbit*
misihêw	*turkey*

Verb in Future Conditional

âtayôhkêci	*if she/he tells a sacred story*

1. tipiskohk nikî-natonawâw nistês.

   _____

2. mowâhkahk kinosêw otâkosiki.

   _____

3. tipiskohk kî-kanawâpamêwak onîmihitowa.

   _____

4. otâkosiki kika-nitawi-natohtawânawak kimosôminawak.

   _____

5. tipiskâki cî kiwî-kocispitâwak wâposwak?

   _____

6. kika-nâtâwâw kimisinaw wâpahki.

_____

7. kî-wâpamêyiwa ohkoma tipiskohk.

_____

8. wî-atoskawêw ohkoma anohc.

_____

9. niwî-natohtawânân nimosôminân âtayôhkêci tipiskâki.

_____

10. kikî-kakwê-kîsiswâwâw misihêw otâkosîhk.

_____

8.3. VTA Paradigms

To complete the paradigm below, the verb stem is placed in the blanks to create the indicative, conjunct, and future conditional forms.

VTA Indicative, Conjunct and Future Conditional Forms

	Indicative	Conjunct	Future Conditional
1	ni_____âw(ak)	ê-_____ak(ik)	_____aki
2	ki_____âw(ak)	ê-_____at(cik)	_____aci
3	_____êw	ê-_____ât	_____âci
3'	_____mêyiwa	ê-_____âyit	_____âyici
1P	ni_____ânân(ak)	ê-_____âyâhk(ik)	_____âyâhki
21	ki_____ânaw(ak)	ê-_____âyahk(ik)	_____âyahki
2P	ki_____âwâw(ak)	ê-_____âyêk(ok)	_____âyêko
3P	_____êwak	ê-_____âcik	_____âtwâwi
3'P	_____êyiwa	ê-_____âyit	_____âyici

Rules for VTAs

1. **Number agreement**: if the object of 1st and 2nd persons is plural, then the verb must show number agreement by adding *ik* or *ok*, as in the above paradigm.

2. **Obviation**: objects of 3rd person verbs are marked for obviation by an *a* at the end of the noun.

8.3.A. TRANSLATION 1

Translate the sentences below into English using the following list of verb stems (*answers are on page 285*).

VTA Verb Stems

otin	*take someone*	nisitawêyim	*recognize someone*
nâs	*fetch someone*	atoskâs	*work for someone*
sâmin	*touch someone*	masinahamaw	*write to someone*
pêhtaw	*hear someone*	postiskaw	*put someone on*
nitawêyim	*want someone*	kêcikoskaw	*take it* off*
mîskon	*feel someone*	kisîpêkin	*wash someone*
natohtaw	*listen to someone*	kîsis	*cook it**
natonaw	*look for someone*	itôtaw	*do it**
miskaw	*find someone*	mêtawâkâs	*disrespect someone*
wâpam	*see someone*	yôhtên	*open it**
kanawâpam	*look at someone*	kipahw-	*close it**
kocispis	*taste it**	ohpin	*lift someone up*
paswâs	*sniff someone*	yahkiwêpin	*push someone*
nisitohtaw	*understand someone*	ocipis	*pull someone*
kiskêyim	*know someone*	nâkatawêyim	*take care of someone*
miyâm	*smell someone*		

1. kîkisêp nikî-otinâwak nitasikanak mohcihk ohci.

   _____

2. kîkisêpâyâki niwî-nâtâwak awâsisak.

   _____

---

*   *it* refers to an animate noun

3. pêyako-kîsikâki nitawi-wîcihâhkêk kimosômiwâw.

    _____

4. nîso-kîsikâki niwî-natonawâw nitêm nôhcimihk.

    _____

5. kotak ispayiki nika-nitawi-kanawâpamâwak opwâtisimowak.

    _____

6. otâhk-ispayiw nikî-pêhtawâwak otâtayôhkêwak.

    _____

7. otâhk-askîwin cî kikî-natohtawâwak nêhiyawi-âtayôhkêwak.

    _____

8. wî-kêcikoskawêw otastisa.

    _____

9. kakwê-nisitohtawâhkan nêhiyawêci.

    _____

10. tahkâyâyiki wî-postiskawêw wâposwayân-asikana.

    _____

8.3.B. TRANSLATION 2

Translate the following sentences into Cree, keeping in mind obviation and number agreement for these VTAS (_answers are on page 285_):

miy	_give it to someone_	wîsâm	_invite someone_
wîcih	_help someone_	asam	_feed someone_
wîcêw	_accompany someone_	mow	_eat it*_
masinahamaw	_write to someone_	miskaw	_find someone_

....

* _it_ refers to an animate noun

1. I gave that book to your older sister.

   _____

2. Did you give your shoes to your cousin (paternal uncle's son)?

   _____

3. He invited your father to the store.

   _____

4. Let's help your younger brother tonight.

   _____

5. She fed the boys ducks.

   _____

6. Are you (sg) going to write to your mother?

   _____

7. I fed my friend bannock.

   _____

8. I ate fish last night.

   _____

9. Did you (sg) accompany the girls to the university this morning.

   _____

10. I will accompany you (pl) to the lake.

    _____

11. He will accompany you (pl) to the store.

    _____

12. Give them your books when you (pl) see them.

    _____

8.3.c. TEXT EXERCISES

Read each text and then answer the corresponding questions using the vocabulary words for each story (*answers are on page 286*).

kâ-mâmawinitohk
A Gathering

Words for the Story

ahpô mîna	*even*	mînisa	*berries*
âmaciwîspimowinihk	*at Stanley Mission*	manôminak	*wild rice*
awâsis	*child*	mêtawâniwin	*there are games*
awâsisîwi	*be a child* (VAI)	mîci	*eat it* (VTI-3)
cîmân	*canoe*	mîciso	*eat* (VAI)
êkospîhk	*at that time*	miy	*give it to someone* (VTA)
êwako	*that one*	môcikan	*it is fun* (VII)
iyiniw	*a First Nations person*	môso-wiyâs	*moose meat*
kâhkêwak	*dried meat*	sôniyâw	*money*
kahkiyaw	*all*	mow	*eat someone* (VTA)
kapê-tipisk	*all night*	nâh-nîmihito	*dance* (VAI)
kihci-okimâwin-simâkanisak	*RCMP*	ê-nîmihitohk	*there is dancing*
		niyânanwâpisk	*five dollars*
kinosêw	*fish*	pahkwêsikan	*bannock*
mâci-	*start*	sôniyâskâw	*it is Treaty Day* (TH- area)
mâh-mawinêhotok	*challenge each other* (2P-VTA Imp.)	tipahamâtowi-sôniyâw	*treaty money*
		tipiskâw	*it is night* (VII)
mâmawinitok	*gather each other* (2P-VTA Imp.)	wâhkômâkan	*a relative*
		kîkisêpâyâw	*it is morning* (VII)

ispîhk kâ-kî-awâsisîwiyân kî-môcikan mâna ispîhk kâ-kî-sôniyâskâk.
When I was a child, it was fun when it was Treaty Day.

kahkiyaw nikî-mâmawinitonân niwâhkômâkanak âmaciwîspimowinihk.
My relatives all gathered together at Stanley Mission.

kâ-kîkisêpâyâk, nânitaw kêkâ-mitâtaht tipahikan ê-ispayik, nikî-mâci-mâh-miyikonânak
    kihci-okimâwin-simâkanisak tipahamâtowi-sôniyâw.
In the morning, starting about nine o'clock, the RCMP started to give us our treaty money.

kahkiyaw iyiniwak niyânanwâpisk miyâwak, ahpô mîna awâsisak.
All the First Nations people were given five dollars, even the children.

mistahi êwako sôniyâw êkospîhk.
That was a lot of money at that time.

kâ-kîsi-miyikawiyâhk nitipahamâtowi-sôniyâminân nikî-mîcisonân.
After we all received our treaty money, we ate.

nikî-mîcinân môso-wiyâs, kâhkêwak, êkwa mînisa. nikî-mowânânak kinosêwak, pahkwêsikan
   êkwa manôminak.
We ate moose meat, dry meat, and berries. We ate fish, bannock, and wild rice.

kâ-kîsi-mîcisoyâhk kî-mêtawâniwin.
After we ate, there were games.

nikî-mâh-mawinêhotonân cîmâna ohci.
We competed with each other with canoes.

kâ-tipiskâk nikî-nâh-nîmihitonân.
At night we danced.

kapê-tipisk mâna kî-nîmihitohk!
There was dancing all night!

mistahi kî-môcikan!
It was a lot of fun!

Note: For the questions in 1P form, answer in the 2P form; for the questions in 3rd person, answer in 3rd person.

1. tânispîhk ôma kâ-kî-itahkamikahk?

   _____

2. tânitê kâ-kî-mâmawinitoyâhk?

   _____

3. tânitahto tipahikan ê-kî-ispayik kâ-kî-mâci-miyikawiyâhk tipahamâtowi-sôniyâw?

   _____

4. awîna kâ-kî-miyikoyâhk tipahamâtowi-sôniyâw?

   _____

5. tânitahtwâpisk kahkiyaw iyiniw kâ-kî-miyiht?

_____

6. kîkwây nikî-mîcinân?

_____

7. nikî-mowânânak cî kinosêwak?

_____

8. tânisi kâ-itahkamikahk kâ-kîsi-mîcisohk?

_____

9. nikî-mâh-mawinêhotonân cî cîmâna ohci?

_____

10. kî-môcikan cî?

_____

Translate the following text using the word list provided, and then answer the questions below (*answers are on page 286*).

kâ-mâmawinitohk kâ-manitowi-kîsikâk
A Christmas Gathering

Words for the Story

askipwâwi	*potato*
awîniki	*who* (pl)
êkwa mîna	*and again*
itôta	*do* (VTI-1)
kîhtwâm	*next time*
kîsahkamikisi	*finish your activity* (VAI)
kîsisa	*cook it* (VTI-1)
kîsitêpotêw	*she/he cooks it** (VTA)
kotakak	*others*

* *it* refers to an animate noun

mahtâmin	*corn*
manitowi-kîsikâw	*Christmas*
manitowi-kîsikâwi-nikamowina	*Christmas songs (carols)*
manitowi-kîsikâw-mêkiwina	*Christmas gifts*
miyitok	*give it to each other* (VTA)
misihêw	*turkey*
nikamo	*sing* (VAI)
nikosis	*my son*
nîpiya	*salad*
nitânis	*my daughter*
niya	*me/I*
ohtohtêho	*travel from* (VAI)
ôki	*these*
okosisiwâwa	*their son*
onâpêma	*her husband*
osîhtâ	*make it* (VTI-2)
oskâtâsk	*carrot*
otawâsimisiwâwa	*their children*
owîkimâkana	*her/his spouse*
pê-	*come* (IPV)
piminawaso	*cook* (VAI)
piponohk	*last winter*
pîswêhkasikanis	*bun*
sîwihkasikan	*pastry*
wâhkômâkanak	*relatives*
wîhkipw-	*like the taste of it** (VTA)
wîhkista	*like the taste of it* (VTI-1)
wîsakîmin-aspahcikan	*cranberry sauce*
wîwa	*his wife*

Translation

1. piponohk niya êkwa niwâhkômâkanak nikî-mâmawinitonân ispîhk kâ-kî-manitowi-kîsikâk.

   _____

   _____

2. nikosis êkwa owîkimâkana mîna otawâsimisiwâwa kî-pê-itohtêwak.

   _____

   _____

....

* *it* refers to an animate noun

3. nitânis êkwa onâpêma mîna okosisiwâwa mîna kî-pê-itohtêwak, Toronto ohci kî-pê-ohtohtêhowak.

_____

_____

4. nikosis êkwa wîwa kî-piminawasowak. kî-kîsitêpotêwak misihêwa, mahtâmina, mîna oskâtâskwa. kî-kîsisamwak askipwâwa mîna kî-osîhtâwak nîpiya mîna wîsakîmin-aspahcikan.

_____

_____

5. pîswêhkasikanisak mîna kotakak sîwihkasikanak mîna nikî-mowânânak. nikî-wîhkipwâw misihêw mîna nikî-wîhkistên nîpiya.

_____

_____

6. kâ-kî-kîsi-mîcisoyâhk nikî-mâh-miyitonân manitowi-kîsikâw-mêkiwina êkwa nikî-nâh-nikamonân manitowi-kîsikâwi-nikamowina.

_____

_____

7. nikî-kîsahkamikisinân pêyakosâp tipahikan ê-kî-ispayik.

_____

_____

8. kîhtwâm manitowi-kîsikâki êkwa-mîna nika-mâmawinitonân, ta-môcikan.

_____

_____

Questions

1. tânispîhk ôki kâ-kî-mâmawinitocik?

_____

2. awîniki kâ-kî-pê-itohtêcik?

_____

3. awîniki kâ-kî-piminawasocik?

_____

4. kîkwây kâ-kî-kîsitêpotâcik?

_____

5. kîkwây kâ-kî-kîsisahkik?

_____

6. kîkwây nikî-wîhkipwâw?

_____

7. kîkwây nikî-wîhkistên?

_____

8. tânitahto tipahikan ê-kî-ispayiyik ispîhk kâ-kî-kîsahkamikisicik?

_____

9. kîhtwâm cî ta-mâmawinitowak manitowi-kîsikâyiki?

_____

10. kî-môcikan cî?

_____

Read the following text using the word list provided, and then answer the questions below (*answers are on page 287*).

âtayôhkêwin kapêsiwin
A Storytelling Camp

Words for the Story

âh-âtayôhkê	*tell sacred stories* (VAI)	osîh	*make someone* (VTA)
aywêpi	*rest* (VAI)	pîkwatahôpânihk	*hole made in the ice for water*
kikasâmohtê	*wear snowshoes* (VAI)		
kîwêhtah	*take someone home* (VTA)	sâh-saskaniyowêw	*there are chinook winds* (VII)
kotawânihk	*in/at/to the campfire*		
mâh-miyo-kîsikâw	*there are good days* (VII)	sakâhk	*in the bush*
mistasiniy-sâkahikanihk		tâpakwâs	*snare someone* (VTA)
	at Big Stone Lake	timikoniw	*the snow is deep* (VII)
nêtê	*over there*	wacaskosak	*muskrats*
ohci-kwâpikê	*draw water from* (VAI)	wâposwak	*rabbits*

ispîhk kâ-kî-aywêpiyâhk kiskinwahamâkosihk ohci nikî-nitawi-âh-âtayôhkân nêtê
   mistasiniy-sâkahikanihk.
When we rested from school, I went to tell sacred stories at Big Stone Lake.

kî-sâh-saskaniyowêw.
There was a chinook wind blowing.

kî-mâh-miyo-kîsikâw.
There were good days.

mistahi kîkway nikî-itôtênân.
We did a lot of things.

pîkwatahôpânihk nikî-ohci-kwâpikânân.
We drew water from a hole in the ice.

wacaskosak nikî-tâpakwâtânânak.
We snared muskrats.

nikî-osîhânânak êkwa nikî-piminawasonân kotawânihk ta-mowâyâhkik.
We prepared them for cooking over a campfire to eat them.

wâposwak mîna nikî-tâpakwâtânânak êkwa nikî-osîhânânak mâka mwêstas kâ-wî-mowâyâhkik.
We also snared rabbits and prepared them, but we are going to eat them later.

nikî-pê-kîwêhtahâwak.
I brought them home with me.

nikî-kikasâmohtânân sakâhk.
We snowshoed in the forest (bush).

kî-timikoniw.
The snow was deep.

kâ-tipiskâk nikî-âh-âtayôhkânân.
At night we told sacred stories.

mistahi kî-môcikan!
It was a lot of fun!

Questions

1. tânispîhk kâ-kî-nitawi-âh-âtayôhkêyân?

   _____

2. tânitê kâ-kî-nitawi-âh-âtayôhkêyân?

   _____

3. tânisi kâ-kî-isiwêpahk?

   _____

4. tânisi kâ-kî-itôtamâhk?

   _____

5. kîkwâyak kâ-kî-tâpakwâtâyâhkik?

   _____

6. nikî-mowânânak cî wacaskosak?

   _____

7. nikî-mowânânak cî wâposwak?

_____

8. nikî-kikasâmohtânân cî sakâhk?

_____

9. tânispîhk kâ-kî-âh-âtayôhkêyâhk?

_____

10. kî-môcikan cî?

_____

CHAPTER 9

· · · · · · · · · · · · ·

TRANSITIVE ANIMATE VERBS

INVERSE AND REFLEXIVE FORMS

9.1. Inverse VTAS

There are two types of inverse forms:

1. the "you and me" set; and
2. the mixed set (for VTA-1 –*ik* forms, VTA-2 -*ok* forms, and VTA-3 -*ak* forms).

9.1.A. THE YOU AND ME (LOCAL) SET

In the "you and me" set, the direct form shows the 1st person as the subject and the 2nd person as the object. The inverse of that would have the 2nd person as the subject and the 1st person as the object. Use the following paradigms for these forms.

Verb stem: asam – *feed someone*

	Imperative	Delayed Imperative
2	_____in	_____ihkan
	asamin	**asam**ihkan
	Feed me.	*Feed me later.*

2P	_____ik	_____ihkêk
	asamik	**asam**ihkêk
	Y'all feed me.	*Y'all feed me later.*

1P	_____inân	_____ihkâhk
	asaminân	**asam**ihkâhk
	Feed us.	*Feed us later.*

Inverse: 1st person subject, 2nd person object

	Indicative	**Conjunct**	**Future Conditional**
1	ki_____itin	ê-_____itân	_____itâni
	kit**asam**itin.	ê-**asam**itân.	**asam**itâni.
	I feed you.	*I feed you.*	*If I feed you.*
1P	ki_____itinân	ê-_____itâhk	_____itâhki
	kit**asam**itinân.	ê-**asam**itâhk.	**asam**itâhki.
	We feed you.	*We feed you.*	*If we feed you.*
2P	ki_____itinâwâw	ê-_____itakok	_____itakoki
	kit**asam**itinâwâw.	ê-**asam**itakok.	**asam**itakoki.
	I feed y'all.	*I feed y'all.*	*If I feed y'all.*

Direct: 2nd person subject, 1st person object

	Indicative	**Conjunct**	**Future Conditional**
1	ki_____in	ê-_____iyan	_____iyani
	kit**asam**in.	ê-**asam**iyan.	**asam**iyani.
	You feed me.	*You feed me.*	*If you feed me.*
1P	ki_____inân	ê-_____iyâhk	_____iyâhki
	kit**asam**inân.	ê-**asam**iyâhk.	**asam**iyâhki.
	You feed us.	*You feed us.*	*If you feed us.*
2P	ki_____inâwâw	ê-_____iyêk	_____iyêko
	kit**asam**inâwâw.	ê-**asam**iyêk.	**asam**iyêko.
	Y'all feed me.	*Y'all feed me.*	*If y'all feed me.*

Translation

Translate the following sentences into English using the vocabulary provided (*answers are on page 287*).

asam	*feed someone* (VTA)	kinosêw	*fish* (NA)
wâpam	*see someone* (VTA)	pahkwêsikan	*bannock* (NA)
sâkih	*love someone* (VTA)		

1. kiwâpamitin.

_____

2. kiwâpamitinân.

_____

3. kiwâpamitinâwâw.

_____

4. kiwâpamin.

_____

5. kiwâpaminân.

_____

6. kiwâpaminâwâw.

_____

7. ê-asamiyan cî awa kinosêw?

_____

8. ê-asamitân awa kinosêw.

_____

9. ê-asamiyêk cî awa pahkwêsikan?

_____

10. ê-asamitâhk awa pahkwêsikan.

_____

11. kisâkihitin.

_____

12. kisâkihitinân.

_____

13. kisâkihitinâwâw.

_____

14. kisâkihin.

_____

15. kisâkihinâwâw.

_____

9.1.B. THE MIXED SET

In previous verb forms we have seen that the person markers _ni_ and _ki_ indicate the subject of the verb, as in _niwâpamâw atim_ "I see a dog." The _ni_ is the subject "I" and the action goes from left to right.

The inverse forms have these person indicators identified as the object, as in _niwâpamik atim_ "The dog sees me." The _ni_ in this case acts as the object, so the action goes from right to left. These are the inverse forms of the transitive animate verbs: third persons are the subjects and the objects are marked by the person indicators.

There are three types of inverse forms: _-ik_ forms, _-ok_ forms and _-âk_ forms.

9.1.C. VTA-INVERSE 1

VTA-Inverse 1 Imperatives

	Regular Imperative	Delayed Imperative
2	_____in	_____ihkan
2P	_____ik	_____ihkêk
2/2P	_____inân	_____ihkahk

VTA-Inverse 1: the -ik forms

	Indicative	Conjunct	Future Conditional
1	ni_____ik(wak)	ê-_____it(cik)	_____ici
2	ki_____ik(wak)	ê-_____isk(ik)	_____iski
3	_____ikow	ê-_____ikot	_____ikoci
3'	_____ikoyiwa	ê-_____ikoyit	_____ikoyici
1P	ni_____ikonân(ak)	ê-_____ikoyâhk(ik)	_____ikoyâhki
21	ki_____ikonaw(ak)	ê-_____ikoyahk(ik)	_____ikoyahki
2P	ki_____ikowâw(ak)	ê-_____ikoyêk(ik)	_____ikoyêko
3P	_____ikowak	ê-_____ikocik	_____ikotwâwi
3'P	_____ikoyiwa	ê-_____ikoyit	_____ikoyici

Part 1: Translation

Translate the following sentences into English (*answers are on page 288*).

1. niwâpamâw nâpêw.

_____

2. niwâpamik nâpêw.

_____

3. niwâpamâwak nâpêwak.

_____

4. niwâpamikwak nâpêwak.

_____

5. nitasamâw nistês kinosêwa.

_____

6. nitasamik nistês kinosêwa.

_____

7. niwîsâmâw nisîmis.

_____

8. niwîsâmik nisîmis.

_____

Part 2: Conjugation

Conjugate the following verbs (_answers are on page 288_).

vTA _natohtaw_ "listen to someone" into the local imperative:

2   _____

2P   _____

2/2P   _____

vTA _kanawâpam_ "look at someone" into the local delayed imperative:

2   _____

2P   _____

2/2P   _____

vTA-inverse 1 _wâpam_ "see someone" into the indicative past tense:

1   _____

2   _____

3   _____

3'   _____

VTA-direct *wâpam* "see someone" into the indicative future intentional:

1 _____

2 _____

3 _____

3' _____

Part 3: Translation

Translate the following into Cree, transforming the following words (if need be) (*answers are on page 288*).

kiwâhkômâkan   *your relative*   kinikamowin   *your song*
nimosôm   *my grandfather*   nôhtê-   *want to* (IPV)
pê-   *come* (IPV)

1. I want to listen to my grandfather.

_____

2. Did you listen to your grandfather?

_____

3. We (exclusive) saw my relatives. (VTA-direct)

_____

4. My relatives (they) saw us (inclusive). (VTA-inverse)

_____

5. He's going to listen to his grandfather.

_____

6. Listen to me (you-sg).

_____

9.1.D. VTA-INVERSE 2

VTA-Inverse 2 Imperatives

Note: subject is 2nd person, object is 1st person

	Regular Imperative	Delayed Imperative
2	_____on	_____ohkan
2P	_____ok	_____ohkêk
2/2P	_____onân	_____ohkahk

VTA-Inverse 2: the -ok forms

	Indicative	Conjunct	Future Conditional
1	ni_____ok(wak)	ê-_____ot(cik)	_____oci
2	ki_____ok(wak	ê-_____osk(ik)	_____oski
3	_____okow	ê-_____okot	_____okoci
3'	_____okoyiwa	ê-_____okoyit	_____okoyici
1P	ni_____okonân(ak)	ê-_____okoyâhk(ok)	_____okoyâhki
21	ki_____okonaw(ak)	ê-_____okoyahk(ok)	_____okoyahki
2P	ki_____okowâw(ak)	ê-_____okoyêk(ok)	_____okoyêko
3P	_____okowak	ê-_____okocik	_____okotwâwi
3'P	_____okoyiwa	ê-_____okoyit	_____okoyici

VTAs in This Class

pakamahw-	*hit someone*
sîkahw-	*comb someone's hair*
wîsakahw-	*hurt someone by hitting*

Part 1: Translation

Translate the following sentences into English (*answers are on page 288*).

1. nipakamahwâw nâpêw.

_____

2. nipakamahok nâpêw.

_____

3. nipakamahwâwak nâpêwak.

_____

4. nipakamahokwak nâpêwak.

_____

5. nisîkahwâw nitânis.

_____

6. nisîkahok nitânis.

_____

7. niwîsakahwâw nitêm.

_____

8. niwîsakahok nitêm.

_____

Part 2: Conjugation

Conjugate the following verbs (_answers are on page 289_).

VTA-direct _pakamah_ "hit someone" into the imperative:

2 _____

2P _____

2/2P _____

VTA-inverse 2 _pakamah_ "hit someone" into the local imperative:

2 _____

2P _____

2/2P _____

VTA-direct *sîkah* "comb someone's hair" into the indicative past tense:

1 _____

2 _____

3 _____

3' _____

VTA-inverse 2 *sîkah* "comb someone's hair" into the indicative future intentional:

1 _____

2 _____

3 _____

3' _____

Part 3: Translation
Translate the following sentences into Cree, transforming the following words (if need be) (*answers are on page 289*).

kiwâhkômâkan	*your relative*	kimis	*your older sister*
kîtisân	*your sibling*	nistês	*my older brother*
nitânis	*my daughter*	nôhtê-	*want to* (IPV)
pê-	*come* (IPV)	pisci-	*accidentally* (IPV)

1. My daughter wants to comb my hair.

_____

2. I want to comb my daughter's hair.

_____

3. Did your younger siblings hurt you?

_____

4. Did you hurt your younger sibling?

_____

5. My younger siblings hit us (exclusive) accidentally.

_____

6. We (exclusive) hurt my younger siblings accidentally.

_____

9.1.E. VTA-INVERSE 3

VTA-Inverse 3 Imperatives

	Regular Imperative	Delayed Imperative
2	_____in	_____ihkan
2P	_____ik	_____ihkêk
2/2P	_____inân	_____ihkahk

VTA-Inverse 3: the -âk *forms*

	Indicative	Conjunct	Future Conditional
1	ni_____âk(wak)	ê-_____it(cik)	_____ici
2	ki_____âk(wak	ê-_____isk(ik)	_____iski
3	_____âkow	ê-_____âkot	_____âkoci
3'	_____âkoyiwa	ê-_____âkoyit	_____âkoyici
1P	ni_____âkonân(ak)	ê-_____âkoyâhk(ok)	_____âkoyâhki
21	ki_____âkonaw(ak)	ê-_____âkoyahk(ok)	_____âkoyahki
2P	ki_____âkowâw(ak)	ê-_____âkoyêk(ok)	_____âkoyêko
3P	_____âkowak	ê-_____âkocik	_____âkotwâwi
3'P	_____âkoyiwa	ê-_____âkoyit	_____âkoyici

VTAs in This Class
(*Note*: the last *aw* gets dropped in the conjugations)

atâwêstam**aw**	*buy something for someone*
pêtam**aw**	*bring something for someone*
nâtam**aw**	*fetch something for someone*
kiskinwaham**aw**	*teach something to someone*

Part 1: Translation

Translate the following sentences into English (*answers are on page 289*).

1. nikî-atâwêstamawâw nistês astotin.

_____

2. nikî-atâwêstamâk nistês maskisina.

_____

3. kikî-pêtamawâw cî kohkom môsowiyâs?

_____

4. kî-pêtamâkow ohkoma pahkwêsikana.

_____

5. kî-nâtamawêw otânisa mihta.

_____

6. kî-nâtamâkow otânisa mihta.

_____

7. nikî-kakwê-kiskinwahamawâw nitôtêm nêhiyawêwin.

_____

8. nikî-kiskinwahamâk nitôtêm nêhiyawêwin.

_____

Part 2: Conjugation

Conjugate the following verbs (*answers are on page 289*).

VTA-direct *masinahamaw* "write to someone" into the imperative:

2   _____

2P   _____

2/2P   _____

VTA-inverse 3 *masinahamaw* "write to someone" into the local imperative:

2 _____

2P _____

2/2P _____

VTA-direct *atâwêstamaw* "buy something for someone" into the indicative past tense:

1 _____

2 _____

3 _____

3' _____

VTA-inverse 3 *atâwêstamaw* "buy something for someone" into the indicative future definite:

1 _____

2 _____

3 _____

3' _____

Part 3: Translation

Translate the following into Cree, transforming the following words (if need be) (*answers are on page 290*).

kiwâhkômâkan	*your relative*	kimis	*your older sister*
nikâwiy	*my mother*	nistês	*my older brother*
nôhtê-	*want to* (IPV)	pê-	*come* (IPV)
pisci-	*accidentally* (IPV)	kîtisân	*your sibling*
cahkâs	*ice cream*		

1. I wanted to buy the book for my mother.

   _____

2. My mother bought a book for me.

   _____

3. Did you buy an ice cream for your younger siblings?

   _____

4. Did your younger siblings buy an ice cream for you?

   _____

5. My younger sister taught me Cree.

   _____

9.2. VTA: Reflexives

Reflexives are verbs in which the subject is also the object. There are three types of reflexive forms: VTA-reflexive 1 -*iso* forms, VTA-reflexive 2 -*oso* forms, and VTA-reflexive 3 -*aso* forms.

9.2.A. VTA-REFLEXIVE 1

Imperatives

	Regular Imperative	**Delayed Imperative**
2	_____iso	_____isohkan
2P	_____isok	_____isohkêk
2/2P	_____isotân	_____isohkahk

VTA-Reflexive 1: the -iso forms

	Indicative	Conjunct	Future Conditional
1	ni_____ison	ê-_____isoyân	_____isoyâni
2	ki_____ison	ê-_____isoyan	_____isoyani
3	_____isow	ê-_____isot	_____isoci
3'	_____isoyiwa	ê-_____isoyit	_____isoyici
1P	ni_____isonân	ê-_____isoyâhk	_____isoyâhki
21	ki_____isonaw	ê-_____isoyahk	_____isoyahki
2P	ki_____isonâwâw	ê-_____isoyêk	_____isoyêko
3P	_____isowak	ê-_____isocik	_____isotwâwi
3'P	_____isoyiwa	ê-_____isoyit	_____isoyici

VTAs in This Class

asam	*feed someone*	wîcih	*help someone*
kanawâpam	*look at someone*	wîcêw	*accompany someone*
wâpam	*see someone*	natom	*invite/call someone*
wîsâm	*invite someone*		

Part 1: Translation

Translate the following sentences (*answers are on page 290*).

1. nikî-wîcihâw nisîmis.

_____

2. nikî-wîcihik nisîmis.

_____

3. nikî-wîcihison.

_____

4. kikî-kanawâpamâw kimosôm.

_____

5. kikî-kanawâpamik kimosôm.

_____

6. kikî-kanawâpamison.

_____

7. kî-wâpamêw ostêsa.

_____

8. kî-wâpamikow ostêsa.

_____

9. kî-wâpamisow.

_____

10. nikî-wîsâmânân nimis.

_____

11. nikî-wîsamikonân nimis.

_____

12. nikî-wîsâmisonân.

_____

13. kikî-natomânaw kohkominaw.

_____

14. kikî-natomikonaw kohkominaw.

_____

15. kikî-natomisonaw.

_____

Part 2: Conjugations

Complete the following chart, paying attention to the subject (*answers are on page 290*).

VTA Stem	VTA-Direct	VTA-Inverse	VTA-Reflexive
asam – *feed someone*	nikî-asamâw		
kanawâpam – *watch someone*		kikî-kanawâpamik	
wâpam – *see someone*			kî-wâpamisow
wîsâm – *invite someone*		kî-wîsâmikoyiwa	
wîcih – *help someone*	nikî-wîcihânân		
wîcêw – *accompany someone*		kikî-wîcêwikonaw	
natom – *call/invite someone*			kikî-natomisonâwâw
nawasôn – *choose someone*		kî-nawasônikowak	
nisitawêyim – *know/ recognize someone*	nisitawêyimêyiwa		
kistêyim – *respect someone*		nikistêyimik	

9.2.B. VTA-REFLEXIVE 2

VTA-Reflexive 2 Imperatives

	Regular Imperative	Delayed Imperative
2	_____oso	_____osohkan
2P	_____osok	_____osohkêk
2/2P	_____osotân	_____osohkahk

VTA-Reflexive 2: the -oso forms

	Indicative		Conjunct		Future Conditional
1	ni_____oson		ê-_____osoyân		_____osoyâni
2	ki_____oson		ê-_____osoyan		_____osoyani
3	_____osow		ê-_____osot		_____osoci
3'	_____osoyiwa		ê-_____osoyit		_____osoyici
1P	ni_____osonân		ê-_____osoyâhk		_____osoyâhki
21	ki_____osonaw		ê-_____osoyahk		_____osoyahki
2P	ki_____osonâwâw		ê-_____osoyêk		_____osoyêko
3P	_____osowak		ê-_____osocik		_____osotwâwi
3'P	_____osoyiwa		ê-_____osoyit		_____osoyici

VTAs in This Class

pakamahw-	*hit someone*	sîkahw-	*comb someone's hair*
wîsakahw-	*hurt someone by hitting*	saskahw-	*ignite/kindle someone*
pasastêhw-	*whip someone*	kipahw-	*imprison someone*
pâskisw-	*shoot someone*	pimitisahw-	*follow someone*
patahw-	*miss (when shooting) someone*	pistahw-	*shoot/hit someone by accident*

Part 1: Translation

Translate the following sentences (*answers are on page 291*).

1. nikî-pakamahwâw nisîmis.

_____

2. nikî-pakamahok nisîmis.

_____

3. nikî-pakamahoson.

_____

4. kikî-sîkahwâw kitânis.

_____

5. kikî-sîkahok kitânis.

_____

6. kikî-sîkahoson.

_____

7. kî-wîsakahwêw ostêsa.

_____

8. kî-wîsakahokow ostêsa.

_____

9. kî-wîsakahosow.

_____

10. nikî-kipahwânân simâkanis.

_____

11. nikî-kipahokonân simâkanis.

_____

12. nikî-kipahosonân.

_____

13. kikî-pimitisahwânaw nimosôm.

_____

14. kikî-pimitisahokonaw nimosôm.

_____

15. kikî-pimitisahosonaw.

_____

Part 2: Conjugations

Complete the following chart with the correct forms (*answers are on page 291*).

VTA Stem	VTA-Direct	VTA-Inverse	VTA-Reflexive
pakamahw- – *hit someone*	nipakamahwâw		
sîkahw- – *comb someone's hair*		kisîkahok	
wîsakahw – *hurt someone by hitting*			wîsakahosow
saskahw- – *ignite someone*		saskahokoyiwa	
pasastêhw- – *whip someone*	nipasastêhwânân		
kipahw- – *imprison someone*		kikipahokonaw	
pâskisw- – *shoot someone*			kipâskisosonâwâw
pimitisahw- – *follow someone*		pimitisahokowak	
patahw- – *miss someone*	patahwêyiwa		
pistahw- – *shoot/hit someone by accident*		nipistahok	

9.2.C. VTA-REFLEXIVE 3

Imperatives

	Regular Imperative	Delayed Imperative
2	_____âso	_____âsohkan
2P	_____âsok	_____âsohkêk
2/2P	_____âsotân	_____âsohkahk

VTA-Reflexive 3: the -âso forms

	Indicative	Conjunct	Future Conditional
1	ni_____âson	ê-_____âsoyân	_____âsoyâni
2	ki_____âson	ê-_____âsoyan	_____âsoyani
3	_____âsow	ê-_____âsot	_____âsoci
3'	_____âsoyiwa	ê-_____âsoyit	_____âsoyici
1P	ni_____âsonân	ê-_____âsoyâhk	_____âsoyâhki
21	ki_____âsonaw	ê-_____âsoyahk	_____âsoyahki
2P	ki_____âsonâwâw	ê-_____âsoyêk	_____âsoyêko
3P	_____âsowak	ê-_____âsocik	_____âsotwâwi
3'P	_____âsoyiwa	ê-_____âsoyit	_____âsoyici

VTAs in This Class
(*Note*: drop the last *aw* for conjugations)

atâwêstama**w**	*buy something for someone*	atoska**w**	*work for someone*
pêtama**w**	*bring something for someone*	natohta**w**	*listen to someone*
nâtama**w**	*fetch something for someone*	masinahama**w**	*write to someone*
kiskinwahama**w**	*teach something to someone*	pêhta**w**	*hear someone*
nisitohta**w**	*understand someone*	nisitawina**w**	*recognize someone*

Part 1: Translation

Translate the following sentences (*answers are on page 291*).

1. nikî-atâwêstamawâw nisîmis mîciwina.

   _____

2. nikî-atâwêstamâk nisîmis mîciwina.

   _____

3. nikî-atâwêstamâson mîciwina.

_____

4. kikî-natohtawâw kimosôm.

_____

5. kikî-natohtâk kimosôm.

_____

6. kikî-natohtâson.

_____

7. kî-nisitohtawêw kimosôma.

_____

8. kî-nisitohtâkow kimosôma.

_____

9. kî-nisitohtâsow.

_____

10. otôtêma kî-masinahamawêyiwa okâwiya.

_____

11. otôtêma kî-masinahamâkoyiwa okâwiya.

_____

12. otôtêma kî-masinahamâsoyiwa.

_____

13. nikî-nisitawinawânân okiskinwahamâkêw.

_____

14. nikî-nisitawinâkonân okiskinwahamâkêw.

_____

15. nikî-nisitawinâsonân.

_____

Part 2: Conjugations

Complete the following chart with the correct forms (*answers are on page 292*).

VTA Stem	VTA-Direct	VTA-Inverse	VTA-Reflexive
atâwêstamaw – *buy something for someone*	nitatâwêstamawâw		
nâtamaw – *fetch something for someone*		kinâtamâk	
pêtamaw – *bring something for someone*			pêtamâsow
atoskaw – *work for someone*		atoskâkoyiwa	
kiskinwahamaw – *teach someone*	nikiskinwahamawânân		
natohtaw – *listen to someone*		kinatohtâkonaw	
masinahamaw – *write to someone*			kimasinahamâsonâwâw
nisitohtaw – *understand someone*		nisitohtâkowak	
nisitawinaw – *recognize someone*	nisitawinawêyiwa		
pêhtaw – *hear someone*		nipêhtâk	

9.3. Text Exercises with vta–Direct, –Inverse, and –Reflexive Forms

Read the following texts and then, using the vocabulary provided, answer the questions below using vta-direct, -inverse, and -reflexive forms.

Shopping with My Children

[1] otâkosîhk nikî-nitawi-papâmi-atâwân ayiwinisa. nicawâsimisak nikî-nôhtê-wîcêwikwak mâka namôya osâm mistahi nikî-osôniyâmin. kiyâm, nika-miskênân ayiwinisa ê-wêhtakihtêki êkwa ta-miywâsiki. nikî-pôsihâwak nisêhkêpayîsimihk ta-nitawi-papâmi-atâwêyâhk.

Yesterday I went about shopping. My children wanted to come with me but I had very little money. No matter, we will find clothes that are inexpensive and in good quality. I loaded them into my car to go about shopping.

[2] nikî-miskênân maskisina nîswâw-mitâtahto-mitanaw tahtwâpisk ê-itakihtêki. osâm âhkwakihtêwa! nikî-natonênân kotaka maskisina nawac ê-wêhtakihtêki. nikî-miskênân maskisina niyânanomitanaw tahtwâpisk ê-itakihtêki. êwakoni nikî-atâwânân.

We found shoes that cost two hundred dollars. They were too expensive. We looked for other shoes which were more inexpensive. We found shoes that cost fifty dollars. We bought those ones.

[3] nikî-miskawânân mitâs mitâtahto-mitanaw tahtwâpisk ê-itakisot. osâm âhkwakisow! nikî-natonawânânak kotakak mitâsak nawac ê-wêhtakisocik. nikî-miskawânânak mitâsak nêwo-mitanaw niyânanosâp tahtwâpisk ê-itakisocik. êwakonik nikî-atâwânânak.

We found pants that cost one hundred dollars. They were too expensive. We looked for other pairs of pants which were more inexpensive. We found pairs of pants that cost forty-five dollars. We bought those ones.

[4] nikî-atâwêstamawâwak nicawâsimisak maskisina mîna mitâsa. nikî-atâwêstamâson maskisina mîna mitâsak.

I bought my children shoes and pairs of pants. I bought myself shoes and pairs of pants.

Words

atâwêstamaw	*buy something for someone* (vta)	itakihtêw	*it costs thus* (vii)
miska	*find it* (vti-1)	itakisow	*she/he costs thus* (vai)
miskaw	*find someone* (vta)	âhkwakihtêw	*it is expensive* (vii)
wêhtakihtêw	*it is inexpensive* (vii)	âhkwakisow	*she/he is expensive* (vai)
wêhtakisow	*she/he is inexpensive* (vai)		

Questions

1. tânispîhk ôki kâ-kî-nitawi-papâmi-atâwêcik?

   _____

2. wîcêwêw cî otawâsimisa?

   _____

3. kîkwâya nîswâw-mitâtahto-mitanaw tahtwâpisk kâ-itakihtêyiki kâ-miskahkik?

   _____

4. atâwêwak cî êwakoni maskisina?

   _____

5. tâniyikohk ê-itakihtêyiki maskisina kâ-atâwêcik?

   _____

6. kîkwâya mitâtahto-mitanaw tahtwâpisk kâ-itakisoyit kâ-miskawâcik?

   _____

7. atâwew cî êwakoni mitâsa?

   _____

8. tâniyikohk ê-itakisoyit mitâsa kâ-atâwêt?

   _____

9. kîkwâyiw kâ-atâwêstamawât ocawâsimisa?

   _____

10. kîkwây kâ-atâwêstamâsot?

   _____

9.4. Indicative and Conjunct Forms of vᴛᴀ-Direct, -Inverse, and -Reflexive

9.4.A. INDICATIVE FORMS

Use the following paradigms to produce the *-iko*, *-oko*, and *-âko* forms of the vᴛᴀ-direct, -inverse, and -reflexive in the indicative.

The -iko *Form*

	vᴛᴀ-Direct	vᴛᴀ-Inverse 1	vᴛᴀ-Reflexive 1
1	ni_____âw(ak)	ni_____ik(wak)	ni_____ison
2	ki_____âw(ak)	ki_____ik(wak)	ki_____ison
3	_____êw	_____ikow	_____isow
3'	_____êyiwa	_____ikoyiwa	_____isoyiwa
1P	ni_____ânân(ak)	ni_____ikonân(ak)	ni_____isonân
21	ki_____ânaw(ak)	ki_____ikonaw(ak)	ki_____isonaw
2P	ki_____âwâw(ak)	ki_____ikowâw(ak)	ki_____isonâwâw
3P	_____êwak	_____ikowak	_____isowak
3'P	_____êyiwa	_____ikoyiwa	_____isoyiwa

The -oko *Form*

	vᴛᴀ-Direct	vᴛᴀ-Inverse 2	vᴛᴀ-Reflexive 2
1	ni_____wâw(ak)	ni_____ok(wak)	ni_____oson
2	ki_____wâw(ak)	ki_____ok(wak)	ki_____oson
3	_____wêw	_____okow	_____osow
3'	_____wêyiwa	_____okoyiwa	_____osoyiwa
1P	ni_____wânân(ak)	ni_____okonân(ak)	ni_____osonân
21	ki_____wânaw(ak)	ki_____okonaw(ak)	ki_____osonaw
2P	ki_____wâwâw(ak)	ki_____okowâw(ak)	ki_____osonâwâw
3P	_____wêwak	_____okowak	_____osowak
3'P	_____wêyiwa	_____okoyiwa	_____osoyiwa

The -âko *Form*

	VTA-Direct	VTA-Inverse 3	VTA-Reflexive 3
1	ni_____âw(ak)	ni_____âk(wak)	ni_____âson
2	ki_____âw(ak)	ki_____âk(wak)	ki_____âson
3	_____êw	_____âkow	_____âsow
3'	_____êyiwa	_____âkoyiwa	_____âsoyiwa
1P	ni_____ânân(ak)	ni_____âkonân(ak)	ni_____âsonân
21	ki_____âyaw(ak)	ki_____âkonaw(ak)	ki_____âsonaw
2P	ki_____âwâw(ak)	ki_____âkowâw(ak)	ki_____âsonâwâw
3P	_____êwak	_____âkowak	_____âsowak
3'P	_____êyiwa	_____âkoyiwa	_____âsoyiwa

9.4.B. CONJUNCT FORMS

Use the following paradigms to produce the *-iko*, *-oko*, and *-âko* forms of the VTA-direct, -inverse, and-reflexive in the conjunct.

The -iko *Form*

	VTA-Direct	VTA-Inverse 1	VTA-Reflexive 1
1	ê-_____ak(ik)	ê-_____it(cik)	ê-_____isoyân
2	ê-_____at(cik)	ê-_____isk(ik)	ê-_____isoyan
3	ê-_____ât	ê-_____ikot	ê-_____isot
3'	ê-_____âyit	ê-_____ikoyit	ê-_____isoyit
1P	ê-_____âyâhk(ik)	ê-_____ikoyâhk(ik)	ê-_____isoyâhk
21	ê-_____âyahk(ik)	ê-_____ikoyahk(ik)	ê-_____isoyahk
2P	ê-_____âyêk(ik)	ê-_____ikoyêk(ik)	ê-_____isoyêk
3P	ê-_____âcik	ê-_____ikocik	ê-_____isocik
3'P	ê-_____âyit	ê-_____ikoyit	ê-_____isoyit

The -oko *Form*

	VTA-Direct	VTA-Inverse 2	VTA-Reflexive 2
1	ê-_____wak(ik)	ê-_____ot(cik)	ê-_____osoyân
2	ê-_____wat(cik)	ê-_____osk(ik)	ê-_____osoyan
3	ê-_____wât	ê-_____okot	ê-_____osot
3'	ê-_____wâyit	ê-_____okoyit	ê-_____osoyit
1P	ê-_____wâyâhk(ik)	ê-_____okoyâhk(ok)	ê-_____osoyâhk
21	ê-_____wâyahk(ik)	ê-_____okoyahk(ok)	ê-_____osoyahk
2P	ê-_____wâyêk(ik)	ê-_____okoyêk(ok)	ê-_____osoyêk
3P	ê-_____wâcik	ê-_____okocik	ê-_____osocik
3'P	ê-_____wâyit	ê-_____okoyit	ê-_____osoyit

The -âko Form

	VTA-**Direct**	VTA-**Inverse 3**	VTA-**Reflexive 3**
1	ê-_____ak(ik)	ê-_____it(cik)	ê-_____âsoyân
2	ê-_____at(cik)	ê-_____isk(ik)	ê-_____âsoyan
3	ê-_____ât	ê-_____âkot	ê-_____âsot
3'	ê-_____âyit	ê-_____âkoyit	ê-_____âsoyit
1P	ê-_____âyâhk(ik)	ê-_____âkoyâhk(ok)	ê-_____âsoyâhk
21	ê-_____âyahk(ik)	ê-_____âkoyahk(ok)	ê-_____âsoyahk
2P	ê-_____âyêk(ik)	ê-_____âkoyêk(ok)	ê-_____âsoyêk
3P	ê-_____âcik	ê-_____âkocik	ê-_____âsocik
3'P	ê-_____âyit	ê-_____âkoyit	ê-_____âsoyit

CHAPTER 10
· · · · · · · · · · · · ·
STORIES

10.1. Stories to Inspire

One of the ways I learned English was hearing English around me all the time and reading constantly. My progress was slow until I was in grade five, when I was introduced to readers with stories and sets of questions to go with the stories. The following set of stories is inspired by that experience, in the hope that students of Cree will find resources such as these to help with their learning.

10.1.A. ACTIVITIES THROUGH THE SEASONS

Making Birch Syrup (answers to the questions are on page 292)

> kayâs, ispîhk kâ-kî-awâsisîwiyân nikî-sâh-sîwâkamisikânân mâna ispîhk kâ-sîkwahk.
> *Long ago, when I was a child, we made birch syrup when it was spring.*
>
> nikî-cîhkêyihtên mâna ispîhk kâ-kî-pôsiyâhk ta-nitawi-sîwâkamisikêyâhk, nîthanân ninîkihikwak êkwa nîtisânak.
> *I liked it when we, my parents, siblings and I, embarked (by canoe) to go make birch syrup.*

1. tânispîhk ôma kâ-kî-itahkamikahk?

    When did this happen?

    _____

2. tânisi mâna kâ-itahkamikisiyâhk ispîhk kâ-kî-sîkwahk?

What did we do when it was spring?

_____

3. nikî-cîhkêyihtên cî ta-sîwâkamisikêyâhk?

Did I like for us to go make birch syrup?

_____

4. awîniki kâ-kî-nitawi-sîwâkamisikêcik?

Who went to make birch syrup?

_____

pêyakwâw ê-niyânano-kîsikâk nikî-pôsinân opahkopîwinihk isi, êkotê ê-kî-nitawi-mânokêyâhk
   ta-sîwâkamisikêyâhk.
One Friday we embarked (by canoe) to The Wading Place to set up a tent to make birch syrup there.

5. kîko kîsikâw ispîhk kâ-kî-pôsiyâhk?

Which day did we embark by canoe?

_____

6. tânitê kâ-kî-nitawi-mânokêyâhk?

Where did we go set up a tent?

_____

7. tânisi kâ-kî-wî-itahkamikisiyâhk?

What were we intending to do?

_____

nikî-nawasônânânak waskwayak ta-mîstasoyâhk.
We chose birch trees to tap.

nikî-mîstasonân waskwayak. pîhcipacikan waskwâhk nikî-astânân êkwa sîpâ pîhcipacikanihk
   nikî-ahânânak askihkosak êkota ta-isi-ohcikawik waskwayâpoy.
*We tapped birch trees. We put a funnel (spout) on the birch, and under the funnel we placed
   little pails to catch the birch sap.*

8. kîkwayak kâ-kî-nawasônâyâhkik ta-mîstasoyâhk?

What did we choose to tap for sap?

_____

9. nikî-mîstasonân cî waskwayak?

Did we tap birch trees for sap?

_____

10. tânisi mîna kâ-kî-itahkamikisiyâhk?

What else did we do?

_____

kapê-kîsik kî-ohcikawin waskwayâpoy. niyanân nâpêsisak nikî-nikohtânân.
The birch sap dripped all day. Us boys made firewood.

kîhtwâm kâ-kîkisêpâyâk nikâwiy êkwa nimisak kî-kisâkamisamwak waskwayâpoy
   ê-sîwâkamisikêcik. nikî-wîhkistên sîwâkamisikan.
The next morning my mother and older sisters boiled the birch sap, making birch syrup.
   I liked the taste of birch syrup.

kî-wîhkasin sîwâkamisikan ta-aspahcikêyân napaki-pahkwêsikanisihk.
Birch syrup tasted good on pancakes.

11. kapê-kîsik cî kî-ohcikawin waskwayâpoy?

Did the birch sap drip all day?

_____

12. tânisi kâ-kî-itahkamikisicik nâpêsisak?

What did the boys do?

_____

13. tânisi kâ-kî-itahkamikisicik nikâwiy êkwa nimisak?

What did my mother and my older sisters do?

_____

14. kî-wîhkasin cî sîwâkamisikan?

Did the birch syrup taste good?

_____

15. kî-wîhkasin cî sîwâkamisikan ta-aspahcikêyân napaki-pahkwêsikanisihk.

Did the birch syrup taste good on pancakes?

_____

10.1.B. ACTIVITIES THROUGH THE DAY

Rabbit Snaring

ispîhk kâ-kî-awâsisîwiyân nikî-cîhkêyihtên ta-papâmi-wîcêwak nohtâwîpan piko itê.
When I was a child, I liked to accompany my late father anywhere.

nikî-mâwaci-cîhkêyihtên ta-nitawi-tâpakwêyâhk, ta-tâpakwâtâyâhkik wâposwak.
I most enjoyed going snaring, to snare rabbits.

pêyakwâw ê-kî-niyânano-kîsikâk nikî-nitawi-papâmi-kapêsinân. kî-ati-otâkosin ispîhk
    kâ-kî-kospîyâhk, nânitaw êtikwê niyânan tipahikan ê-kî-ispayik.
One Friday we went camping. It was getting on toward evening when we went into the forest,
    maybe about five o'clock.

kinwêsk nôhcimihk nikî-pimohtânân ê-kî-natonamâhk wâposo-mêskanâsa.
We walked for a long time in the forest looking for rabbit trails.

nânitaw êtikwê pêyak tipahikan nikî-pimohtânân ispîhk kâ-miskamâhk wâposo-mêskanâsa.
Maybe we walked for an hour when we found rabbit trails.

nikî-tâh-tâpakwânân. mêtoni mihcêt tâpakwâna nikî-akotânân.
We set snares. We hung quite a lot of snares.

nikî-ati-kîwânân mêtoni kêkâc ê-kî-ati-pahkisimok.
We headed home when it was almost sundown.

nânitaw êtikwê ayinânêw tipahikan mîna âpihtaw ê-kî-ispayik kâ-kî-matâwisiyâhk
    nikapêsiwininâhk.
It was about eight thirty when we emerged (from the forest) onto our campsite.

nikî-otâkwani-mîcisonân êkwa nikî-ati-kawisimonân ayisk ê-kî-tipiskâk, nânitaw êtikwê
   mitâtaht tipahikan ê-kî-ispayik.
We ate supper and laid down to sleep as it was night, maybe it was about ten o'clock.

wîpac ê-kîkisêpâyâk nikî-waniskânân, nânitaw êtikwê têpakohp tipahikan ê-kî-ispayik.
Early in the morning we got up, maybe it was about seven o'clock.

nikî-papâsi-kîkisêpâ-mîcisonân pâmwayês ta-kospîyâhk.
We quickly ate breakfast before going into the forest.

nikî-kospînân nânitaw ayinânêw tipahikan mîna âpihtaw ê-kî-ispayik, ta-nâtakwêyâhk.
We went into the forest at around eight thirty to fetch our snares.

mihcêt wâposwak nikî-tâpakwâtânânak.
We snared a lot of rabbits.

wâposo-mîcimâpohkân kî-piminawasow nikâwîpan. niya êkwa nîtisânak nikî-takahki-mîcisonân
   ispîhk kâ-âpihtâ-kîsikâk. takahkispakosiwak wâposwak.
My late mother cooked rabbit stew. Me and my siblings had a wonderful meal at noon.
   Rabbits are tasty.

Questions (answers are on page 293)

1. tânispîhk ôma kâ-kî-itahkamikahk?

   _____

2. kîkway nikî-cîhkêyihtên ta-itôtamân?

   _____

3. nikî-mâwaci-cîhkêyihtên cî ta-nitawi-tâpakwâtâyâhkik wâposwak?

   _____

4. tânispîhk ôma kâ-kî-nitawi-papâmi-kapêsiyâhk?

   _____

5. tânitahto tipahikan ê-kî-ispayik kâ-kî-kospîyâhk?

   _____

6. kinwêsk cî nôhcimihk nikî-pimohtânân ê-kî-natonamâhk wâposo-mêskanâsa?

_____

7. mihcêt cî tâpakwâna nikî-âh-akotânân?

_____

8. tânispîhk kâ-kî-ati-kîwêyâhk?

_____

9. tânitahto tipahikan ê-kî-ispayik kâ-kî-matâwisiyâhk nikapêsiwininâhk?

_____

10. tânitahto tipahikan ê-kî-ispayik kâ-kî-ati-kawisimoyâhk?

_____

11. wîpac cî ê-kîkisêpâyâk nikî-waniskânân?

_____

12. tânitahto tipahikan ê-kî-ispayik kâ-kî-waniskâyâhk?

_____

13. nikî-papâsi-kîkisêpâ-mîcisonân cî pâmwayês ta-kospîyâhk?

_____

14. tânitahto tipahikan ê-kî-ispayik kâ-kî-kospîyâhk ta-nâtakwêyâhk?

_____

15. mihcêt cî wâposwak nikî-tâpakwâtânânak?

_____

10.2. Stories with Audio

The following seven texts are a collection of original stories I wrote relating to traditional Cree cultural teachings. They have been posted online with audio and word lists on Cree Language Literacy (creeliteracy.org). You can hear the audio and read the text together by going to the following webpage: *creeliteracy.org/cree-cultural-teachings*.

10.2.A. kistêyihtamowin – RESPECT

nêhiyaw-isîhcikêwin – **Cree Cultural Teachings**
by Solomon Ratt

[1] ispîhk kâ-kî-awâsisîwiyâhk niya êkwa nimis nikî-kanâcihtânân yîkwahaskân akâmihk ita ohci kâ-kî-wîkiyâhk. cîmânihk nikî-pôsinân ê-âsowahamâhk sîpiy. kî-miyo-kîsikâw.

When I was a child, me and my older sister cleaned the graveyard that was across the water from where we lived. We boarded a canoe and crossed the river. It was a good day.

[2] nikî-mâci-kanâcihtânân yîkwahaskân. kapê-kîsik nikî-kanâcihcikânân. kêtahtawê, ê-pôni-âpihtâ-kîsikâk, kâ-ati-sôhkiyowêk êkwa ê-pêtânaskwâk. kwayask kî-kaskitêwânaskwâw êkwa mîna kwayask kî-sôhkiyowêw! piyêsiwak kî-kâh-kitowak êkwa kî-wâh-wâsaskotêpayin!

We started to clean the cemetery. We cleaned all day. All of a sudden it was afternoon when a big wind picked up and clouds rolled in. They were very dark clouds and it was very windy. Thunder started to roll and lightning flashed.

[3] mâka mîna niya nikî-nôhtê-mâyêyihtên ôma kâ-isi-wêpahk. nikî-kaskimâw nimis kita-kakwê-âsowahamâhk kiyâm ôma kâ-isi-wêpahk. êkwâni nikî-pôsinân. wahwâ! kwayask kî-mâh-misi-mamahkâhan mâka kêyâpic nipimiskânân, ê-nanimahamâhk! kwayask nikî-nayêhtâwêhikonân yôtin êyikohk ê-mâh-misi-mamahkâhk mâka piyisk nimisakânân nîkinâhk. nikî-mâh-mamihcihisonân kâ-kî-isi-mâyêyihcikêyâhk...mâka nohtâwînân nikî-kîhkâmikonân, ê-kî-itikoyâhk ta-kî-kistêyihtamahk anima kâ-kî-isi-wêpahk, namôya konita ta-kî-pôsiyâhk ispîhk kâ-sôhkiyowêk mîna kâ-mâh-misi-kîstihk.

As usual, I wanted to challenge the weather. I convinced my older sister for us to try to go across the water in spite of the weather! We got on board (the canoe). Holy! The waves were huge, but still we paddled on, we paddled against the wind! The wind gave us a real tough time because of the big waves, but we eventually arrived on shore where we lived. We were so proud of ourselves for meeting the challenge...but our father scolded us, told us to respect the weather when it was very windy, to not go on board a canoe for any reason when it was storming.

Words

akâmihk	*across the water*
anima	*that one*
âsowaha	*go across the water* (VTI-1)
cîmânihk	*in the canoe*
ê-kî-itikoyâhk	*she/he told us* (VTA-inv)
êkwâni	*and then*
êyikohk	*so much, so far, as much*
kâh-kitowak	*thunderbirds call, there is thunder*
kâ-isiwêpahk	*the way the weather is*
kâ-mâh-misi-kîstihk	*there was a big windstorm* (VII)
kanâcihcikê	*clean up* (VAI)
kanâcihtâ	*clean it* (VTI-2)
kapê-kîsik	*all day*
kaskim	*convince someone* (VTA)
kaskitêwânaskwâw	*there are dark clouds* (VII)
kêyâpic	*still*
kîhkâmikow	*she/he is scolded by someone* (VTA-inv)
kî-mâh-misi-mamahkâhan	*there were big waves* (VII)
kiyâm	*never mind, it doesn't matter, may as well*
kwayask	*right, correct*
nayêhtâwêhikow	*she/he struggles with it* (VTA-inv)
mâh-misi-mamahkâhan	*there are big waves* (VII)
mâka piyisk	*but eventually*
mâyêyihcikê	*be disrespectful* (VAI)
mâyêyihta	*disrespect it* (VTI-1)
misakâ	*arrive on shore by canoe/boat* (VAI)
miyo-kîsikâw	*it is a nice day* (VII)
namôya konita	*it is not for nothing*
nanimaha	*go (paddle canoe) against the wind* (VTI-1)
nikî-mâh-mamihcihisonân	*we really were proud of ourselves* (VAI)
nîkinâhk	*at our home*
nimis	*my older sister*
nohtâwînân	*our father*
pêtânaskwâw	*the clouds are coming* (VII)
pimiskâ	*paddle* (VAI)
piyêsiwak	*thunder*
pôni-âpihtâ-kîsikâw	*it is afternoon* (VII)
sîpiy	*river*
sôhkiyowêw	*it is very windy* (VII)
ta-kî-kistêyihtamahk	*we should respect something* (VTI-1)
ta-kî-pôsiyâhk	*we should get on board* (VAI)
wâh-wâsaskotêpayin	*there is lightning* (VII)

wîki	reside (VAI)
yîkwahaskân	cemetery
yôtin	it is windy (VII)

Questions (answers are on page 293)

1. tânispîhk ôma kâ-kî-itahkamikahk?

_____

2. tânisi ôki kâ-kî-wî-itahkamikisicik?

_____

3. tânisi kâ-kî-isiwêpahk ispîhk kâ-kî-âsowahahkik sîpiy?

_____

4. tânisi kâ-kî-ati-isiwêpahk ispîhk kâ-pôni-âpihtâ-kîsikâk?

_____

5. piyêsiwak cî kî-kitowak?

_____

6. kî-ati-sôhkiyowêw cî?

_____

7. kî-wâh-wâsaskotêpayin cî?

_____

8. tânisi awa kâ-kî-itôtahk?

_____

9. kî-kakwê-âsowahamwak cî sîpiy?

_____

10. tânisi ohtâwîwâwa kâ-kî-itôtamiyit?

_____

10.2.B. ka-ispitisihk isîhcikêwin – PROTOCOL: AGE-APPROPRIATE CONDUCT

[1] kayâs mâna mihcêtwâw nikî-nitawiminânân natimihk ita ohci kâ-kî-wîkiyâhk. niya, nîtisânak, nikâwiy êkwa pêyak nohkom nikî-pôsinân mâna cîmânihk natimihk ê-isicimêyâhk ta-nitawiminêyâhk nôhcimihk ita ê-ispatinâk. nikî-kospînân mâna êkwa nikî-mâh-mawisonân. namôya mâna kinwêsk âsay kâ-iskatêyihtamâhk ta-mawisoyâhk, niya, nistês êkwa pêyak nisîmis. nikî-mâh-mâci-mêtawânân êskwâ ê-mawisocik nikâwiy, nohkom êkwa nisîmisak, aniki iskwêsisak. mêtoni mâna kapê-kîsik ê-mâh-mêtawêyâhk. piyisk kâ-ati-otâkosik nitêpwâtikonân nikâwiy êkwa kâ-takopahtâyâhk nititikonân ta-nayahtamâhk mînisa nâsipêtimihk isi. mêtoni mâna mistahi miscikowacisa ê-kî-sâh-sâkaskinahtâcik iyinimina ohci. kî-kosikwanwa mâna anihi mînisa êkwa wâhyaw ta-isi-nayahtamâhk nâsipêtimihk isi mâka namôya nânitaw nikî-itêyihtênân ayisk êkosi mâna kapê ê-kî-isi-atoskêhikawiyâhk niyanân nâpêsisak.

A long time ago there were a lot of times we'd go berry-picking upriver from where we lived. Me, my siblings, my mother and one of my grandmothers went on board a canoe and paddled upriver to go berry-picking inland where there are high hills. We went inland into the bush and picked berries. It wasn't long before I, my older brother, and one of my younger siblings got tired of picking berries. We played while my mother, my grandmother, and my younger siblings, those girls, picked berries. We played practically all day. Eventually, in the late afternoon our mother called for us, and when we arrived running, she told us to carry the berries on our backs to the shore of the lake. There were a lot of little boxes filled with blueberries. Those berries were heavy, and we had to carry them far to the shore, but we thought nothing of it because this is the way we boys were always made to work.

Words

anihi	*those ones*
aniki	*those ones*
âsay	*already*
wâhyaw	*far*
ê-kî-isi-atoskêhikawiyâhk	*the way we were made to work*
wîki	*reside* (VAI)
êkosi mâna	*that's the way it was usually*
êskwâ	*while*
kapê	*always*
isicimê	*canoe toward that way* (VAI)
iskatêyihta	*be bored (with something)* (VTI-1)
iskwêsis	*girl*
ispatinaw	*hill*
ita ohci	*from where*
niyanân	*us*
itêyihta	*think thus* (VTI-1)
iyinimina	*blueberries*
takopahtâ	*arrive running* (VAI)

kapê-kîsik	*all day*
kayâs	*long ago*
kinwêsk	*a long time*
nâpêsis	*boy*
kosikwanwa	*they are heavy* (VII)
kospî	*go into the forest (inland)* (VAI)
mâh-mawiso	*pick berries* (VAI)
mêtawê	*play* (VAI)
mêtoni mâna mistahi	*there were so many*
mihcêtwâw	*many times*
mînisa	*berries*
miscikowacis	*small box*
namôya mâna	*not usually*
nâsipêtimihk isi	*toward the shore*
natimihk	*upriver*
nayahta	*carry on your back* (VTI-1)
nikâwiy	*my mother*
nisîmis	*my younger sibling*
nistês	*my older brother*
nitawiminê	*go in search of berries* (VAI)
nîtisânak	*my siblings*
otâkosin	*it is evening* (VII)
nitêpwâtikonân	*she/he calls us* (VTA-inv)
nititikonân	*she/he tells us* (VTA-inv)
nôhcimihk	*inland, into the forest*
nohkom	*my grandmother*
sâkaskinahtâ	*fill it up* (VTI-2)
nitawiminê	*go berry-picking* (VAI)

Questions (answers are on page 293)

1. tânisi mâna kâ-kî-itahkamikisicik ôki?

   _____

2. tânitê mâna kâ-kî-nitawiminêcik?

   _____

3. awîniki mâna kâ-kî-nitawi-minêcik?

   _____

4. ispatinâhk cî kâ-kî-nitawiminêcik?

_____

5. kî-ati-iskatêyihtamwak cî ta-mawisocik ôki nâpêsisak?

_____

6. tânisi kâ-kî-ati-itôtahkik?

_____

7. kapê-kîsik cî mâna kî-mâh-mêtawêwak ôki nâpêsisak?

_____

8. tânisi kâ-kî-itôtahkik ispîhk kâ-otâkosiniyik?

_____

9. mistahi cî mâna kî-mawisowak ôki iskwêwak?

_____

10. tânisi mâna nâpêsisak kâ-kî-isi-atoskêhikawicik?

_____

10.2.c. tapahtêyimisowin – HUMILITY

This is a story I heard as a child, I think...but I may have stolen it.

[1] pêyakwâw êsa wîsahkêcâhk kî-pêhtam âcimowin, ê-âcimimiht oskinîkiwa mistahi ê-itêyimisoyit, ê-kî-kihcêyimot awa oskinîkiw. ê-kakwê-wîkimihiht êsa awa oskinîkiw, ê-kakwê-mêkiskwêwêhikot iyiniwa, mâka tahtwâw kâ-pê-asotamâht iskwêwa ta-wîkimât, âtawêyimêw! êwako ôma âcimowin kâ-pêhtahk wîsahkêcâhk.

Once Wîsahkêcâhk heard a story about a young man who thought highly of himself; this young man was conceited. People were trying to marry him off; the people were trying to offer him young women to marry, but every time a young woman was offered for marriage, he would reject her. This is the story Wîsahkêcâhk hears.

[2] êkwâni, nitawâpênikêw awa, mahti êsa tâpwê. takosin ihtâwinihk ita awa kâ-kî-âcimiht oskinîkiw. sakâhk ohci kâ-kîmôtâpit, kâ-wâpamât oskinîkiwa akâmi-sîpîhk, wâsakâm sîpîhk ê-matwê-kanawâpamisoyit nipîhk. mêtoni kinwêsk kanawâpamêw ôhi oskinîkiwa, osâm piko kapê-kîsik. mâmaskâtêw ôhi oskinîkiwa kâ-itahkamikisiyit, kapê-kîsik nipîhk ê-kitâpamisoyit, êyikohk mistahi ê-itêyimisoyit! nama nânitaw kotak kîkway atoskâtamiyiwa, nama nânitaw itâpatisiyiwa. êkwâni êkota ohci pasikôw wîsahkêcâhk ê-mâmitonêyihtahk tânisi ta-kî-isi-wawiyasihât ôhi oskinîkiwa.

So then he sets off to check up on this, to see if it was true. He arrives at the place where the people were living where the young man lived, according to the story. From a bush he looks on in secret, when he sees the young man across the river, along the shore of the river, he sees him looking at himself in the water. For a long time he watches this young man, almost all day! He wonders about the young man, about his actions, all day looking at himself in the water, thinking so highly of himself. He works at nothing else, he is good for nothing! From there Wîsahkêcâhk gets up, wondering what he can do to play a trick on the young man.

[3] kêtahtawê pêyak kîsikâw, êskwâ ê-kâh-kitâpamisot nipîhk awa oskinîkiw kâ-wâpamât pêyak oskinîkiskwêwa akâmi-sîpîhk ê-matwê-kanâcihoyit. wahwâ! akâwâtêw ôhi oskinîkiskwêwa êyikohk ê-kî-miyonâkosiyit. sêmâk nâtêw ohtâwiya ta-itwêstamâkot ayisk ê-nôhtê-wîkimât anihi oskinîkiskwêwa. mêtoni kinwêsîs êyikohk kâ-kaskimiht awa oskinîkiskwêw ta-wîkimât ôhi oskinîkiwa. êkwâni mâka, piyisk wîkihtowak ôki. kwayask miywêyihtam awa oskinîkiw ê-wîkimât ôhi kâ-mâwaci-miyonâkosiyit oskinîkiskwêwa. êkwa ispîhk kâ-wîkihtocik ati-ocêmêw oski-wîwa, mwêhci kâ-ocêmât kâ-ati-mîskotinâkosiyit, ê-ati-nâpêwinâkosiyit! wahwâ! nisitawinawêw wîsahkêcâhkwa! wîsahkêcâhk êsa ê-kî-iskwêwisîhot ta-wîkimât ôhi oskinîkiwa mistahi kâ-itêyimisoyit.

As it came about, one day, while the young man was looking at himself in the water, he sees a young woman across the river, cleansing herself. Holy! He desires this young woman, so beautiful was she! Immediately he goes to get his father to speak for him because he wants to marry this young woman. It takes a long time for the young woman to be convinced for her to marry the young man. Eventually, however, they marry. The man was very happy for marrying this most beautiful young woman. And when it was time for the wedding, he begins to kiss his new wife, just when he was going to kiss her, she begins to change her looks, she begins to look like a man! Holy! He recognizes Wîsahkêcâhk. Apparently Wîsahkêcâhk had dressed like a woman to marry this young man who thought so highly of himself.

Words

âcimowin	*story*
akâmi-sîpîhk	*across the river*
akâwâtêw	*she/he desires someone* (VTA)
âtawêyimêw	*she/he rejects someone* (VTA)
atoskâta	*work at it* (VTI-1)
ê-âcimimiht	*stories are told about someone*

ê-kâh-kitâpamisot	*she/he looks at her/himself* (VTA-refl)
ê-kakwê-mêkiskwêwêhikot	*they try to give him a woman to marry* (VAI)
ê-kakwê-wîkimihiht	*they try to marry her/him off* (VTA)
êkota	*there*
êkwa ispîhk	*and when*
êkwâni	*then*
êkwâni mâka	*but then*
ê-nôhtê-wîkimât	*she/he wants to marry someone* (VTA)
êsa	*evidently*
êskwâ	*while*
êwako	*that one*
ê-wîkimât	*she/he marries someone* (VTA)
ihtâwinihk	*village*
iskwêw	*woman*
iskwêwisîho	*dress as a woman* (VAI)
itâpatisi	*be useful in some way* (VAI)
êyikohk	*so much that*
itêyimiso	*think yourself that way* (VAI)
kâ-kaskimiht	*she/he is convinced* (VTA)
kâ-kî-âcimiht	*stories were told about someone* (VTA)
kâ-mâwaci-miyonâkosiyit oskinîkiskwêwa	
	the most beautiful young woman
kanâciho	*clean self* (VAI)
kanawâpam	*look at someone* (VTA)
kanawâpamiso	*look at yourself* (VTA-refl)
kâ-pê-asotamâht	*that which is promised someone* (VTA)
kâ-wîkihtocik	*when they marry* (VAI)
kêtahtawê	*suddenly*
kihcêyimo	*brag* (VAI)
kîmôtâpi	*sneak a peek* (VAI)
kinwêsîs	*for quite awhile*
kinwêsk	*a long time*
kîsikâw	*it is day* (VII)
kitâpamiso	*look at yourself* (VTA-rfl)
kotak kîkway	*another thing*
kwayask miywêyihtam	*she/he is very happy* (VTA)
mahti êsa	*let's see then*
mâmaskâtêw	*she/he wonders about someone* (VTA)
mâmitonêyihta	*think about it* (VTI-1)
matwê-	*something happens in the distance*
mîskotinâkosi	*looks different* (VAI)
mistahi	*a lot*
mistahi ê-itêyimisoyit	*she/he thinks highly of her/himself*

miyonâkosiw	*she/he is beautiful* (VAI)
mwêhci	*just when*
nama nânitaw	*nothing about*
nâpêwinâkosi	*look like a man* (VAI)
nâtêw	*she/he fetches (goes toward) someone* (VTA)
nipîhk	*in the water*
nisitawinawêw	*she/he recognizes someone* (VTA)
nitawâpênikê	*go check it out* (VAI)
ocêm	*kiss someone* (VTA)
ôhi	*these*
ohtâwiya	*her/his father*
ôki	*these*
ôma	*this*
osâm piko	*mostly, mainly*
oskinîkiskwêw	*young woman*
oskinîkiw	*young man*
oski-wîwa	*his new wife*
pasikô	*stand up* (VAI)
pêhta	*hear it* (VTI-1)
sêmâk	*right away*
sîpîhk	*in the river*
tahtwâw	*every time*
ta-itwêstamâkot	*to speak for him, on his behalf* (VTA-inv)
ta-kî-isi-wawiyasihât	*to be able to play a trick on someone* (VTA)
takosin	*she/he arrives* (VAI)
tâpwê	*true*
ta-wîkimât	*to marry someone*
wâsakâm	*around/along the shore*
wîkihtowak	*they marry* (VAI)

Questions (answers are on page 294)

1. kîko âcimowina awa wîsahkêcâhk kâ-kî-pêhtahk?

   _____

2. tânisi mâna awa oskinîkiw kâ-itôtahk ispîhk kâ-asotamâht iskwêwa ta-wîkimât?

   _____

3. tânitê ohci kâ-kîmôtâpit wîsahkêcâhk?

   _____

4. tânitê kâ-wâpamât oskinîkiwa?

_____

5. tânisi kâ-itôtamiyit oskinîkiwa?

_____

6. kîkwây kâ-mâmitonêyihtahk wîsahkêcâhk?

_____

7. tânita awa oskinîkiw kâ-kitâpimisot ispîhk kâ-wâpamât oskinîkiskwêwa?

_____

8. akâwâtêw cî ôhi oskinîkiskwêwa?

_____

9. tânisi ohtâwiya kâ-itôtamiyit?

_____

10. wîkimêw cî wîsahkêcâhk ôhi oskinîkiwa mistahi kâ-itêyimisot?

_____

10.2.D. nikwatisowin êkwa mâtinamâkêwin – SHARING AND GENEROSITY

nikiskisin kâ-kî-awâsisîwiyâhk nikî-nitomikawinân niya mîna nistês ta-nitawi-nikwatisoyâhk. pêyak awa niwâhkômâkaninân ê-kî-nipahât môswa êkwa wâhyaw nôhcimihk sakâhk ê-kî-nakatât ê-kî-pê-nâtât owâhkômâkana ta-nikwatisoyit, êkosi mâna kayâs omâcîwak ê-kî-itôtahkik. tahto-wîtisânîhitowinihk nitomêw kanakê pêyak nâpêsisa ta-nitawi-nikwatisoyit. nistês kî-wîsâmâw niwîtisânîhitowininâhk ohci êkwa nîsta nikî-wîsâmikawin ta-nâtamawak môso-wiyâs pêyak nohkom kâ-pêyako-wîkit. wîpac ê-kîkisêpâyâk nikî-sipwêhtânân, niyanân nâpêsisak mîna nâpêwak. kinwêsk nôhcimihk sakâhk nikî-pimohtânân. nikî-môcikihtânân, ê-âh-âcimocik nâpêwak mîna ê-nâh-nanôyacihikoyâhkik. piyisk nitakohtânân minahowinihk. nâpêwak kî-mâh-manisâwâtêwak anihi môswa êkwa nikî-âh-asiwatânân môso-wiyâs nimaskimotinâhk. kâwi nikî-kîwânân. ispîhk kâ-takohtêyâhk nikapêsiwininâhk nikî-wîhkohkânân. ana nohkom kâ-kî-pêtamawak wiyâs nikî-kîsisamâk môso-wiyâs, ê-kî-nawacîstamawit. wahwâ! kwayask nikî-wîhkistên êwako môso-wiyâs! kwayask mîna nikî-môcikihtân êkospîhk kâ-kî-nitawi-nikwatisoyâhk.

I remember when we were children, me and my older brother were invited to go fetch meat from a kill. One of my relatives had killed a moose, and it was deep in the forest where he had left it to come get his relatives to go fetch the meat; this is what hunters did a long time ago. From every family he invited at least one boy to go fetch meat. My older brother was invited from my family, and I was also invited so I can fetch moose meat for a grandmother who lived alone. Early in the morning we left, us boys and the men. We walked in the forest for a long time. We had fun, the men would tell stories and they would tease us boys. We eventually arrived at the kill site. The men cut up the moose and we filled our bags with moose meat. We went back home. When we arrived at our camp, we made a feast. That grandmother for whom I brought moose meat cooked moose meat for me, she had roasted it for me on a stick. Holy! I really liked the taste of that moose meat. I had lots of fun at that time when we went to fetch meat at the killing site.

Words

âh-âcimo	*tell stories* (VAI)
âh-asiwatâ	*place in a bag* (VTI-2)
êkosi mâna	*that is the way usually*
êkospîhk	*at that time*
kanakê	*at least*
kayâs	*long ago*
kîkisêpâyâw	*it is morning* (VII)
kîsisamaw	*cook something for someone* (VTA)
kiskisi	*remember* (VAI)
mâh-manisâwât	*cut someone* (VTA)
maskimot	*bag*
minahowinihk	*at the place of the kill*
môcikihtâ	*have fun* (VAI)
môswa	*moose*
ê-nâh-nanôyacihikoyâhkik	*they tease us* (VTA-inv)
nakat	*leave someone* (VTA)
nâpêw	*man*
nât	*fetch someone* (VTA)
nâtamaw	*fetch it for someone* (VTA)
nawacîstamaw	*roast something for someone* (VTA)
nikapêsiwininâhk	*at our camp*
nikwatiso	*fetch meat from a killing place* (VAI)
nipah	*kill someone* (VTA)
nîsta	*me too*
nistês	*my older brother*
nitom	*invite* (VTA)
nôhcimihk	*inland, in the forest*
nohkom	*my grandmother*
omâcîwa	*hunter*

pêtamaw	*bring something for someone* (VTA)
pêyako-wîki	*live alone* (VAI)
pimohtê	*walk* (VAI)
sipwêhtê	*eave* (VAI)
tahto-wîtisânîhitowinihk	*from every family*
takohtê	*arrive by foot* (VAI)
wâhyaw	*far*
wîhkista	*like the taste of something* (VTI-1)
wîhkohkê	*put on a feast* (VAI)
wîsâm	*invite someone* (VTA)

Questions (answers are on page 294)

1. tânispîhk ôma kâ-kî-itahkamikahk?

_____

2. awîniki kâ-kî-nitomihcik ta-nitawi-nikwatisocik?

_____

3. awîna kâ-kî-nipahât môswa?

_____

4. tânitê kâ-kî-nakatât môswa?

_____

5. tânêhki kâ-kî-nakatât êkotê môswa?

_____

6. tânisi mâna kayâs omâcîwak kâ-kî-itôtahkik?

_____

7. awîna kâ-kî-wîsâmiht ta-nâtamawât ohkoma môso-wiyâs?

_____

8. tânispîhk kâ-kî-sipwêhtêcik ôki?

_____

9. kinwêsk cî mâna sakâhk kî-pimohtêwak?

_____

10. tânisi kâ-kî-isi-môcikihtâcik ôki?

_____

10.2.E. tâpokêyihtamowin – FAITH

kayâs kâ-kî-awâsisîwiyân nikî-pâh-pimohtêhonân mâna misiwê itê mâhtâwi-sîpîhk. pêyakwâw ê-sîkwahk nikî-wâpamânân môswa ê-âsowahahk sâkahikan. kêsiskaw kî-otihtinam pîminahkwân nohcâwîs êkwa kî-ati-tâpakwêwêpinêw êwakoni môswa. mâka ana môswa kwayask nikî-sêkihik ayisk mêtoni kêhciwâk cîmânihk ita kâ-apiwak ê-pê-isicimêt. piyisk âtawiya kî-nipahêw êwakoni môswa nohcâwîs ê-mwayî-kwatapiskamwak cîmânis ispîhk kâ-kî-kakwê-tapasîhak ana môswa. awîna êtikwê nawac kî-sêkisiw, niya awêkâ cî ana môswa? matwân cî ê-kî-nitawi-wâpamât nôsê-môswa ministikohk ita kâ-kî-nihtâwikiyit osk-âyisisa?

A long time ago when I was a child, we travelled all over the Churchill River. One time, in the spring, we saw a moose crossing the waters of a lake. Quickly my uncle grabbed a rope and lassoed that moose. But that moose scared me because he would swim close to where I was sitting in the canoe. Eventually my uncle killed that moose before I tipped the canoe from my attempts at getting away from it. I wonder who was more scared, me or the moose? I wonder if it was going to go see a female moose on the island where the young moose was born?

Words

api	_sit_ (VAI)
âtawiya	_at least_
awêkâ cî	_or else_
awîna êtikwê	_wonder who_
cîmânis	_small canoe_
êwakoni	_that one_
isicimê	_go toward_ (VAI)
kêhciwâk	_close to something_
kêsiskaw	_in a hurry_
kwatapiska	_tip it over by sudden movement_ (VTI-1)
mâhtâwi-sîpîhk	_at the Churchill River_
matwân cî	_maybe_
ministik	_island_
misiwê	_all over_
mwayî-	_before_ (IPV)

nawac	*more so*
nihtâwiki	*be born* (VAI)
nipah	*kill someone* (VTA)
nohcâwîs	*my uncle*
nôsê-môswa	*cow moose*
osk-âyisisa	*young moose, yearling*
otihtina	*grab something* (VTI-1)
pah-pimohtêho	*travel about* (VAI)
pîminahkwân	*rope*
sâkahikan	*lake*
sêkih	*scare someone* (VTA)
sêkisi	*be scared* (VAI)
sîkwan	*it is spring* (VII)
tâpakwêwêpin	*rope/snare someone with a rope* (VTA)
tapasîh	*flee from someone* (VTA)

Questions (answers are on page 294)

1. tânispîhk ôma kâ-kî-itahkamikahk?

_____

2. tânitê kâ-kî-pâh-pimohtêhocik ôki?

_____

3. tânisi ê-ihkiniyik ispîhk kâ-wâpamâcik môswa?

_____

4. tânisi ana môswa ê-itôtahk?

_____

5. tânisi ohcâwîsa awa kâ-itôtamiyit?

_____

6. tânisi ê-wî-isi-âpacihtât pîminahkwân?

_____

7. tâpakwê-wêpinêw cî môswa pîminahkwân ohci?

_____

8. kî-sêkihikow cî môswa ana nâpêsis?

_____

9. tânêhki ôhi môswa kâ-sêkihikot?

_____

10. kêkâc cî kî-kwatapiskam cîmânis awa?

_____

10.2.F. kisêwâtisiwin – KINDNESS

kayâs kâ-kî-awâsisîwiyâhk nikî-wîcihinân nohtâwîpan ta-nikohtawât atâwêwikimâwa.
osâm piko kapê-nîpin nikî-nikohtânân natimihk nîkinâhk ohci. nohtâwîpan
kî-kâh-kîskatahâhtikwêw êkwa niyanân nikî-nâsipêyâwatânân anihi mihta.
nikî-sôhki-atoskânân mâna. piyisk mihcêt mihta nikî-âwatânân êkwa mihtot nikî-osîhtânân.
nîstâw nikî-pê-wîcihikonân ta-pimitâpihpâhtwât otôtihk ohci, ta-sakahpitahk anima mihtot
otôtihk. nikî-itikawinân ta-pôsiyâhk ôsihk mâka nikî-akâwâtênân tahkohc mihtotihk
ta-pôsiyâhk. kî-pâhpisiw nohtâwîpaninân mâka nikî-pakitinikonân tahkohc mihtotihk
ta-pôsiyâhk. wahwâ! kwayask kî-môcikan!

_A long time ago when we were children, we helped my late father to cut wood for the store manager.
We worked almost all summer at cutting wood upriver from our home. My father would chop down
the trees and we would haul them down to the river. We worked hard. Eventually we had a lot of
wood, so we made a raft. My brother-in-law came to help us to drag the raft with his motorboat, to
tie the raft to his boat. We were told to get into the boat, but we wanted to ride on top of the raft. My
father smiled but he let us ride on top of the raft. Holy! It was a lot of fun._

Words

akâwâta	_desire something_ (VTI-1)
anima	_that_
atâwêwikimâw	_store manager_
âwatâ	_haul something_ (VAI-2)
kâh-kîskatahâhtikwê	_cut down trees_ (VAI)
kapê-nîpin	_all summer_
mihcêt	_many_
mihta	_firewood_ (pl)
mihtot	_raft_
mihtotihk	_in the raft_
nâsipêyâwatâ	_haul it to the shore_ (VAI-2)
natimihk	_upriver_
nikî-itikawinân	_we were told_ (VTA-inv)
nîkinâhk	_at our home_
nikohtaw	_make firewood for someone_ (VTA)

nikohtê	*make firewood* (VAI)
nîstâw	*my brother-in-law*
nohtâwîpan	*my late father*
nohtâwîpaninân	*our late father*
osâm piko	*almost like*
ôsihk	*in the boat*
osîhtâ	*make it* (VAI-2)
otôtihk	*in her/his boat*
pâhpisi	*smile* (VAI)
pakitin	*allow someone* (VTA)
pimitâpihpâhtwâ	*drag it in the water* (VAI-2)
sakahpita	*tie something* (VTI-1)
sôhki-	*hard* (IPV)
tahkohc	*on top of*
ta-pôsiyâhk	*to board, to go on a boat/canoe* (VAI)
wîcih	*help someone* (VTA)

Questions (answers are on page 295)

1. tânispîhk ôma kâ-kî-itahkamikahk?

_____

2. tânisi kâ-wî-isi-wîcihâcik ohtâwîwâwa ôki?

_____

3. awîna kâ-kî-atoskêhiwêt?

_____

4. osâm piko cî kapê-nîpin kî-nikohtêwak?

_____

5. awîna kâ-kî-kîskatahâhtikwêt?

_____

6. awîniki kâ-kî-nâsipêyâwatâcik mihta?

_____

7. kî-sôhki-atoskêwak cî mâna?

_____

8. kîkwây kâ-kî-osîhtâcik?

_____

9. awîna kâ-pê-wîcihiwêt?

_____

10. kîkwây kâ-akâwâtahkik ta-itôtahkik ôki nâpêsisak?

_____

10.2.G. âniskô-kiskinwahamâkêwin – PASSING ON TEACHINGS

[1] pêyakwâw ê-nîpîhk nikî-nitawi-papâmiskânân mâmihk âmaciwîspimowinihk ohci, ê-pimitisahamâhk mâhtâwi-sîpiy. nikî-cîmâwak nitôtêmak. nikî-ati-kapêsinân pâwiscikosihk nistam kâ-tipiskâk êkwa ê-ati-wâpahk kîhtwâm nikî-pôsinân, ê-âsowahamâhk sâkahikanisis. piyisk wapâsihk nikî-takocimânân, kâ-mâyiciwasik isiyihkâtêw anima wapâs. kêtahtawê kâ-matwê-têpwêcik nitôtêmak. "ohcistin kitôtinaw!"

One summer we went canoeing downriver from Stanley Mission, following the Churchill River. I went with my friends. We camped at Little Stanley Rapids the first night and went on our way the next day, crossing the little lake, eventually arriving at a narrows, known as "place of difficult currents" (Frog Narrows). All of a sudden my friends hollered, "Our boat is leaking!"

[2] nikî-itâpin mostihtakohk, wahwâ! tâpwê ôt âni, nikî-ohcistinisinân.

I looked at the bottom of the canoe, and, sure enough, we were leaking!

[3] "âhâw, cêskwa. kika-sêskipitênaw cîmân miniscikosihk misakâyahki," nikî-itâwak.

"Okay, just wait. We'll pull the canoe to shore at a little island when we arrive there," I told them.

[4] ispîhk kâ-misakâyâhk miniscikosihk nikî-sêskipitênân cîmân êkwa nikî-kwatapinênân. nikî-itâwak nitôtêmak ta-kotawêcik êkwa niya nikî-kospîn ê-nitonawak pikiw minahikohk. nikî-miskawâw.

When we arrived at the little island, we pulled the canoe to shore and tipped it over. I told my friends to build a campfire, and I went inland looking for spruce gum on a spruce tree. I found some.

[5] ispîhk kâ-pê-nâsipêhtêyân kî-takahki-kwâhkotêw kotawân. êkota nikî-ati-tihkiswâw ana minahik-pikiw. kâ-kî-kîsi-tihkisot ana pikiw nikî-ati-mîsahên nicîmâniminân êwako pikiw ê-âpacihak. nikitâpamikwak nitôtêmak tâpiskôc nawac piko ê-ânwêhtahkik ôma kâ-itahkamikisiyân. nipêhonân ta-pâsot ana pikiw, piyisk pâsow êkwa kîhtwâm nipôsinân. kâ-mâtwê-têpwêcik nitôtêmak.

When I went to the shore, there was a good fire going. I began to melt the spruce gum. When the pine-pitch was done melting I began to patch our canoe using that spruce gum. My friends looked at me as if they doubted that I knew what I was doing. We waited for the spruce gum to dry, eventually it dried and once again we boarded the canoe. My friends called out.

[6] "namôya awasimê ohcistin! wahwâ! tânisi ôma ê-isi-kiskêyihtaman ta-mîsahaman cîmân?"

"There is no more leak! Holy! How did you know how to do that to patch the canoe?"

[7] "kayâs iyiniw mamahtâwisiwin anima. kayâs iyiniw ê-kî-kiskinwahamawit, nohtâwîpan."

"It's an old Indian trick. An old Indian taught me, my late father."

Words

âhâw	okay
ânwêhta	disbelieve something (VTI-1)
âpacih	use someone (VTA)
âsowaha	go across water (VTI-1)
cêskwa	wait
cîm	accompany someone on vehicle (VTA)
isiyihkâtêw	it is called (VII)
itâpi	look toward a direction (VAI)
kâ-mâyiciwasik	place of difficult currents
kapêsi	camp (VAI)
kiskêyihta	know something (VTI-1)
kiskinwahamaw	teach someone (VTA)
kitôtinaw	our boat
kospî	go inland (VAI)
kotawân	campfire
kotawê	make a campfire (VAI)
kwâhkotêw	it flares up (VII)
kwatapina	flip something over (VTI-1)
mâhtâwi-sîpiy	Churchill River
mamahtâwisiwin	skill
mâmihk	downriver
minahikohk	amongst the spruce
minahik-pikiw	spruce gum

miniscikosihk	*on a small island*
mîsaha	*mend something* (VTI-1)
misakâ	*arrive by boat/canoe* (VAI)
miskaw	*find someone* (VTA)
mostihtakohk	*on the bottom of the canoe*
namôya awasimê	*no longer*
nâsipêhtê	*walk to the shore, walk downhill* (VAI)
nawac piko	*more likely*
nicîmâniminân	*our canoe*
nikî-itâwak	*I said to them* (VTA)
nikî-itikwak	*they said to me* (VTA-inv)
nikitâpamikwak	*they look at me* (VTA-inv)
nîpîn	*it is summer*
nistam	*first*
nitonaw	*look for someone* (VTA)
nitôtêmak	*my friends*
ohcistin	*it leaks* (VII)
papâmiskâ	*canoe about, paddle about* (VAI)
pâso	*dry* (VAI)
pâwiscikosihk	*at the small rapids*
pêho	*wait* (VAI)
pikiw	*gum*
pimitisaha	*follow something* (VTI-1)
sâkahikanisis	*small lake*
sêskipita	*pull it ashore* (VTI-1)
takahki	*great*
takocimê	*arrive by boat/canoe* (VAI)
tâpiskôc	*just like*
tâpwê ot âni	*for sure it is true*
têpwê	*yell* (VAI)
tihkis	*melt someone* (VTA)
tihkiso	*melt* (VAI)
tipiskâw	*it is night* (VII)
wâpan	*it is dawn* (VII)
wapâs	*narrows*
wapâsihk	*at the narrows*

Questions (answers are on page 295)

1. tânispîhk ôma kâ-kî-itahkamikahk?

   _____

2. tânitê kâ-kî-nitawi-papâmiskâcik ôki?

   _____

3. tânitê kâ-kî-ati-kapêsicik nistam kâ-tipiskâyik?

   _____

4. tânispîhk kîhtwâm kâ-kî-ati-pôsicik?

   _____

5. tânitê kâ-takocimêcik?

   _____

6. tânisi kâ-isi-têpwêyit otôtêma?

   _____

7. ohcistin cî cîmân?

   _____

8. kîkwây kâ-ohci-mîsahahk cîmân?

   _____

9. ânwêhtamiyiwa cî otôtêma êwakoni pikiwa ta-mîsahamiyit cîmâna?

   _____

10. awînihi kâ-kî-kiskinwahamâkot ta-isi-mîsahikâkêyit pikiwa?

    _____

ANSWERS

CHAPTER 1 EXERCISES

1.1.D. Translation

aciyaw,...	For a bit, for a bit, come to work for a bit.
ispimihk,...	Up, up, run upstairs.
otina,...	Take it, take it, take his shoes.
âstam,...	Come, come, come tell a story.
êkosi,...	That way, that way, say it that way.
yiyîkicihcîs,...	Little finger, little finger, point with the little finger.
ôta,...	Here, here, here in the town of Regina.
cêskwa,...	Wait, wait, wait, a little lower.
hâw,...	Okay, okay, okay crow, okay.
kiyipa,...	Hurry, hurry, hurry home you.
mahti,...	Please, please, please think about this.
nikamo,...	Sing, sing, that man sings well.
pahkwên,...	Break it off, break it off, break off (a bit of) bannock.
sîwisiw,...	It is sweet, it is sweet, the candy is sweet.
têpakohp,...	Seven, seven, there are seven chairs here.
wâpan,...	It is dawn, it is dawn, get up, it is dawn.
yôskâw,...	It is soft, it is soft, the rubber overshoe is soft.

1.2.B. Introducing Yourself

The answers below provide my information, which you can replace with your own information. The verb forms will remain the same.

Solomon nitisiyihkâson. – *My name is Solomon.*

nikotwâsikomitanaw têpakohposâp nititahtopiponân. – *I am 67 years old.*

âmaciwîspimowinihk ohci niya kayâhtê. – *I am originally from Stanley Mission.*

oskana kâ-asastêki mêkwâc niwîkin. – *I currently live/reside in Regina.*

mâhtâwi-sîpîhk nikî-nihtâwikin, apisis kîwêtinohk âmaciwîspimowinihk ohci. –
   I was born on the Churchill River, a bit north from Stanley Mission.

kî-mikiskon ispîhk kâ-kî-nihtâwikiyân. – *It was late fall when I was born.*

ihkopîwi-pîsim mâna kâ-akimiht ispîhk kâ-tipiskamân. – *I have a birthday in November.*

nîsitanaw nistosâp ê-akimiht êwako pîsim mâna kâ-tipiskamân. –
   I have a birthday on the 23rd of that month.

namôya, namôya okiskinwahamâkan niya.* – *No, I am not a student.*

nicîhkêyihtên ta-nêhiyawêyân. – *I like to speak Cree.*

CHAPTER 2 EXERCISES

2.2.A. Kinship Chart Exercise

Kinship	1st Person	2nd Person	3rd Person
ohkomimâw	—	kohkom	ohkoma
omosômimâw	nimosôm	—	omosôma
ohtâwîmâw	nohtâwiy	kohtâwiy	—
okâwîmâw	nikâwiy	kikâwiy	—
ostêsimâw	nistês	—	ostêsa
omisimâw	—	kimis	omisa
osîmimâw	nisîmis	—	osîmisa
otânisimâw	nitânis	kitânis	—
okosisimâw	nikosis	—	okosisa
ohcâwîsimâw	—	kohcâwîs	ohcâwîsa

* Answers to the polarity question indicator *cî* can take three forms:

- You can anwer with an *âha* "yes": âha, okiskinawahamâkan niya. – *Yes, I am a student.*

- You can answer with a *namôya* and state that you are not a student: namôya, namôya okiskinawahamâkan niya. – *No, I am not a student.*

- You can answer with a *namôya* and state that you are something other than a student: namôya, okiskinwahamâkêw ôma niya. – *No, I am a teacher.*

okâwîsimâw	nikâwîs	—	okâwîsa
osikosimâw	nisikos	kisikos	—
osisimâw	nisis	—	osisa
ociwâmimâw	—	kiciwâm	ociwâma
ociwâmiskwêmâw	niciwâmiskwêm	—	ociwâmiskwêma
otawêmâw	nitawêmâw	kitawêmâw	—
wîtimowâw	nîtim	—	wîtimwa
wîstâwimâw	—	kîstâw	wîstâwa
ocâhkosimâw	nicâhkos	—	ocâhkosa
atim	nitêm	kitêm	—

2.2.B. Vital Statistics Exercise I

Name

A in 1: Paul nitisiyihkâson.

A in 3: Paul isiyihkâsow wiya.

Age

A in 1: nistomitanaw nititahtopiponân.

A in 3: nistomitanaw itahtopiponêw wiya.

Place of Origin

A in 1: mistahi sâkahikanihk ohci niya.

A in 3: mistahi sâkahikanihk ohci wiya.

Present Residence

A in 1: oskana kâ-asastêki mêkwâc niwîkin.

A in 3: oskana kâ-asastêki mêkwâc wîkiw wiya.

Birth Place

A in 1: mistahi sâkahikanihk kâ-kî-nihtâwikiyân.

A in 3: mistahi sâkahikanihk kâ-kî-nihtâwikit.

Season of Birth

A in 1: kî-ati-pipon ispîhk kâ-kî-nihtâwikiyân.

A in 3: kî-ati-piponiyiw ispîhk kâ-kî-nihtâwikit wiya.

Birth Month

A in 1: ihkopîwipîsim mâna kâ-tipiskamân?

A in 3: ihkopîwipîsimwa mâna kâ-tipiskahk wiya.

Birth Date

    A in 1:   nîsitanaw nistosâp ê-akimiht êwako pîsim mâna kâ-tipiskamân.

    A in 3:   nîsitanaw nistosâp ê-akimimiht êwakoni pîsimwa mâna kâ-tipiskahk wiya.

Family Size

    A in 1:   mâmawi têpakohp nitihtasinân.

    A in 3:   mâmawi têpakohp ihtasiwak.

Youngest Sibling

    A in 1:   namôya, namôya osîmimâw niya.

    A in 3:   namôya, namôya osîmimâw wiya.

Eldest Sister

    A in 1:   namôya, namôya omisimâw niya.

    A in 3:   namôya, namôya omisimâw wiya.

Eldest Brother

    A in 1:   âha, ostêsimâw niya.

    A in 3:   âha, ostêsimâw wiya.

Younger Siblings

    A in 1:   nikotwâsik nitosîmisin.

    A in 3:   nikotwâsik osîmisiw.

Older Sisters

    A in 1:   namôya kîkway nitomisin.

    A in 3:   namôya kîkway omisiw.

Older Brothers

    A in 1:   namôya kîkway nitostêsin.

    A in 3:   namôya kîkway ostêsiw.

2.2.C. Vital Statistics Exercise II

Name

    A in 3:   Mary isiyihkâsow nitânis.

    A in 3:   Mary isiyihkâsoyiwa otânisa wiya.

Age

    A in 3:   nêwosâp itahtopiponêw nitânis.

    A in 3:   nêwosâp itahtopiponêyiwa otânisa wiya.

Place of Origin

    A in 3:   mistahi sâkahikanihk ohcîw nitânis.

    A in 3:   mistahi sâkahikanihk ohcîyiwa otânisa wiya.

Present Residence

    A in 3:   oskana kâ-asastêki mêkwâc wîkiw nitânis.

    A in 3:   oskana kâ-asastêki mêkwâc wîkiyiwa otânisa wiya.

Birth Place

    A in 3:   mistahi sâkahikanihk kâ-kî-nihtâwikit nitânis.

    A in 3:   mistahi sâkahikanihk kâ-kî-nihtâwikiyit otânisa wiya.

Season of Birth

    A in 3:   kî-ati-sîkwaniyiw ispîhk kâ-kî-nihtâwikit? nitânis.

    A in 3:   kî-ati-sîkwaniyiw ispîhk kâ-kî-nihtâwikiyit otânisa wiya.

Birth Month

    A in 3:   mikisiwipîsimwa mâna kâ-tipiskahk nitânis.

    A in 3:   mikisiwipîsimwa mâna kâ-tipiskamiyit otânisa wiya.

Birth Date

    A in 3:   nîsitanaw ê-akimimiht êwakoni pîsimwa mâna kâ-tipiskahk nitânis.

    A in 3:   nîsitanaw ê-akimimiht êwakoni pîsimwa mâna kâ-tipiskamiyit otânisa wiya.

Student?

    A in 3:   âha, okiskinwahamâkan nitânis.

    A in 3:   âha, okiskinwahamâkan otânisa wiya.

What do you like to do?

    A in 3:   cîhkêyihtam ta-ayamihcikêt nitânis.

    A in 3:   cîhkêyihtamiyiwa ta-ayamihcikêyit otânisa.

2.2.E. Talking about Travel

Text 1

1. ê-kî-têpakohpo-kîsikâyik, pêyak kisêyiniw kî-ispayiw pimihâkan-twêhowinihk isi.
2. ayisk ê-kî-nitawi-môsâhkinât otânisa.
3. Toronto ohci ê-kî-pê-ohtâcihoyit.
4. nânitaw têpakohp tipahikan ê-kî-ispayiyik.

Text 2

1. pîhcâyihk pimihâkan-twêhowinihk pa-pêhow kisêyiniw.
2. atâwêstamâsow pihkahtêwâpoy. -or- pihkahtêwâpoy kâ-atâwêstamâsot.*
3. âha, ati-ayêski-pêhow.**
4. kâ-pimihâhk 357 Toronto ohci ê-otamipayiyik kanakê pêyak tipahikan.***

Text 3

1. kî-otamipayiw pêyak tipahikan kâ-pimihâhk 357 Toronto ohci.
2. piyisk mitâtaht tipahikan ê-ispayiyik kâ-twêhômakaniyik kâ-pimihâhk 357 Toronto ohci.
3. pêhêw otânisa awa kisêyiniw nîhc-âyihk nîhtaciwêpicikanihk.
4. cîhkêyihtam awa kisêyiniw ayisk êkwâni nistam ta-nakiskawât ôsisima.

CHAPTER 3 EXERCISES

3.3.A. Questions

> **Day of the week:** pêyako-kîsikâw anohc
> **Present month:** pinâskowipîsim akimâw mêkwâc.
> **Today's date:** nîstanaw ayinânêwosâp akimâw awa pîsim.
> **Weather:** yôtin êkwa misposin.

3.3.B. Translation

1. Last winter we went skiing in the mountains.
2. In the summer I am going to go fishing at the lake.
3. Last fall I went cross-country skiing in the mountains.
4. In the spring we are going to go hiking in the mountains.
5. Last spring we went travelling to the mountains.
6. In the winter we are going to go sliding in the mountains.
7. Last summer we went dancing powwow on the reserve.
8. In the fall we are going hunting in the mountains.
9. It was winter when I was born.
10. It is spring when I have a birthday.

---

* *Hint*: replace the content question word with what is being asked for and use the rest of the question in your answer.
** *Hint*: *cî* is a polarity question, so use *âha* or *namôya, namôya*.
   Note: *pêho!* "wait!"; *pêhin!* "Wait for me!"; *pêhinân* "wait for us."
***Note: If *ê-ispayik* or *ê-ispayiyik* were in the sentence, then it would be 1:00, not a duration of one hour.

3.4.A. Exercises

Days of the Week

English	Conjunct	Future Conditional
Sunday	ê-ayamihêwi-kîsikâk	ayamihêwi-kîsikâki
Monday	ê-pêyako-kîsikâk	pêyako-kîsikâki
Tuesday	ê-nîso-kîsikâk	nîso-kîsikâki
Wednesday	ê-nisto-kîsikâk	nisto-kîsikâki
Thursday	ê-nêwo-kîsikâk	ê-nêwo-kîsikâk
Friday	ê-niyânano-kîsikâk	niyânano-kîsikâki
Saturday	ê-nikotwâso-kîsikâk	nikotwâso-kîsikâki

Past Tense

English	Indicative Past Tense	Conjunct Past Tense
Monday	kî-pêyako-kîsikâw.	ê-kî-pêyako-kîsikâk
Tuesday	kî-nîso-kîsikâw.	ê-kî-nîso-kîsikâk
Wednesday	kî-nisto-kîsikâw.	ê-kî-nisto-kîsikâk
Thursday	kî-nêwo-kîsikâw.	ê-kî-nêwo-kîsikâk
Friday	kî-niyânano-kîsikâw.	ê-kî-niyânano-kîsikâk
Saturday	kî-nikotwâso-kîsikâw.	ê-kî-nikotwâso-kîsikâk

3.5.A. Translation

1. kîkisêpâyâki nika-itohtânân sâkahikanihk.
2. kî-kîkisêpâyâyiw ispîhk kâ-kî-takosihk ôta.
3. ta-kîkisêpâyâw ispîhk kîsahkamikisiyahko.
4. sipwêhtêtân êkwa, kîkisêpâyâw.
5. kotawê, kîkisêpâyâw.

3.5.B. Temporal Words

Temporal Words	Conjunct	Future Conditional
wâpan	ê-wâpahk	wâpahki – *if/when it is dawn/tomorrow*
kîkisêpâyâw	ê-kîkisêpâyâk	kîkisêpâyâki – *if/when it is morning*
âpihtâ-kîsikâw	ê-âpihtâ-kîsikâk	âpihtâ-kîsikâki – *if/when it is noon*
pôni-âpihtâ-kîsikâw	ê-pôni-âpihtâ-kîsikâk	pôni-âpihtâ-kîsikâki – *if/when it is afternoon*
otâkosin	ê-otâkosik	otâkosiki – *if/when it is evening*
pahkisimon	ê-pahkisimok	pahkisimoki – *if/when it is sundown*
wawâninâkwan	ê-wawâninâkwahk	wawâninâkwahki – *if/when it is twilight*
tipiskâw	ê-tipiskâk	tipiskâki – *if/when it is night/tonight*
âpihtâ-tipiskâw	ê-âpihtâ-tipiskâk	âpihtâ-tipiskâki – *if/when it is midnight*

CHAPTER 4 EXERCISES

4.1.A. Questions

1. têpakohp tipahikan mâna ê-ispayik kâ-waniskâyân ispîhk kâ-kîkisêpâyâk
2. têpakohp tipahikan mîna âpihtaw mâna ê-ispayik kâ-kîkisêpâ-mîcisoyân.
3. ayinânêw tipahikan mâna ê-ispayik kâ-nitawi-kiskinwahamâkosiyân.
4. nîstanaw cipahikanis miyâskam ayinânêw tipahikan mâna ê-ispayik kâ-takosiniyân kiskinwahamâtowikamikohk.
5. kêkâ-mitâtaht tipahikan mâna ê-ispayik kâ-mâci-kiskinwahamâkosiyân nêhiyawêwin.
6. nîsosâp tipahikan mîna âpihtaw mâna ê-ispayik kâ-âpihtâ-kîsikani-mîcisoyân.
7. niyânanosâp miyâskam mitâtaht tipahikan mâna ê-ispayik kâ-kîsi-kiskinwahamâkosiyân.
8. nîsitanaw cipahikanis pâmwayês nêwo tipahikan mâna ê-ispayik kâ-ati-kîwêyân.
9. nikotwâsik tipahikan mâna ê-ispayik kâ-otâkwani-mîcisoyân.
10. nisêsâwohtân mâna ispîhk kâ-otâkosik.
11. pêyakosâp tipahikan mâna ê-ispayik kâ-kawisimoyân.

4.2.A. VAIs in 1st Person

Temporal Words	Time	Activity
kîkisêp	nânitaw niyânanosâp cipahikanis pâmwayês ayinânêw tipahikan ê-kî-ispayik,	nikî-waniskân.
anohc	nânitaw niyânanosâp cipahikanis miyâskam pêyak tipahikan ispayiki,	niwî-sôhki-atoskân.
ispîhk kâ-pêtâpahk,	nânitaw niyânan tipahikan mâna ê-ispayik,	ninisîhkâci-pihkahtêwâpôhkân.
ispîhk kâ-sâkâstêk,	nânitaw niyânan tipahikan mîna âpihtaw mâna ê-ispayik,	nitati-piminawason.
ispîhk kâ-wâpahk,	nânitaw mitâtaht cipahikanis pâmwayês nikotwâsik tipahikan mâna ê-ispayik,	nikîsi-piminawason.
ispîhk kâ-kîkisêpâyâk,	nânitaw nikotwâsik tipahikan mâna ê-ispayik,	nikîkisêpâ-mîcison.
ispîhk kâ-âpihtâ-kîsikâk,	nânitaw nîsosâp tipahikan mîna âpihtaw mâna ê-ispayik,	nitâpihtâ-kîsikani-mîcison.
ispîhk kâ-pôni-âpihtâ-kîsikâk,	nânitaw nisto tipahikan mâna ê-ispayik,	nitaywêpisin.
ispîhk kâ-otâkosik,	nânitaw nikotwâsik tipahikan mîna âpihtaw mâna ê-ispayik,	nitotâkwani-mîcison.
ispîhk kâ-pahkisimok,	nânitaw têpakohp tipahikan mâna ê-ispayik,	nisêsâwohtân.

ispîhk kâ-wawâninâkwahk,	nânitaw têpakohp tipahikan mîna âpihtaw mâna ê-ispayik,	nitayapin.
ispîhk kâ-tipiskâk,	nânitaw pêyakosâp tipahikan mâna ê-ispayik,	nikakwê-nipân.

4.2.B. VAIs in 1st Person in Future Conditional

Temporal Words	Time	Activity
wâpahki,	nânitaw mitâtaht cipahikanis pâmwayês nikotwâsik tipahikan ispayiki,	niwî-kîsi-piminawason.
kîkisêpâyâki,	nânitaw nikotwâsik tipahikan ispayiki,	niwî-kîkisêpâ-mîcison.
âpihtâ-kîsikâki,	nânitaw nîsosâp tipahikan mîna âpihtaw ispayiki,	niwî-âpihtâ-kîsikani-mîcison.
pôni-âpihtâ-kîsikâki,	nânitaw nisto tipahikan ispayiki,	niwî-aywêpisin.
otâkosiki,	nânitaw nikotwâsik tipahikan mîna âpihtaw ispayiki,	niwî-otâkwani-mîcison.
pahkisimoki,	nânitaw têpakohp tipahikan ispayiki,	niwî-sêsâwohtân.
wawâninâkwahki,	nânitaw têpakohp tipahikan mîna âpihtaw ispayiki,	niwî-ayapin.
tipiskâki,	nânitaw pêyakosâp tipahikan ispayiki,	niwî-kakwê-nipân.

4.2.C. VAIs in 3rd Person

Note: Use *mâna* when the VAI is in present tense to refer to the usual time of doing an activity.

Temporal Words	Time	Activity
kîkisêp	nânitaw niyânanosâp cipahikanis pâmwayês ayinânêw tipahikan ê-kî-ispayiyik	kî-waniskâw.
anohc	nânitaw niyânanosâp cipahikanis miyâskam pêyak tipahikan ispayiyiki,	wî-sôhki-atoskêw.
ispîhk kâ-pêtâpaniyik,	nânitaw mâna niyânan tipahikan ê-ispayiyik,	nisîhkâci-pihkatêwâpôhkêw.
ispîhk kâ-sâkâstêyik,	nânitaw mâna niyânan tipahikan mîna âpihtaw ê-ispayiyik,	ati-piminawasow.
ispîhk kâ-wâpaniyik,	nânitaw mâna mitâtaht cipahikanis pâmwayês nikotwâsik tipahikan ê-ispayiyik,	kîsi-piminawasow.

ispîhk kâ-kîkisêpâyâyik,	nânitaw mâna nikotwâsik tipahikan ê-ispayiyik,	kîkisêpâ-mîcisow.
ispîhk kâ-âpihtâ-kîsikâyik,	nânitaw mâna nîsosâp tipahikan mîna âpihtaw ê-ispayiyik,	âpihtâ-kîsikani-mîcisow.
ispîhk kâ-pôni-âpihtâ-kîsikâyik,	nânitaw mâna nisto tipahikan ê-ispayiyik,	aywêpisiw.
ispîhk kâ-otâkosiniyik,	nânitaw mâna nikotwâsik tipahikan mîna âpihtaw ê-ispayiyik,	otâkwani-mîcisow.
ispîhk kâ-pahkisimoyik,	nânitaw mâna têpakohp tipahikan ê-ispayiyik,	sêsâwohtêw.
ispîhk kâ-wawâninâkwaniyik,	nânitaw mâna têpakohp tipahikan mîna âpihtaw ê-ispayiyik,	ayapiw.
ispîhk kâ-tipiskâyik,	nânitaw mâna pêyakosâp tipahikan ê-ispayiyik,	kakwê-nipâw.

4.2.D. VAIs in 3rd Person in Future Conditional

Temporal Words	Time	Activity
wâpaniyiki	nânitaw mitâtaht cipahikanis pâmwayês nikotwâsik tipahikan ispayiyiki,	wî-kîsi-piminawasow.
kîkisêpâyâyiki,	nânitaw nikotwâsik tipahikan ispayiyiki,	wî-kîkisêpâ-mîcisow.
âpihtâ-kîsikâyiki,	nânitaw nîsosâp tipahikan mîna âpihtaw ispayiyiki,	wî-âpihtâ-kîsikani-mîcisow.
pôni-âpihtâ-kîsikâyiki,	nânitaw nisto tipahikan ispayiyiki,	wî-aywêpisiw.
otâkosiniyiki,	nânitaw nikotwâsik tipahikan mîna âpihtaw ispayiyiki,	wî-otâkwani-mîcisow.
pahkisimoniyiki,	nânitaw têpakohp tipahikan ispayiyiki,	wî-sêsâwohtêw.
wawâninâkwaniyiki,	nânitaw têpakohp tipahikan mîna âpihtaw ispayiyiki,	wî-ayapiw.
tipiskâyiki,	nânitaw pêyakosâp tipahikan ispayiyiki,	wî-kakwê-nipâw.

4.3.A. Translation

1. niwî-nitawi-yahki-sôskoyâpawin otâkosiki.
2. wî-nitawi-yahki-sôskoyâpawiw otâkosiniyiki.
3. kiwî-nitawi-mâcîn cî wâpahki?
4. wî-nitawi-mâcîw cî wâpaniyiki?
5. kiwî-itohtânaw ôtênâhk kîkisêpâyâki.
6. wî-itohtêwak ôtênâhk kîkisêpâyâyiki.
7. kiwî-nitawi-pakâsimonâwâw cî kîspin miyo-kîsikâki?
8. wî-nitawi-pakâsimoyiwa cî otôtêma kîspin miyo-kîsikâyiki?
9. niwî-nitawi-mîcisonân mîcisowikamikohk âpihtâ-kîsikâki.
10. wî-nitawi-mîcisow mîcisowikamikohk âpihtâ-kîsikâyiki.
11. kiwî-itohtânâwâw cî cikâstêpayihcikanihk pôni-âpihtâ-kîsikâki.
12. wî-itohtêwak cî cikâstêpayihcikanihk pôni-âpihtâ-kîsikâyiki.
13. niwî-nitawi-pîcicîn tipiskâki.
14. wî-nitawi-pîcicîw tipiskâyiki.
15. nikawisimon mâna âpihtâ-tipiskâki.
16. kawisimow mâna âpihtâ-tipiskâyiki.
17. nika-pê-kîwân pâmwayês wawâninâkwahki.
18. wî-pê-kîwêw pâmwayês wawâninâkwaniyiki.
19. kiwî-nitawi-papâmiskân cî nîpihki?
20. wî-nitawi-papâmiskâw cî nîpiniyiki?

4.4.B. Exercises with Time and Times of Day

1. nîsta! nikotwâsik tipahikan mâna ê-ispayik niwaniskân kâ-kîkisêpâyâk?
2. têpakohp tipahikan mâna ê-ispayik nipostayiwinisân kâ-kîkisêpâyâk.
3. namôya mâna nimîcison ispîhk kâ-kîkisêpâyâk.
4. namôya mâna nisêsâwîn kâ-kîkisêpâyâk.
5. ayinânêw tipahikan mîna âpihtaw mâna ê-ispayik nikisîpêkinastân.
6. kêkâ-mitâtaht tipahikan mîna âpihtaw mâna ê-ispayik ninitawi-nîmihiton ispîhk kâ-tipiskâk.
7. niyânanosâp cipahikanis pâmwayês nisto tipahikan mâna ê-ispayik nitati-nôhtêhkwasin.
8. niyânanosâp cipahikanis miyâskam nisto tipahikan mâna ê-ispayik nitati-nipân.

CHAPTER 5 EXERCISES

5.1.A. VAI Imperatives

Imperative Forms for 2 (2nd Person Singular You)

English	Imperative	Negative Imperative	Delayed Imperative
Wake up/Get up	—	êkâwiya waniskâ	waniskâhkan
Pray	kâkîsimo	—	kâkîsimohkan
Wash your face	kâsihkwê	êkâwiya kâsihkwê	—
Get dressed	—	êkâwiya postayiwinisê	postayiwinisêhkan
Cook	piminawaso	—	piminawasohkan
Be hungry	nôhtêhkatê	êkâwiya nôhtêhkatê	—
Eat	—	êkâwiya mîciso	mîcisohkan
Drink	minihkwê	—	minihkwêhkan
Get up/Stand up	pasikô	êkâwiya pasikô	—
Sit/Be at home	api	—	apihkan
Read	—	êkâwiya ayamihcikê	ayamihcikêhkan
Write	masinahikê	—	masinahikêhkan
Be sleepy	nôhtêhkwasi	êkâwiya nôhtêhkwasi	—
Lie down	kawisimo	—	kawisimohkan
Sleep	—	êkâwiya nipâ	nipâhkan

Imperative Forms for 2P (2nd Person Plural You):

English	Imperative	Negative Imperative	Delayed Imperative
Wake up/Get up	—	êkâwiya waniskâk	waniskâhkêk
Pray	kâkîsimok	—	kâkîsimohkêk
Wash your face	kâsihkwêk	êkâwiya kâsihkwêk	—
Get dressed	—	êkâwiya postayiwinisêk	postayiwinisihkêk
Cook	piminawasok	—	piminawasohkêk
Be hungry	nôhtêhkatêk	êkâwiya nôhtêhkatêk	—
Eat	—	êkâwiya mîcisok	mîcisohkêk
Drink	minihkwêk	—	minihkwêhkêk
Get up/Stand up	pasikôk	êkâwiya pasikôk	—
Sit/Be at home	apik	—	apihkêk
Read	—	êkâwiya ayamihcikêk	ayamihcikêhkêk
Write	masinahikêk	—	masinahikêhkêk
Be sleepy	nôhtêhkwasik	êkâwiya nôhtêhkwasik	—
Lie down	kawisimok	—	kawisimohkêk
Sleep	—	êkâwiya nipâk	nipâhkêk

Imperative Forms for 21 (2nd Person Inclusive Let's):

English	Imperative	Negative Imperative	Delayed Imperative
Wake up/Get up	—	êkâwiya waniskâtân	waniskâhkahk
Pray	kâkîsimotân	—	kâkîsimohkahk
Wash your face	kâsihkwêtân	êkâwiya kâsihkwêtân	—
Get dressed	—	êkâwiya postayiwinisêtân	postayiwinisêhkahk
Cook	piminawasotân	—	piminawasohkahk
Be hungry	nôhtêhkatêtân	êkâwiya nôhtêhkatêtân	—
Eat	—	êkâwiya mîcisotân	mîcisohkahk
Drink	minihkwêtân	—	minihkwêhkahk
Get up/Stand up	pasikôtân	êkâwiya pasikôtân	—
Sit/Be at home	apitân	—	apihkahk
Read	—	êkâwiya ayamihcikêtân	ayamihcikêhkahk
Write	masinahikêtân	—	masinahikêhkahk
Be sleepy	nôhtêhkwasitân	êkâwiya nôhtêhkwasitân	—
Lie down	kawisimotân	—	kawisimohkahk
Sleep	—	êkâwiya nipâtân	nipâhkahk

5.2.A. Exercises with VAIs

	Verb Stem		Indicative	Conjunct
2	wâniskâ	1st pres	niwaniskân	ê-waniskâyân
		1st past	nikî-waniskân	ê-kî-waniskâyân
		1st fut int	niwî-waniskân	ê-wî-waniskâyân
		1st fut def	nika-waniskân	
2	kîkisêpâ-mîciso	2nd pres	kikîkisêpâ-mîcison	ê-kîkisêpâ-mîcisoyan
2P	kîkisêpâ-mîcisok	2nd past	kikî-kîkisêpâ-mîcison	ê-kî-kîkisêpâ-mîcisoyan
21	kîkisêpâ-mîcisotân	2nd fut int	kiwî-kîkisêpâ-mîcison	ê-wî-kîkisêpâ-mîcisoyan
		2nd fut def	kika-kîkisêpâ-mîcison	
2	itohtê	3rd pres	itohtêw	ê-itohtêt
2P	itohtêk	3rd past	kî-itohtêw	ê-kî-itohtêt
21	itohtêtân	3rd fut int	wî-itohtêw	ê-wî-itohtêt
		3rd fut def	ta-itohtêw	
2	kiskinwahamâkosi	3' pres	kiskinwahamâkosiyiwa	ê- kiskinwahamâkosiyit
2P	kiskinwahamâkosik	3' past	kî-kiskinwahamâkosiyiwa	ê-kî- kiskinwahamâkosiyit
21	kiskinwahamâkositân	3' fut int	wî-kiskinwahamâkosiyiwa	ê-wî- kiskinwahamâkosiyit
		3' fut def	ta-kiskinwahamâkosiyiwa	

2	âpihtâ-kîsikani-mîciso	1P pres	nitâpihtâ-kîsikani-mîcisonân	ê-âpihtâ-kîsikani-mîcisoyâhk
2P	âpihtâ-kîsikani-mîcisok			
21	âpihtâ-kîsikani-mîcisotân	1P past	nikî-âpihtâ-kîsikani-mîcisonân	ê-kî-âpihtâ-kîsikani-mîcisoyâhk
		1P fut int	niwî-âpihtâ-kîsikani-mîcisonân	ê-wî-âpihtâ-kîsikani-mîcisoyâhk
		1P fut def	nika-âpihtâ-kîsikani-mîcisonân	

2	kîwê	21 pres	kikîwânaw	ê-kîwêyahk
2P	kîwêk	21 past	kikî-kîwânaw	ê-kî-kîwêyahk
21	kîwêtân	21 fut int	kiwî-kîwânaw	ê-wî-kîwêyahk
		21 fut def	kika-kîwânaw	

2	otâkwani-mîciso	2P pres	kitotâkwani-mîcisonâwâw	ê-otâkwani-mîcisoyêk
2P	otâkwani-mîcisok	2P past	kikî-otâkwani-mîcisonâwâw	ê-kî-otâkwani-mîcisoyêk
21	otâkwani-mîcisotân	2P fut int	kiwî-otâkwani-mîcisonâwâw	ê-kî-otâkwani-mîcisoyêk
		2P fut def	kika-otâkwani-mîcisonâwâw	

2	kawisimo	3P pres	kawisimowak	ê-kawisimocik
2P	kawisimok	3P past	kî-kawisimowak	ê-kî-kawisimocik
21	kawisimotân	3P fut int	wî-kawisimowak	ê-wî-kawisimocik
		3P fut def	ta-kawisimowak	

5.2.B. VAI Conjugations

Part 1: Conjugations

Subject/Actor		Imperative	Negative Imperative	Delayed Imperative
2	you (sg)	—	êkâwiya nipâ	nipâhkan
2P	you (pl)	pimipâhtâk	—	pimipâhtâhkêk
21	Let's (you and I)	atoskêtân	êkâwiya atoskêtân	—
2	you (sg)	mêtawê	—	mêtawêhkan
2P	you (pl)	masinahkikêk	êkâwiya masinahkikêk	—)
21	Let's (you and I)	—	êkâwiya ayamihcikêtân	ayamihcikêhkahk
2	you (sg)	mîciso	êkâwiya mîciso	—
2P	you (pl)	—	êkâwiya sêsâwîk	sêsâwîhkêk
21	Let's (you and I)	minihkwêtân	—	minihkwêhkahk

Singular Subject

Subject/Actor	Indicative	Conjunct
1 I	—	ê-kî-apiyân
2 you	kitatoskân	—
3 she/he	atoskêw	ê-kî-apit
3' her/his (friend)	—	ê-kî-apiyit

Plural Subject

Subject/Actor	Indicative	Conjunct
1P we (excl)	nika-nôhtê-mêtawânân	—
21 we (incl)	—	ê-wî-waniskâyahk
2P you (pl)	kika-nôhtê-mêtawânâwâw	ê-wî-waniskâyêk
3P they	—	ê-wî-waniskâcik

Part 2: Translation

1. Last night my older brother had a good sleep.
2. Try to get up early in the morning.
3. Last night I read good. (As in "I enjoyed reading.")
4. We (incl) will go and exercise this evening.
5. Tonight my elder sister and younger sibling will have a good run.
6. We (excl) will go and work early tomorrow.
7. Her/his younger sibling played good last night.
8. Are you (sg) going to eat early today?
9. Did you (pl) drink coffee this (past) morning?
10. Their friends try to write.

5.3.B. Self Test

A. Fill in the Blanks

Base Numbers	11–19	20–100
nîso – 2	nîsosâp – 12	—
nisto – 3	—	nistomitanaw – 30
nêwo – 4	nêwosâp –14	—
niyânan – 5	niyânanosâp – 15	niyânanomitanaw – 50
nikotwâsik – 6	—	nikotwâsikomitanaw – 60
têpakohp – 7	têpakohposâp – 17	—
ayinânêw – 8	—	ayinânêwomitanaw – 80
kêkâ-mitâtaht – 9	—	kêkâ-mitâtahtomitanaw – 90

B. Check/Fill the Best Possible Answer

1. a)
2. c) *[your name here]* nitisiyihkâson.
3. b) *[originally from place]* ohci niya kayahtê.
4. b) *[present place of residence here]* mêkwâc niwîkin.
5. c) *[write your age here]* niya nititahtopiponân.
6. b) *[date]* ê-akimiht *[month]* mâna kâ-tipiskamân.
7. As appropriate
8. b) *[date]* akimâw awa pîsim.

C. Conjunct and Future Conditional Forms: Seasons

Last Season	Present Season	Future Season
sîkwanohk	ê-sîkwahk	sîkwahki
miyoskamîhk	ê-miyoskamik	miyoskamiki
nîpinohk	ê-nîpihk	nîpihki
takwâkohk	ê-takwâkik	takwâkiki
mikiskohk	ê-mikiskohk	mikiskohki
piponohk	ê-pipohk	pipohki

D. Conjunct and Future Conditional Forms: Days of the Week

Indicative	Conjunct	Future conditional
ayamihêwi-kîsikâw	ê-ayamihêwi-kîsikâk	ayamihêwi-kîsikâki
pêyako-kîsikâw	ê-pêyako-kîsikâk	pêyako-kîsikâki
nîso-kîsikâw	ê-nîso-kîsikâk	nîso-kîsikâki
nisto-kîsikâw	ê-nisto-kîsikâk	nisto-kîsikâki
nêwo-kîsikâw	ê-nêwo-kîsikâk	nêwo-kîsikâki
niyânano-kîsikâw	ê-niyânano-kîsikâk	niyânano-kîsikâki
nikotwâso-kîsikâw	ê-nikotwâso-kîsikâk	nikotwâso-kîsikâki

E. Choose the Correct Answers

1. b)
2. d)
3. a)
4. b)
5. d)
6. c)
7. c)
8. d)

F. Answer the Questions

1. âha, ispîhk mâna kâ-sîkwahk nicîhkêyihtên ta-papâmi-tihtipiskamân cihcipayapisikanis.
2. âha, cîhkêyihtam kistês ta-papâmi-tihtipiskahk cihcipayapisikanis ispîhk kâ-sîkwaniyik.
3. âha, ispîhk mâna kâ-nîpihk nicîhkêyihtên ta-papâmiskâyân.

4. âha, cîhkêyihtam kimis ta-papâmiskât ispîhk kâ-nîpiniyik.
5. âha, ispîhk mâna kâ-takwâkik nicîhkêyihtên ta-papâmi-sêsâwohtêyân.
6. âha, cîhkêyihtam kimosôm ta-papâmi-sêsâwohtêt ispîhk kâ-takwâkiniyik.
7. âha, ispîhk mâna kâ-pipohk nicîhkêyihtên ta-yahki-sôskoyâpawiyân.
8. âha, cîhkêyihtam kisîmis ta-yahki-sôskoyâpawit ispîhk kâ-piponiyik.

G. Answer the Questions

1. a) waniskâw awa môswa têpakohp tipahikan mâna ê-ispayiyik.
   b) nânitaw têpakohp tipahikan mâna ê-ispayik kâ-waniskâyân.

2. a) ati-kîsitêpow awa môswa têpakohp tipahikan mîna âpihtaw mâna ê-ispayiyik.
   b) nânitaw têpakohp tipahikan mîna âpihtaw mâna ê-ispayik kâ-ati-kîsitêpoyân.

3. a) niyânanosâp cipahikanis pâmwayês ayinânêw tipahikan mâna ê-ispayiyik kâ-kîkisêpâ-mîcisot awa môswa.
   b) niyânanosâp cipahikanis pâmwayês ayinânêw tipahikan mâna ê-ispayik kâ-kîkisêpâ-mîcisoyân.

4. a) kîsi-kiskinwahamâkosiw awa môswa nîsitanaw cipahikanis miyâskam kêkâ-mitâtaht tipahikan mâna ê-ispayiyik.
   b) nânitaw nîsitanaw cipahikanis miyâskam kêkâ-mitâtaht tipahikan mâna ê-ispayik kâ-kîsi-kiskinwahamâkosiyân.

5. a) ati-nipâw awa môswa nânitaw pêyakosâp tipahikan mâna ê-ispayiyik.
   b) nânitaw pêyakosâp tipahikan mâna ê-ispayik kâ-ati-nipâyân.

5.5.A. Subordinate Clause Exercise

1. mwayî-nitawi-atoskêyâni.
2. ta-nitawi-mîcisoyân.
3. ê-nôhtêhkatêt.
4. kâ-nitawi-atoskêt.
5. ta-kî-pê-itohtêyan ôta wâpahki.

5.5.B. Sentence Structures with VAIs and VIIs

1. anohc nititohtân sâkahikanihk.
2. otâkosîhk cî kikî-sôhki-atoskân?*
3. awasi-otâkosîhk kî-pimohtêw mêskanâhk.
4. wâpaniyiw, papâmohtêyiwa asinî-wacîhk.
5. wâpahki nika-sêsâwohtânân ispatinâhk.
6. awasi-wâpahki kika-pimipahtânaw wayawîtimihk.
7. kotak ispayiki cî kiwî-sêsâwipahtânâwâw mêskanâsihk.

....

* Note: Usually sentences in the 2nd person are in the forms of questions.

8. kîkisêpâyâyiki ta-nitawi-kiyokêwak iskonikanihk.
9. otâhk ispayiw kî-pimipayiyiwa asinî-wacîhk isi.
10. otâhk askîwin nikî-papâmiskân sîpîhk.
11. kotak askîwiki cî kiwî-yahki-sôskoyâpawin kîwêtinohk?
12. otâkosiniyiki ta-kisîpêkiyâkanêw.
13. sîkwanohk kî-kiskinwahamâkosiyiwa kihci-kiskinwahamâtowikamikohk.
14. sîkwahki nika-kiyôtênân iskonikanihk.
15. nîpinohk kikî-pakâsimonaw sîpîsisihk.
16. takwâkin, ati-wâstêpakâw.
17. takwâkiki cî kiwî-mâcînâwâw?
18. piponiyiki wî-pîcicîwak.
19. âpihtâ-kîsikâyiki ta-âpihtâ-kîsikani-mîcisoyiwa.
20. âpihtâ-tipiskâw, nikîsahkamikisin.
21. pôni-âpihtâ-tipiskâw, kiwî-nikamon cî?
22. tipiskâyiw wî-nîmihitow.
23. tipiskâyiki wî-kîsitêpoyiwa.
24. tipiskohk nikî-sôniskwâtahikânân.
25. awasi-tipiskohk kikî-papâmi-atâwânaw.

5.5.C. Daily Activity Exercises

kîkisêp kî-kisinâw.

Q to 2nd   kîkisêp kî-kisinâw.
This past morning it was very cold.

Q about 3rd   kî-kisinâyiw kîkisêp.
It was extremely cold this past morning.

têpakohp tipahikan mîna âpihtaw ê-ispayik nikî-waniskân.

Q to 2nd   têpakohp tipahikan mîna âpihtaw ê-ispayik nikî-waniskân.
I got up at seven thirty.

Q about 3rd   têpakohp tipahikan mîna âpihtaw ê-ispayiyik kî-waniskâw.
He got up at seven thirty.

nikî-pihkahtêwâpôhkân.

Q to 2nd   âha, nikî-pihkahtêwâpôhkân.
Yes, I made coffee.

Q about 3rd   âha, kî-pihkahtêwâpôhkêw awa.
Yes, he made coffee.

nikî-minihkwân pihkahtêwâpoy.

Q to 2nd   âha, nikî-minihkwân pihkahtêwâpoy.
Yes, I drank coffee.

Q about 3rd   âha, kî-minihkwêw pihkahtêwâpoy awa.
Yes, he drank coffee.

nikî-piminawason.

Q to 2nd	âha, nikî-piminawason.
	Yes, I cooked.
Q about 3rd	âha, kî-piminawasow awa.
	Yes, he cooked.

nikî-kîkisêpâ-mîcison.

Q to 2nd	âha, nikî-kîkisêpâ-mîcison.
	Yes, I ate breakfast.
Q about 3rd	âha, kî-kîkisêpâ-mîcisow awa.
	Yes, he ate breakfast.

ispîhk kâ-kîsi-mîcisoyân nikî-itohtân kihci-kiskinwahamâtowikamikohk.

Q to 2nd	ispîhk kâ-kîsi-mîcisoyân nikî-itohtân kihci-kiskinwahamâtowikamikohk.
	When I finished eating, I went to the university.
Q about 3rd	ispîhk kâ-kîsi-mîcisot kî-itohtêw kihci-kiskinwahamâtowikamikohk.
	When he finished eating, he went to the university.

pêyakosâp tipahikan ê-ispayik nikî-itohtân kihci-kiskinwahamâtowikamikohk.

Q to 2nd	pêyakosâp tipahikan ê-ispayik nikî-itohtân kihci-kiskinwahamâtowikamikohk.
	I went to the university at eleven o'clock.
Q about 3rd	pêyakosâp tipahikan ê-ispayiyik kî-itohtêw kihci-kiskinwahamâtowikamikohk.
	He went to the university at eleven o'clock.

Other possible answers to the previous exercise:

1. If the answer to a *cî* question is "yes," use *âha* followed by the verb in 1st person if the question is in the 2nd person. If the question is in the 3rd person, then have the verb in the 3rd person.

2. If the answer to a *cî* question is "no," use:

    a) *namôya, namôya* (one *namôya* for "no" and the other negates the verb), followed by the verb in 1st person if the question is in the 2nd person. If the question is in the 3rd person, then have the verb in the 3rd person.

    b) *namôya, namôya mâna*, followed by the verb in 1st person if the question is in the 2nd person. If the question is in the 3rd person, then have the verb in the 3rd person. For example:
        Question: kikî-piminawason cî? – *Did you cook?*
        Question: namôya, namôya mâna nipiminawason. – *No, I don't usually cook.*

    c) If you don't do a certain activity but do another, then use *namôya* once, followed by another verb in 1st person if the question is in the 2nd person. If the question is in the 3rd person, then have the other verb in the 3rd person. For example:
        Question: kikî-minihkwân cî pihkahtêwâpoy? – *Did you drink coffee?*
        Question: namôya, nikî-minihkwân nihtiy. – *No, I drank tea.*

Other possible answers with namôya:

namôya wîhkâc – *never*
e.g., namôya wîhkâc niminihkwân pihkahtêwâpoy. – *I never drink coffee.*

namôya mwâsi – *hardly ever*
e.g., namôya mwâsi niminihkwân pihkahtêwâpoy. – *I hardly ever drink coffee.*

namôya cêskwa – *not yet*
e.g., namôya cêskwa niminihkwân pihkahtêwâpoy. – *I did not drink coffee yet.*

namôya mâna – *not usually*
e.g., namôya mâna niminihkwân pihkahtêwâpoy. – *I don't usually drink coffee.*

5.5.D. Daily Activities Translation and Questions

Translation

When it is spring, early in the morning on Saturdays I go cycling about. I try to ride far on the bike. If it is not very windy, I try to ride the bike for fourteen kilometres to the little lake and ride back home. Altogether I ride the bike for twenty-eight kilometres. When it is very windy, I don't usually ride far. I go at least for a while on the bike when it is very windy. Sometimes it is very windy here on the prairies.

I like to go riding the bike in the spring. When I am out and about, I see all sorts of birds: pelicans, blackbirds, geese, crows, and all sorts of ducks. I also see pussywillows when the leaves start coming out. The Earth is very beautiful when it's spring.

Questions

1. ispîhk mâna kâ-sîkwaniyik papâmi-tihtipiskam cihcipayapisikanis.
2. âha, wâhyaw mâna kakwê-papâmi-tihtipiskam cihcipayapisikanis.
3. nîsitanaw ayinânêwosâp cipahaskânisa mâna tihtipiskam cihcipayapisikanis kîspin êkâ mistahi sôhkiyowêyiki.
4. sâkahikanisihk mâna kâ-isi-tihtipiskahk cihcipayapisikanis.
5. namôya, namôya mâna wâhyaw papâmi-tihtipiskam cihcipayapisikanis ispîhk ê-sôhkiyowêyik.
6. âha, têpiyâhk mâna aciyaw têhtipiskam cihcipayapisikanis ispîhk sôhkiyowêyiki.
7. âha, âskaw mâna mistahi sôhkiyowêw ôta maskotêhk.
8. âha, cîhkêyihtam ta-papâmi-tihtipiskahk cihcipayapisikanis ispîhk kâ-sîkwaniyik.
9. âha, nicîhkêyihtên ta-papâmi-tihtipiskamân cihcipayapisikanis ispîhk kâ-sîkwahk.
10. wâpamêw mâna cahcahkayôsa, cahcahkiwa, niska, âhâsiwa, êkwa nanâtohk sîsîpa.

CHAPTER 6 EXERCISES

6.1.A. VTI-1 Imperatives

English	2nd Person Singular	2nd Person Plural	2nd Person Inclusive
Look at it.	—	kanawâpahtamok	kanawâpahtêtân
Don't look at it.	êkâwiya kanawâpahta	—	êkâwiya kanawâpahtêtân
Look at it later.	kanawâpahtamohkan	kanawâpahtamohkêk	—
See it.	wâpahta	—	wâpahtêtân
Don't see it.	—	êkâwiya wâpahtamok	êkâwiya wâpahtêtân
See it later.	wâpahtamohkan	—	wâpahtamohkahk
Look for it.	natona	natonamok	—
Don't look for it.	êkâwiya natona	—	êkâwiya natonêtân
Look for it later.	—	natonamohkêk	natonamohkahk
Find it.	miska	—	miskêtân
Don't find it.	êkâwiya miska	êkâwiya miskamok	—
Find it later.	miskamohkan	—	miskamohkahk
Do it.	—	itôtamok	itôtêtân
Don't do it.	êkâwiya itôta	—	êkâwiya itôtêtân
Do it later.	itôtamohkan	itôtamohkêk	—

6.2.A. Exercises with VTI-1s

Verb Stem		Indicative	Conjunct
otina	1st pres	nitotinên	ê-otinamân
	1st past	nikî-otinên	ê-kî-otinamân
	1st fut int	niwî-otinên	ê-wî-otinamân
	1st fut def	nika-otinên	
nâta	2nd pres	kinâtên	ê-nâtaman
	2nd past	kikî-nâtên	ê-kî-nâtaman
	2nd fut int	kiwî-nâtên	ê-wî-nâtaman
	2nd fut def	kika-nâtên	
natona	3rd pres	natonam	ê-natonahk
	3rd past	kî-natonam	ê-kî-natonahk
	3rd fut int	wî-natonam	ê-wî-natonahk
	3rd fut def	ta-natonam	
miska	3' pres	miskamiyiwa	ê-miskamiyit
	3' past	kî-miskamiyiwa	ê-kî-miskamiyit
	3' fut int	wî-miskamiyiwa	ê-wî-miskamiyit
	3' fut def	ta-miskamiyiwa	

natohta	1P pres	ninatohtênân	ê-natohtamâhk
	1P past	nikî-natohtênân	ê-kî-natohtamâhk
	1P fut int	niwî-natohtênân	ê-wî-natohtamâhk
	1P fut def	nika-natohtênân	
pêhta	21 pres	kipêhtênaw	ê-pêhtamahk
	21 past	kikî-pêhtênaw	ê-kî-pêhtamahk
	21 fut int	kiwî-pêhtênaw	ê-wî-pêhtamahk
	21 fut def	kika-pêhtênaw	
nisitohta	2P pres	kinisitohtênâwâw	ê-nisitohtamêk
	2P past	kikî-nisitohtênâwâw	ê-kî-nisitohtamêk
	2P fut int	kiwî-nisitohtênâwâw	ê-wî-nisitohtamêk
	2P fut def	kika-nisitohtênâwâw	
wâpahta	3P pres	wâpahtamwak	ê-wâpahtahkik
	3P past	kî-wâpahtamwak	ê-kî-wâpahtahkik
	3P fut int	wî-wâpahtamwak	ê-wî- wâpahtahkik
	3P fut def	ta-wâpahtamwak	

6.2.B. VTI-1 Conjugations

Part 1

	Subject/Actor	Imperative	Negative Imperative	Delayed Imperative
2	you (sg)	—	êkâwiya wâpahta	wâpahtamohkan
2P	you (pl)	natonamok	—	natonamohkêk
21	Let's (you and I)	natohtêtân	êkâwiya natohtêtân	—
2	you (sg)	mêtawâkâta	—	mêtawâkâtamohkan
2P	you (pl)	atoskâtamok	êkâwiya atoskâtamok	—
21	Let's (you and I)	—	êkâwiya kanawâpahtêtân	kanawâpahtamohkahk
2	you (sg)	kîsisa	êkâwiya kîsisa	—
2P	you (pl)	—	êkâwiya kocispitamohk	kocispitamohkêk
21	Let's (you and I)	nâtêtân	—	nâtamohkahk

Singular Subject

	Subject/Actor	Indicative	Conjunct
1	I	nitatoskâtên	—
2	you	—	ê-kî-wâpahtaman
3	she/he	atoskâtam	ê-kî-kanawâpahtahk
3'	her/his (friend)	atoskâtamiyiwa	—

Plural Subject

	Subject/Actor	Indicative	Conjunct
1P	we (excl)	—	ê-wî-natonamâhk
21	we (incl)	kika-natohtênaw	—
2P	you (pl)	kika-natohtênâwâw	ê-wî-natonamêk
3P	they	—	ê-wî-natonahkik

Part 2

1. Last night we (excl) listened to songs.
2. Cook eggs in the morning.
3. Last night they watched television.
4. In the evening we will go and look for your shoes.
5. Tonight I am going to taste berries.
6. You will go and get your books tomorrow.
7. Their younger siblings saw a movie last night.
8. Are you (pl) going to work on Cree soon today?
9. Let's listen to sacred stories tonight.
10. My friend tried to cook meat yesterday.

6.3.A. Translation

1. This past morning I took my books from the table.
2. In the morning we (excl) are going to get firewood.
3. On Monday, begin to work on your books.
4. On Tuesday I'm going to look for my coat.
5. Next week I will go and watch a movie.
6. Last week I heard that song.
7. Did you listen to Cree sacred stories last year?
8. She/he is going to take off her/his shoes at the door.
9. She/he tries to understand Cree.
10. If it is cold she/he is going to put on her/his parka.

6.3.B. Conversion

1. nâtamohkan kimaskisina nôhtê-atoskâtamani nêhiyawêwin.
2. otinamohkêk kimasinahikaniwâwa pôni-masinahamêko âcimowina.
3. kêcikoskamohkahk astotina kipahamahki iskwâhtêm.
4. postiskamohkan kiskotâkay nâtamani mihta.
5. nitawi-kanawâpahtamohkêk cikâstêpayihcikana kîsi-kisîpêkinamêko oyâkana.
6. postiskamohkan astotin tahkâyâki.
7. kipahamohkan iskwâhtêm tahkâyâki.
8. natohtamohkahk anima nêhiyawêwin ispîhk ana iskwêw kocihtâci.
9. otinamohkêk anima wiyâs kîsi-manisahki.
10. kanawâpahtamohkan anima masinahikêwin pôni-ayamihtâci.

CHAPTER 7 EXERCISES

7.1.B. Possessive Forms

Common Items

pôsinâpâsk
a) nipôsinâpâsk
b) kipôsinâpâsk
c) opôsinâpâskwa

âwatawâsiswâkan
a) nitâwatawâsiswâkan
b) kitâwatawâsiswâkan
c) otâwatawâsiswâkana

otinikêwi-têhamân
a) nitotinikêwi-têhamân
b) kitotinikêwi-têhamân
b) ototinikêwi-têhamân

masinahikêwi-têhamân
a) nimasinahikêwi-têhamân
b) kimasinahikêwi-têhamân
c) omasinahikêwi-têhamâna

âhkosîwasinahikan
a) nitâhkosîwasinahikan
b) kitâhkosîwasinahikan
c) otâhkosîwasinahikan

otinikêwi-âwacikan
a) nitotinikêwi-âwacikan
b) kitotinikêwi-âwacikan
c) ototinikêwi-âwacikan

miskîsikohkâna
a) niskîsikohkâna
b) kiskîsikohkâna
c) oskîsikohkâna

pimihâkan
a) nipimihâkan
b) kipimihâkan
c) opimihâkan

iskotêwitâpân
a) nitiskotêwitâpân
b) kitiskotêwitâpân
c) otiskotêwitâpâna

sîhci-pakwahtêhon
a) nisîhci-pakwahtêhon
b) kisîhci-pakwahtêhon
c) osîhci-pakwahtêhon

sôskopayîs
a) nisôskopayîs
b) kisôskopayîs
c) osôskopayîsa

cihcipayapisikanis
a) nicihcipayapisikanis
b) kicihcipayapisikanis
c) ocihcipayapisikanis

sôniskwâtahikan
a) nisôniskwâtahikan
b) kisôniskwâtahikan
c) osôniskwâtahikan

sôniskwâtahikanâhtik
a) nisôniskwâtahikanâhtik
b) kisôniskwâtahikanâhtik
c) osôniskwâtahikanâhtik

pâkahatowân
a) nipâkahatowân
b) kipâkahatowân
c) opâkahatowâna

On the Land: Out and About

pâskisikan
a) nipâskisikan
b) kipâskisikan
c) opâskisikan

môswasiniy
a) nimôswasiniy
b) kimôswasiniy
c) omôswasiniy

cîkahikan
a) nicîkahikan
b) kicîkahikan
c) ocîkahikan

kîskipocikan
a) nikîskipocikan
b) kikîskipocikan
c) okîskipocikan

ayapiy
a) nitayapiy
b) kitayapiy
c) otayapiya

pîminahkwân
a) nipîminahkwân
b) kipîminahkwân
c) opîminahkwân

tâpakwân
a) nitâpakwân
b) kitâpakwân
c) otâpakwân

tâpakwânêyâpiy
a) nitâpakwânêyâpiy
b) kitâpakwânêyâpiy
c) otâpakwânêyâpiy

asâm
a) nitasâm
b) kitasâm
c) otasâma

mâtahikan
a) nimâtahikan
b) kimâtahikan
c) omâtahikan

mihkihkwan
a) nimihkihkwan
b) kimihkihkwan
c) omihkihkwan

mânihtoyâsk
a) nimânihtoyâsk
b) kimânihtoyâsk
c) omânihtoyâsk

mîkiwâhp
a) nimîkiwâhp
b) kimîkiwâhp
c) omîkiwâhp

pakwânikamik
a) nipakwânikamik
b) kipakwânikamik
c) opakwânikamik

kotawân
a) nikotawân
b) kikotawân
c) okotawân

akwâwân
a) nitakwâwân
b) kitakwâwân
c) otakwâwân

cîmân
a) nicîmân
b) kicîmân
c) ocîmân

apoy
a) nitapoy
b) kitapoy
c) otapoya

waskitipêsimon
a) niwaskitipêsimon   b) kiwaskitipêsimon   c) owaskitipêsimon

In the Classroom

maskimot
a) nimaskimot
b) kimaskimot
c) omaskimot

masinahikan
a) nimasinahikan
b) kimasinahikan
c) omasinahikan

masinahikanêkin
a) nimasinahikanêkin
b) kimasinahikanêkin
c) omasinahikanêkin

masinahikanâhtik
a) nimasinahikanâhtik
b) kimasinahikanâhtik
c) omasinahikanâhtikwa

masinahikanâhcikos
a) nimasinahikanâhcikos
b) kimasinahikanâhcikos
c) omasinahikanâhcikos

masinahikêwinâhtik
a) nimasinahikêwinâhtik
b) kimasinahikêwinâhtik
c) omasinahikêwinâhtik

ayamâkanis
a) nitayamâkanis
b) kitayamâkanis
c) otayamâkanis

mâhtâw-âpacihcikan
a) nimâhtâw-âpacihcikan
b) kimâhtâw-âpacihcikan
c) omâhtâw-âpacihcikan

cikâstêpayihcikanis
a) nicikâstêpayihcikanis
b) kicikâstêpayihcikanis
c) ocikâstêpayihcikanis

In the House

wâskahikan
a) niwâskahikan
b) kiwâskahikan
c) owâskahikan

mîkiwâm
a) nimîkiwâm
b) kimîkiwâm
c) omîkiwâm

mîcisowinâhtik
a) nimîcisowinâhtik
b) kimîcisowinâhtik
c) omîcisowinâhtik

têhtapiwin
a) nitêhtapiwin
b) kitêhtapiwin
c) otêhtapiwin

yôski-têhtapiwin
a) niyôski-têhtapiwin
b) kiyôski-têhtapiwin
c) oyôski-têhtapiwin

kihci-yôski-têhtapiwin
a) nikihci-yôski-têhtapiwin
b) kikihci-yôski-têhtapiwin
c) okihci-yôski-têhtapiwin

âkôpicikan
a) nitâkôpicikan
b) kitâkôpicikan
c) otâkôpicikan

nipêwin
a) ninipêwin
b) kinipêwin
c) onipêwin

akohp
a) nitakohp
b) kitakohp
c) otakohp

aspiskwêsimon
a) nitaspiskwêsimon
b) kitaspiskwêsimon
c) otaspiskwêsimon

wâsaskotênikan
a) niwâsaskotênikan
b) kiwâsaskotênikan
c) owâsaskotênikan

In the Kitchen

tahkascikan
a) nitahkascikan
b) kitahkascikan
c) otahkascikan

âhkwatihcikan
a) nitâhkwatihcikan
b) kitâhkwatihcikan
c) otâhkwatihcikan

kotawânâpisk
a) nikotawânâpisk
b) kikotawânâpisk
c) okotawânâpisk

sêkowêpinâpisk
a) nisêkowêpinâpisk
b) kisêkowêpinâpisk
c) osêkowêpinâpisk

kêsiskawihkasikan
a) nikêsiskawihkasikan
b) kikêsiskawihkasikan
c) okêsiskawihkasikan

sâsâpiskisikan
a) nisâsâpiskisikan
b) kisâsâpiskisikan
c) osâsâpiskisikana

askihk
a) nitaskihk
b) kitaskihk
c) otaskihkwa

oyâkan
a) nitoyâkan
b) kitoyâkan
c) otoyâkan

môhkomân
a) nimôhkomân
b) kimôhkomân
c) omôhkomân

êmihkwân
a) nitêmihkwân
b) kitêmihkwân
c) otêmihkwâna

cîstahâsêpon
a) nicîstahâsêpon
b) kicîstahâsêpon
c) ocîstahâsêpon

minihkwâkan
a) niminihkwâkan
b) kiminihkwâkan
c) ominihkwâkan

mîciwin
a) nimîciwin   b) kimîciwin   c) omîciwin

Sewing

kaskikwâswâkan
a) nikaskikwâswâkan
b) kikaskikwâswâkan
c) okaskikwâswâkan

asapâp
a) nitasapâpim
b) kitasapâpim
c) otasapâpima

kawiyak
a) nikawiyak
b) kikawiyak
c) okawiyakwa

kaskikwâsowinâpisk
a) nikaskikwâsowinâpisk
b) kikaskikwâsowinâpisk
c) okaskikwâsowinâpiskwa

paskwahamâtowin
a) nipaskwahamâtowin
b) kipaskwahamâtowin
c) opaskwahamâtowin

mîkis
a) nimîkisim
b) kimîkisim
c) omîkisima

sâponikan	*pahkêkin*	*ayânis*	
a) nisâponikan	a) nipahkêkin	a) nitayânis	
b) kisâponikan	b) kipahkêkin	b) kitayânis	
c) osâponikan	c) opahkêkin	c) otayânis	
sênipân	*sênipânêkin*	*sênipânisapâp*	
a) nisênipân	a) nisênipânêkin	a) nisênipânisapâp	
b) kisênipân	b) kisênipânêkin	b) kisênipânisapâp	
c) osênipâna	c) osênipânêkin	c) osênipânisapâpa	

7.2.A. Body Parts Exercise

noun	my	your	her/his
mahkwan	—	kahkwan	wahkwan
manaway	nanaway	—	wanaway
masakay	nasakay	kasakay	—
maskasiy	—	kaskasiy	waskasiya
mâskikan	nâskikan	—	wâskikan
matay	natay	katay	—
mêstakay	nêstakay	kêstakay	—
micihcîwi-ânisawikanân	—	kicihcîwi-ânisawikanân	ocihcîwi-ânisawikanân
micihciy	nicihciy	—	ocihciy
mihcikwan	nihcikwan	kihcikwan	—
mihkwâkan	—	kihkwâkan	wihkwâkan
mihtawakay	nihtawakay	—	ohtawakay
mikohtaskway	nikohtaskway	kikohtaskway	—
mikot	—	kikot	okot
mikwâskoniy	kikwâskoniy	—	okwâskoniy
mikwayaw	nikwayaw	kikwayaw	—
mipwâm	—	kipwâm	opwâm
miyêsâpiwinân	niyêsâpiwinân	—	oyêsâpiwinân
misit	nisit	kisit	—
miskâhtik	—	kiskâhtik	oskâhtik
miskât	niskât	—	oskât
misicihcân	nimisicihcân	kimisicihcân	—
misisitân	nimisisitân	—	omisisitân
miskîsik	niskîsik	kiskîsik	—
misôkan	—	kisôkan	osôkan
mispiskwan	nispiskwan	—	ospiskwan
mispiton	nispiton	kispiton	—
mistikwân	nistikwân	—	ostikwân
mitâpiskan	nitâpiskan	kitâpiskan	—
mitihtiman	—	kitihtiman	otihtiman

mitêyikom	nitêyikom	—	otêyikom
mitohtôsim	nitohtôsim	kitohtôsim	—
mitokan	—	kitokan	otokan
mitôn	nitôn	—	otôn
mitôskwan	nitôskwan	kitôskwan	—
miyaw	—	kiyaw	wiyaw
yiyîkicihcân	niyiyîkicihcân	—	oyiyîkicihcân
yiyîkisitân	niyiyîkisitân	kiyiyîkisitân	—

7.2.C. Text Exercises

A Visit to the Doctor

1. namôya, kî-nisîhkâci-waniskâw awa.
2. âha, mêtoni misiwê kî-têyisiw.
3. kanâcihowikamikohk awa kâ-itohtêt.
4. wâpamonihk kî-kanawâpamisow.
5. âha, kî-koskwâpisin awa.
6. kî-wâpahtam misiwê wihkwâkanihk êkwa wiyawihk ê-kî-miyawêsit!
7. âha, kî-kakwê-kâskipâsow.
8. âha, kêyâpic kî-miyawêsiw.
9. âha, kî-nitawi-wâpamêw maskihkîwiyiniwa.
10. âha, mêtoni kinwêsk kî-pêhow.
11. ê-miyawêyâspinêt awa.
12. nôhcimihk kâ-itohtêt ta-nitawi-wîcâyâmât mistâpêwa.

Tadpole's Visit to the Doctor

1. misiwê wiyawihk wîsakêyihtam.
2. nitawi-wâpamêw maskihkîwiyiniwa ayisk ê-wîsakêyihtahk wiyaw.
3. "tânita kâ-wîsakêyihtaman?" kâ-isi-kakwêcimikot maskihkîwiyiniwa.
4. âha, wiyaw wîsakêyihtam ayîkisis.
5. "namôya anima nânitaw ê-itâspiniyan," itikow. êkwa mîna itikow "ê-ati-kîsi-ohpikiyan anima."
6. nipâwi-maskihkiy miyikow.
7. âha, mîciw nipâwi-maskihkiy ayîkisis.
8. âha, onipêwinihk ohci-kwâskohtiw.
9. âha, kanawâpamisow.
10. âha, ayîkisiwiw êkwa.

7.3.A. Possessives

noun	my	your	her/his
asikan	—	kitasikan	otasikana
astotin	nitastotin	—	otastotin
cîpwastotin	nicîpwastotin	kicîpwastotin	—
iskwêwasâkay	nitiskwêwasâkay	—	otiskwêwasâkay
iskwêwitâs	—	kitiskwêwitâs	otiskwêwitâsa
kîskasâkay	nikîskasâkay	—	okîskasâkay
kîskinakwêwayân	nikîskinakwêwayân	kikîskinakwêwayân	—
maskisin	nimaskisin	—	omaskisin
miskotâkay	—	kiskotâkay	oskotâkay
mitâs	nitâs	—	otâsa
pahkêkinwêsâkay	nipahkêkinwêsâkay	kipahkêkinwêsâkay	—
pahkêkinwêskisin	nipahkêkinwêskisin	—	opahkêkinwêskisin
pakwahtêhon	—	kipakwahtêhon	opakwahtêhon
papakiwayân	nipapakiwayân	—	opapakiwayân
piponasâkay	nipiponasâkay	kipiponasâkay	—
pîhconês	nipîhconês	—	opîhconês
sênipânasâkay	—	kisênipânasâkay	osênipânasâkay
sênipânipapakiwayân	nisênipânipapakiwayân	—	osênipânipapakiwayân
sîpêkiskâwasâkay	nisîpêkiskâwasâkay	kisîpêkiskâwasâkay	—
tâpiskâkan	nitâpiskâkan	—	otâpiskâkana

7.3.B. Shopping Trips

Shopping for Clothes and Groceries

2. atâwêwikamikohk anima kâ-kî-nitawi-papâmi-atâwêyan.
3. kikî-otinâw ê-sîpihkosit mitâs.
4. kikî-otinâwak ê-kaskitêsicik asikanak.
5. kikî-otinên ê-mihkwâk papakiwayân.
6. kikî-otinên ê-nîpâmâyâtahk miskotâkay.
7. kikî-otinên wâwa, askipwâwa, nanâtohk mînisa, êkwa nîpiya.
8. atâwêwikamik-simâkanis kâ-kî-pimitisahosk.
9. sôskwâc piko kîkway kikî-ati-asiwatân kitotinikêwi-âwacikanihk.
10. namôya, namôya katâc kîkway kikî-atâwân êkota ohci.

Shopping for Groceries

2. mîciwin awa kâ-kî-nôhtê-atâwêt.
3. sôpirstôrihk awa kâ-kî-nitawi-papâmi-atâwêt.
4. wiyâs awa kâ-kakwê-otinahk.
5. nîstosâp-tahtwâpisk mîna nîso sôniyâs itakihtêw pêyak kosikwanis mostosowiyâs.

6. âha, osâm âhkwakihtêw mostosowiyâs.
7. mitâtahtwâpisk mîna nisto sôniyâs itakihtêw pêyak kosikwanis kohkôsiwiyâs.
8. âha, osâm âhkwakihtêw kohkôsiwiyâs.
9. kêkâ-mitâtaht-tahtwâpisk itakihtêw pêyak kosikwanis pâhkahâhkwâniwiyâs.
10. wêhtakihtêyiwa sisikopicikaniwiyâs, otakisîhkâna, spâm êkwa palônî, êwakoni kâ-otinahk.

7.3.C. *Colour Terms*

Colour Prenoun	Inanimate Nouns	Animate Nouns
mihko-	mihkwâw	mihkosiw
wâposâwi	wâposâwâw	wâposâwisiw
sîpihko	sîpihkwâw	sîpihkosiw
osâwi-	osâwâw	osâwisiw
askihtako-	askihtakwâw	askihtakosiw
nîpâmâyâci-	nîpâmâyâtan	nîpâmâyâtisiw
wâpiski-	wâpiskâw	wâpiskisiw
kaskitêwi-	kaskitêwâw	kaskitêsiw
kaskitêwi-osâwi-	kaskitêwi-osâwâw	kaskitêwi-osâwisiw
cîpêhtako-	cîpêhtakwâw	cîpêhtakosiw
mihkosâwi-	mihkosâwâw	mihkosâwisiw
wâposâwisâwi-	wâposâwisâwâw	wâposâwisâwisiw
wâposâwi-askihtako-	wâposâwi-askihtakwâw	wâposâwi-askihtakosiw
osâwasko-	osâwaskwâw	osâwaskosiw
mihko-sîpihko-	mihko-sîpihkwâw	mihko-sîpihkosiw

Colour Prenoun	"It Looks Like…" for Inanimate Nouns	"It Looks Like…" for Animate Nouns
mihko-	mihkonâkwan	mihkonâkosiw
wâposâwi-	wâposâwinâkwan	wâposâwinâkosiw
sîpihko-	sîpihkonâkwan	sîpihkonâkosiw
osâwi-	osâwinâkwan	osâwinâkosiw
askihtako-	askihtakonâkwan	askihtakonâkosiw
nîpâmâyâci-	nîpâmâyâcinâkwan	nîpâmâyâcinâkosiw
wâpiski-	wâpiskinâkwan	wâpiskinâkosiw
kaskitêwi-	kaskitêwinâkwan	kaskitêwinâkosiw
kaskitêwi-osâwi-	kaskitêwi-osâwinâkwan	kaskitêwi-osâwinâkosiw
cîpêhtako-	cîpêhtakonâkwan	cîpêhtakonâkosiw
mihkosâwi-	mihkosâwinâkwan	mihkosâwinâkosiw
wâposâwisâwi-	wâposâwisâwinâkwan	wâposâwisâwinâkosiw
wâposâwi-askihtako-	wâposâwi-askihtakonâkwan	wâposâwi-askihtakonâkosiw
osâwasko-	osâwaskonâkwan	osâwaskonâkosiw
mihko-sîpihko-	mihko-sîpihkonâkwan	mihko-sîpihkonâkosiw

CHAPTER 8 EXERCISES

8.1.A. VTA Imperatives

English	2P Singular	2P Plural	2P Inclusive
Look at someone	—	kanawâpamihk(ok)	kanawâpamâtân(ik)
Don't look at someone.	êkâwiya kanawâpam(ik)	—	êkâwiya kanawâpamâtân(ik)
Look at someone later.	kanawâpamâhkan(ik)	kanawâpamâhkêk(ok)	—
See someone.	wâpam(ik)	—	wâpamâtân(ik)
Don't see someone.	—	êkâwiya wâpamihk(ok)	êkâwiya wâpamâtân(ik)
See someone later.	wâpamâhkan(ik)	—	wâpamâhkahk(ik)
Look for someone.	natonaw(ik)	natonawihk(ok)	—
Don't look for someone.	êkâwiya natonaw(ik)	—	êkâwiya natonawâtân(ik)
Look for someone later.	—	natonawâhkêk(ok)	natonawâhkahk(ik)
Find someone.	miskaw(ik)	—	miskawâtân(ik)
Don't find someone.	êkâwiya miskaw(ik)	êkâwiya miskawihk(ok)	—
Find someone later.	miskawâhkan(ik)	—	miskawâhkahk(ik)

8.2.A. Exercises with VTAs

Verb Stem		Indicative	Conjunct
otin(ik)	1st pres	nitotinâw(ak)	ê-otinak(ik)
	1st past	nikî-otinâw(ak)	ê-kî-otinak(ik)
	1st fut int	niwî-otinâw(ak)	ê-wî-otinak(ik)
	1st fut def	nika-otinâw(ak)	
nâs(ik)	2nd pres	kinâtâw(ak)	ê-nâtat(cik)
	2nd past	kikî-nâtâw(ak)	ê-kî-nâtat(cik)
	2nd fut int	kiwî-nâtâw(ak)	ê-wî-nâtat(cik)
	2nd fut def	kika-nâtâw(ak)	
natonaw(ik)	3rd pres	natonawêw	ê-natonawât
	3rd past	kî-natonawêw	ê-kî-natonawât
	3rd fut int	wî-natonawêw	ê-wî-natonawât
	3rd fut def	ta-natonawêw	
miskaw(ik)	3' pres	miskawêyiwa	ê-miskawâyit
	3' past	kî-miskawêyiwa	ê-kî-miskawâyit
	3' fut int	wî-miskawêyiwa	ê-wî-miskawâyit
	3' fut def	ta-miskawêyiwa	
natohtaw(ik)	1P pres	ninatohtawânân(ak)	ê-natohtawâyâhk(ik)

	1P past	nikî-natohtawânân(ak)	ê-kî-natohtawâyâhk(ik)
	1P fut int	niwî-natohtawânân(ak)	ê-wî-natohtawâyâhk(ik)
	1P fut def	nika-natohtawânân(ak)	
pêhtaw(ik)	21 pres	kipêhtawânaw(ak)	ê-pêhtawâyahk(ik)
	21 past	kikî-pêhtawânaw(ak)	ê-kî-pêhtawâyahk(ik)
	21 fut int	kiwî-pêhtawânaw(ak)	ê-wî-pêhtawâyahk(ik)
	21 fut def	kika-pêhtawânaw(ak)	
nisitohtaw(ik)	2P pres	kinisitohtawâwâw(ak)	ê-nisitohtawâyêk(ok)
	2P past	kikî-nisitohtawâwâw(ak)	ê-kî-nisitohtawâyêk(ok)
	2P fut int	kiwî-nisitohtawâwâw(ak)	ê-wî-nisitohtawâyêk(ok)
	2P fut def	kika-nisitohtawâwâw(ak)	
wâpam(ik)	3P pres	wâpamêwak	ê-wâpamâcik
	3P past	kî-wâpamêwak	ê-kî-wâpamâcik
	3P fut int	wî-wâpamêwak	ê-wî- wâpamâcik
	3P fut def	ta-wâpamêwak	

8.2.B. VTA Conjugations

Part 1

	Subject/Actor	Imperative	Negative Imperative	Delayed Imperative
2	you (sg)	—	êkâwiya wâpam	wâpamâhkan
2P	you (pl)	natonawihk	—	natonawâhkêk
21	Let's (you and I)	natohtawâtân	êkâwiya natohtawâtân	—
2	you (sg)	mêtawâkâs	—	mêtawâkâtâhkan
2P	you (pl)	atoskawihk	êkâwiya atoskawihk	—
21	Let's (you and I)	—	êkâwiya kanawâpamâtân	kanawâpamâhkahk
2	you (sg)	kîsis	êkâwiya kîsis	—
2P	you (pl)	—	êkâwiya kocispisihk	kocispitâhkêk
21	Let's (you and I)	nâtâtân	—	nâtâhkahk

Singular Subject

	Subject/Actor	Indicative	Conjunct
1	I	—	ê-kî-kanawâpamak
2	you	kitatoskawâw	—
3	she/he	atoskawêw	ê-kî-kanawâpamât
3'	her/his (friend)	—	ê-kî-kanawâpamâyit

Plural Subject

	Subject/Actor	Indicative	Conjunct
1P	we (excl)	nika-nôhtê-mowânân	—
21	we (incl)	—	ê-wî-natonawâyahk
2P	you (pl)	kika-nôhtê-mowâwâw	ê-wî-natonawâyêk
3P	they	ta-nôhtê-mowêwak	—

Part 2

1. Last night I looked for my older brother.
2. Let's eat the fish this evening.
3. Last night they looked at the dancers.
4. This evening we (incl) will go and listen to our (incl) grandfathers.
5. Are you (sg) going to taste the rabbits tonight?
6. You (pl) will go fetch our older sister tomorrow.
7. Her/his (friend) saw her/his grandmother last night.
8. She/he is going to work for her/his grandmother today.
9. We (excl) are going to listen to our (excl) grandfather telling sacred stories tonight.
10. You (pl) tried to cook the turkey yesterday.

8.3.A. Translation 1

1. This past morning I picked up my socks from the floor.
2. In the moring I am going to fetch the children.
3. On Monday go and help your (pl) grandfather.
4. On Tuesday I am going to look for my dog in the forest.
5. Next week I will go and watch the powwow dancers.
6. Last week I listened to storytellers.
7. Last year, did you listen to the Cree storytellers?
8. She/he is going to take off her/his gloves.
9. Try to understand her/him when/if she/he speaks Cree.
10. If it is cold, she/he is is going to wear rabbit-fur socks.

8.3.B. Translation 2

1. nikî-miyâw kimis anima masinahikan.
2. kikî-miyâw cî kiciwâm (kitawîmâw if talking to a female) kimaskisina?
3. kî-wîsâmêw kohtâwiya atâwêwikamikohk isi.
4. wîcihâhkahk kisîmis tipiskâki.
5. kî-asamêw nâpêsisa sîsîpa.
6. kiwî-masinahamawâw cî kikâwiy?
7. nikî-asamâw nitôtêm pahkwêsikana.
8. nikî-mowâw kinosêw tipiskohk.
9. kikî-wîcêwâwak cî iskwêsisak kihci-kiskinwahamâtowikamikohk isi kîkisêp?

10. kika-wîcêwitinâwâw sâkahikanihk isi.
11. kika-wîcêwikowâw atâwêwikamikohk isi.
12. miyâhkanik kimasinahikana wâpamitwâwi.

8.3.C. Text Exercises

A Gathering

1. kâ-kî-awâsisîwiyan, ispîhk kâ-sôniyâskâk.
   When you were a child, when it was Treaty Day.
2. âmaciwîspimowinihk kâ-kî-mâmawinitoyêk.
   Y'all gathered at Stanley Mission.
3. kêkâ-mitâtaht tipahikan ê-kî-ispayik kâ-kî-mâci-miyikawiyêk tipahamâtowi-sôniyâw.
   It was at nine o'clock when you started getting your treaty money.
4. kihci-okimâwin-simâkanisak kâ-kî-miyikoyêk tipahamâtowi-sôniyâw.
   The RCMP gave you the treaty money.
5. niyânawâpisk kahkiyaw iyiniw kâ-kî-miyiht.
   Five dollars was given to every person.
6. kikî-mîcinâwâw môswa-wiyâs, kahkêwak, êkwa mînisa.
   You ate moose meat, dry meat, and berries.
7. âha, kikî-mowâwâwak kinosêwak.
   Yes, you ate fish.
8. kâ-kîsi-mîcisohk kî-mêtawâniwin.
   When the eating was done, there were games.
9. âha, kikî-mâh-mawinêhotonâwâw cîmâna ohci.
   Yes, you competed with canoes.
10. âha, kî-môcikan.
    Yes, it was fun.

A Christmas Gathering: Translation

1. Last winter me and my relatives gathered together at Christmas.
2. My son and his wife and their children came.
3. My daughter and her husband and their son also came, they travelled from Toronto.
4. My son and his wife cooked. They cooked turkey, corn and carrots. They cooked potatoes and they made salad and cranberry sauce.
5. We ate buns and other pastry. I like the taste of turkey and I like the taste of salad.
6. After eating we gave each other Christmas presents and we sang Christmas carols.
7. We finished up at around eleven o'clock.
8. Next Christmas we will gather together again, it will be fun.

A Christmas Gathering: Questions

1. piponohk ôki kâ-kî-mâmawinitocik.
2. kiwâhkômâkanak kî-pê-itohtêwak.
3. kikosis êkwa wîwa kî-piminawasowak.
4. kî-kîsitêpwêwak misihêwa, mahtâmina, mîna oskâtâskwa.
5. kî-kîsisamwak askipwâwa mîna kî-osihtâwak nîpiya mîna wîsakîmin-aspahcikan.
6. kikî-wîhkipwâw misihêw.
7. kikî-wîhkistên nîpiya.
8. kikî-kîsahkamikisinâwâw pêyakosâp tipahikan ê-kî-ispayik.
9. âha, kîhtwâm ta-mâmawinitowak manitowi-kîsikâyiki.
10. âha, kî-môcikan.

A Storytelling Camp

1. ispîhk kâ-kî-aywêpiyêk kiskinwahamâkosihk ohci kâ-kî-nitawi-âh-âtayohkêyan.
2. mistasiniy-sâkahikanihk kâ-kî-nitawi-âh-âtayôhkêyan.
3. kî-sâh-saskaniyowêw.
4. mistahi kîkway kâ-kî-itôtaman.
5. wacaskosak kâ-kî-tâpakwâtacik.
6. âha, kikî-mowâwâwak wacaskosak.
7. namôya, namôya kikî-mowâwâwak wâposwak.
8. âha, kikî-kikasâmânâwâw sakâhk.
9. kâ-tipiskâk kâ-kî-âh-âtayôhkêyêk.
10. âha, mistahi kî-môcikan!

CHAPTER 9 EXERCISES

9.1.A. Translation

1. I see you.
2. We see you.
3. I see y'all.
4. You see me.
5. You see us.
6. Y'all see me.
7. Are you feeding me this fish?
8. I am feeding you this fish.
9. Are y'all feeding me this bannock?
10. We are feeding you this bannock.
11. I love you.
12. We love you.
13. I love y'all.
14. You love me.
15. Y'all love me.

9.1.C. VTA-Inverse 1

Part 1: Translation

1. I see a man.
2. A man sees me.
3. I see men.
4. Men see me.
5. I feed my older brother fish.
6. My older brother feeds me fish.
7. I invite my younger sibling.
8. My younger sibling invites me.

Part 2: Conjugation

VTA: *natohtaw*

2	natohtawin
2P	natohtawik
2/2P	natohtawinân

VTA: *kanawâpam*

2	kanawâpamihkan
2P	kanawâpamihkêk
2/2P	kanawâpamihkahk

VTA-inverse: *wâpam*

1	nikî-wâpamik
2	kikî-wâpamik
3	kî-wâpamikow
3'	kî-wâpamikoyiwa

VTA-direct: *wâpam*

1	niwî-wâpamâw
2	kiwî-wâpamâw
3	wî-wâpamêw
3'	wî-wâpamêyiwa

Part 3: Translation

1. ninôhtê-natohtawâw nimosôm.
2. kikî-natohtawâw cî kimosôm.
3. nikî-wâpamânânak niwâhkômâkanak.
4. niwâhkômâkanak kika-wâpamikonawak.
5. wî-natohtawêw omosôma.
6. natohtawin.

9.1.D. VTA-Inverse 2

Part 1: Translation

1. I hit a man.
2. A man hits me.
3. I hit the men.
4. The men hit me.
5. I comb my daughter's hair.
6. My daughter combs my hair.
7. I hurt my dog.
8. My dog hurt me.

Part 2: Conjugation

VTA-direct: *pakamah*

2	pakamah
2P	pakamahohk
2/2P	pakamahwâtân

VTA-inverse 2: *pakamah*

2	pakamahon
2P	pakamahok
2/2P	pakamahonân

VTA-direct: *sîkah*

1	nikî-sîkahwâw
2	kikî-sîkahwâw
3	kî-sîkahwêw
3'	kî-sîkahwêyiwa

VTA-inverse 2: *sîkah*

1	niwî-sîkahok
2	kiwî-sîkahok
3	wî-sîkahokow
3'	wî-sîkahokoyiwa

Part 3: Translation

1. nitânis ninohtê-sîkahok.
2. ninôhtê-sîkahwâw nitânis.
3. kikî-wîsakahokwak cî kisîmisak?
4. kikî-wîsakahwâwak cî kisîmisak?
5. nisîmisak nikî-pisci-pakamahokonânak.
6. nisîmisak nikî-pisci-pakamahwânânak.

9.1.E. VTA-Inverse 3

Part 1: Translation

1. I bought a hat for my older brother.
2. My older brother bought shoes for me.
3. Did you bring moose meat for your grandmother?
4. Her/his grandmother brought bannock for her/him.
5. She/he fetched firewood for her/his daughter.
6. Her/his daughter fetched firewood for her/him.
7. I tried to teach Cree to my friend.
8. My friend taught me Cree.

Part 2: Conjugation

VTA-direct: *masinahamaw*

2	masinahamaw
2P	masinahamawihk
2/2P	masinahamawâtân

VTA-inverse 3: *masinahamaw*

2	masinahamawin
2P	masinahamawik
2/2P	masinahamawinân

vTA-direct: *atâwêstamaw*		vTA-inverse 3: *atâwêstamaw*	
1	nikî-atâwêstamawâw	1	nika-atâwêstamâk
2	kikî-atâwêstamawâw	2	kika-atâwêstamâk
3	kî-atâwêstamawêw	3	ta-atâwêstamâkow
3'	kî-atâwêstamawêyiwa	3'	ta-atâwêstamâkoyiwa

Part 3: Translation

1. ninôhtê-atâwêstamawâw nikâwiy masinahikan.
2. nikâwiy nikî-atâwêstamâk masinahikan.
3. kikî-atâwêstamawâwak cî kisîmisak cahkâs?
4. kikî-atâwêstamâkwak cî kisîmisak cahkâs?
5. nisîmis nikî-kiskinwahamâk nêhiyawêwin.

9.2.A. VTA-Relexive 1

Part 1: Translation

1. I helped my younger sibling.
2. My younger sibling helped me.
3. I helped myself.
4. You watched your grandfather.
5. Your grandfather watched you.
6. You watched yourself.
7. She/he saw her/his older brother.
8. Her/his older brother saw her/him.
9. She/he saw her/himself.
10. We invited my older sister.
11. My older sister invited us.
12. We invited ourselves.
13. We called/invited our grandmother.
14. Our grandmother called/invited us.
15. We called/invited ourselves.

Part 2: Conjugations

vTA Stem	vTA-Direct	vTA-Inverse	vTA-Reflexive
asam	—	nikî-asamik	nikî-asamison
kanawâpam	kikî-kanawâpamâw	—	kikî-kanawâpamison
wâpam	kî-wâpamêw	kî-wâpamikow	—
wîsâm	kî-wîsâmêyiwa	—	kî-wîsâmisoyiwa
wîcih	—	nikî-wîcihikonân	nikî-wîcihisonân
wîcêw	kikî-wîcêwânaw	—	kikî-wîcêwisonaw
natom	kikî-natomâwâw	kikî-natomikowâw	—
nawasôn	kî-nawasônêwak	—	kî-nawasônisowak
nisitawêyim	—	nisitawêyimikoyiwa	nisitawêyimisoyiwa
kistêyim	nikistêyimâw	—	nikistêyimison

9.2.B. VTA-Reflexive 2

Part 1: Translation

1. I hit my younger sibling.
2. My younger sibling hit me.
3. I hit myself.
4. You combed your daughter's hair.
5. Your daughter combed your hair.
6. You combed your own hair.
7. She/he hurt her/his older brother.
8. Her/his older brother hurt her/him.
9. She/he hurt her/himself.
10. We imprisoned the policeman.
11. The policeman imprisoned us.
12. We imprisoned ourselves.
13. We followed my grandfather.
14. My grandfather followed us.
15. We followed ourselves.

Part 2: Conjugations

VTA Stem	VTA-Direct	VTA-Inverse	VTA-Reflexive
pakamahw-	—	nipakamahok	nipakamahoson
sîkahw-	kisîkahwâw	—	kisîkahoson
wîsakahw	wîsakahwêw	wîsakahokow	—
saskahw-	saskahwêyiwa	—	saskahosoyiwa
pasastêhw-	—	nipasastêhokonân	nipasastêhosonân
kipahw-	kikipahwânaw	—	kikipahosonaw
pâskisw-	kipâskiswâwâw	kipâskisokowâw	—
pimitisahw-	pimitisahwêwak	—	pimitisahosowak
patahw-	—	patahokoyiwa	patahosoyiwa
pistahw-	nipistahwâw	—	nipistahoson

9.2.C. VTA-Reflexive 3

Part 1: Translation

1. I bought groceries for my younger sibling.
2. My younger sibling bought groceries for me.
3. I bought groceries for myself.
4. You listened to your grandfather.
5. Your grandfather listened to you.
6. You listened to yourself.
7. She/he understood your grandfather.
8. Your grandfather understood her/him.
9. She/he understood her/himself.
10. Her/his friend wrote to her/his mother.
11. Her/his mother wrote to her/his friend.
12. Her/his friend wrote to her/himself.
13. We recognized the teacher.
14. The teacher recognized us.
15. We recognized ourselves.

VTA Stem	VTA-Direct	VTA-Inverse	VTA-Reflexive
atâwêstamaw	—	nitatâwêstamâk	nitatâwêstamâson
nâtamaw	kinâtamawâw	—	kinâtamâson
pêtamaw	pêtamawêw	pêtamâkow	—
atoskaw	atoskawêyiwa	—	atoskâsoyiwa
kiskinwahamaw	—	nikiskinwahamâkonân	nikiskinwahamâsonân
natohtaw	kinatohtawânaw	—	kinatohtâsonaw
masinahamaw	kimasinahamawâwâw	kimasinahamâkowâw	—
nisitohtaw	nisitohtawêwak	—	nisitohtâsowak
nisitawinaw	—	nisitawinâkoyiwa	nisitawinâsoyiwa
pêhtaw	nipêhtawâw	—	nipêhtâson

9.3. Text Exercises

1. otâkosîhk ôki kâ-kî-nitawi-papâmi-atâwêcik.
2. âha, wîcêwêw ocawâsimisa.
3. kî-miskamwak maskisina nîswâw-mitâtahto-mitanaw tahtwâpisk ê-itakihtêyiki.
4. namôya, namôya atâwêwak êwakoni maskisina.
5. niyânanomitanaw tahtwâpisk ê-itakihtêyiki maskisina kâ-kî-atâwêcik.
6. mitâsa mitâtahtomitanaw tahtwâpisk ê-itakisoyit kâ-kî-miskawâcik.
7. namôya, namôya atâwêwak êwakoni mitâsa.
8. nêwomitanaw niyânanosâp tahtwâpisk ê-itakisoyit mitâsa kâ-atâwêcik.
9. mitâsa êkwa maskisina kâ-atâwêstamawât ocawâsimisa.
10. wîstas mitâsa êkwa maskisina kî-atâwêstamâsow.

CHAPTER 10 EXERCISES

10.1.A. Activities through the Seasons

Making Birch Syrup

1. kayâs ispîhk kâ-kî-awâsisîwiyan ôma kî-itahkamikan.
2. kikî-pôsinâwâw mâna ta-nitawi-sîwâkamisikêyêk.
3. âha, kikî-cîhkêyihtên mâna ta-sîwâkamisikêyêk.
4. kiya, kinîkihikwak, êkwa kîtisânak kikî-nitawi-sîwâkamisikânâwâw.
5. pêyakwâw ê-niyânano-kîsikâk kikî-pôsinâwâw.
6. opahkopîwinihk kâ-kî-nitawi-mânokêyêk.
7. ê-wî-nitawi-sîwâkamisikêyêk.
8. kikî-nawasônâwâwak waskwayak ta-mîstasoyêk.
9. âha, kikî-mîstasonâwâw waskwayak.
10. pîhcipacikan waskwâhk kikî-astânâwâw êkwa sîpâ pîhcipacikanihk kikî-ahânâwâwak askihkosak êkota ta-isi-ohcikawik waskwayâpoy.

11. âha, kapê-kîsik kî-ohcikawin waskwayâpoy.
12. kî-nikohtêwak nâpêsisak.
13. kikâwiy êkwa kimisak kî-kisâkamisamwak waskwayâpoy ê-sîwâkamisikêcik.
14. âha, kî-wîhkasin sîwâkamisikan.
15. âha, kî-wîhkasin sîwâkamisikan ta-aspahcikiyan napaki-pahkwêsikanisihk.

10.1.B. *Activities through the Day*

Rabbit Snaring

1. ispîhk kâ-kî-awâsisîwiyan ôma kâ-kî-itahkamikahk.
2. kikî-cîhkêyihtên ta-papâmi-wîcêwat kohtâwîpan.
3. âha, kikî-mâwaci-cîhkêyihtên ta-nitawi-tâpakwâtâyêkik wâposwak.
4. pêyakwâw ôma ê-kî-niyânano-kîsikâk kâ-kî-nitawi-papâmi-kapêsiyêk
5. nânitaw êtikwê niyânan tipahikan ê-kî-ispayik, ê-otâkosik, kâ-kî-kospîyêk.
6. âha, kinwêsk nôhcimihk kikî-pimohtânâwâw ê-kî-natonamêk wâposo-mêskanâsa.
7. âha, mihcêt tâpakwâna kikî-âh-akotânâwâw.
8. mêtoni kêkâc ê-kî-ati-pahkisimok kâ-kî-ati-kîwêyêk.
9. ayinânêw tipahikan mîna âpihtaw ê-kî-ispayik kâ-kî-matâwisiyêk kikapêsiwiniwâhk.
10. mitâtaht tipahikan ê-kî-ispayik kâ-kî-ati-kawisimoyêk.
11. âha, wîpac ê-kîkisêpâyâk kikî-waniskânâwâw.
12. nânitaw têpakohp tipahikan ê-kî-ispayik kâ-kî-waniskâyêk.
13. âha, kikî-papâsi-kîkisêpâ-mîcisonâwâw pâmwayês ta-kospîyêk.
14. ayinânêw tipahikan mîna âpihtaw ê-kî-ispayik kâ-kî-kospîyêk ta-nâtakwêyêk.
15. âha, mihcêt wâposwak kikî-tâpakwâtâwâwak.

10.2.A. kistêyihtamowin – *Respect*

1. ispîhk kâ-kî-awâsisîwiyêk.
2. ê-kî-wî-kanâcihtâcik anima yîkwahaskân.
3. kî-miyo-kîsikâyiw ispîhk kâ-kî-âsowahahkik sîpiy.
4. kî-ati-sôhkiyowêw êkwa kî-ati-kaskitêwânaskwâw ispîhk kâ-pôni-âpihtâ-kîskâk.
5. âha, piyêsiwak kî-kitowak.
6. âha, kî-ati-sôhkiyowêw.
7. âha, kî-wâh-wâsaskotêpayin.
8. kî-kakwê-âsowahamwak ôki.
9. âha, kî-kakwê-âsowahamwak sîpiy.
10. kî-kihkâmikowak ohtâwîwâwa.

10.2.B. ka-ispitisihk isîhcikêwin – *Protocol: Age-Appropriate Conduct*

1. kî-nâh-nitawiminêwak mâna.
2. natimihk mâna kâ-kî-nitawiminêcik.
3. kiya, kîtisânak, kikâwiy, êkwa pêyak kohkom mâna kâ-kî-nitawiminêyêk.
4. âha, ispatinâhk mâna kâ-kî-nitawiminêcik.

5. âha, kî-ati-iskatêyihtamwak ta-mawisocik ôki nâpêsisak?
6. kî-ati-mâh-mêtawêwak nâpêsisak.
7. âha, kapê-kîsik mâna kî-mâh-mêtawêwak ôki nâpêsisak.
8. kî-takopahtâwak mâna ispîhk kâ-otâkosiniyik.
9. âha, mistahi mâna kî-mawisowak ôki iskwêwak.
10. kî-itâwak ta-nayahtahkik mînisa nâsipêtimihk isi.

10.2.C. tapahtêyimisowin – *Humility*

1. kî-pêhtam ê-âcimimiht oskinîkwa mistahi ê-itêyimisoyit.
2. kî-âtawêyimêw anihi iskwêwa kâ-asotamâht.
3. sakâhk ohci kâ-kîmôtâpit wîsahkêcâhk.
4. akâmi-sîpîhk kâ-wâpamât oskinîkiwa.
5. kapê-kîsik nipîhk ê-kitâpamisoyit ôhi oskinîkiwa.
6. wîsahkêcâhk mâmitonêyihtam nânitaw ta-isi-wawiyasihât oskinîkiwa.
7. nipîhk awa oskinîkiw kâ-kitâpimisot ispîhk kâ-wâpamât oskinîkiskwêwa.
8. âha, akâwâtêw ôhi oskinîkiskwêwa.
9. ohtâwiya itwêstamâkow ta-wîkimât oskinîkiskwêwa.
10. âha, wîkimêw wîsahkêcâhk ôhi oskinîkiwa mistahi kâ-itêyimisot.

10.2.D. nikwatisowin êkwa mâtinamâkêwin – *Sharing and Generosity*

1. ispîhk kâ-kî-awâsisîwiyan.
2. kiya êkwa kistês kikî-nitomikawinâwâw ta-nitawi-nikwatisoyêk.
3. pêyak kiwâhkômâkaniwâw ana kâ-kî-nipahât môswa.
4. wâhyaw nôhcimihk sakâhk kâ-kî-nakatât môswa.
5. ayisk êkosi mâna omâcîwak kayâs ê-kî-itôtahkik, ta-nikwatisoyit owâhkômâkaniwâwa.
6. kayâs mâna omâcîwak kî-nakatêwak môswa nôhcimihk ta-nikwatisoyit owâhkômâkaniwâwa.
7. kiya kâ-kî-wîsâmikawiyan ta-nâtamawat kohkom môso-wiyâs.
8. wîpac ê-kîkisêpâyâyik kî-sipwêhtêwak ôki nâpêwak êkwa nâpêsisak.
9. âha, kinwêsk mâna sakâhk kî-pimohtêwak.
10. kî-âh-âcimowak nâpêwak êkwa kî-nâh-nanôyacihêwak nâpêsisa.

10.2.E. tâpokêyihtamowin – *Faith*

1. kayâs kâ-kî-awâsisîwiyan.
2. misiwê itê mâhtâwi-sîpîhk kâ-kî-pâh-pimohtêhocik ôki.
3. kî-sîkwaniyiw ispîhk kâ-wâpamâcik môswa.
4. môswa awa ê-âsowahahk sâkahikan.
5. kêsiskaw otihtinamiyiw pîminahkwân ohcâwîsa.
6. ê-wî-tâpakwêwêpinât anihi môswa pîminahkwân ohci.
7. âha, tâpakwêwêpinêw môswa pîminahkwân ohci.
8. âha, kî-sêkihikow môswa ana nâpêsis.
9. ayisk mêtoni kêhciwâk cîmânihk ita kâ-apit ê-pê-isicimêyit môswa.
10. âha, kêkâc kî-kwatapiskam cîmânis awa.

10.2.F. kisêwâtisiwin – *Kindness*

1. kayâs kâ-kî-awâsisîwiyan ôma kî-itahkamikan.
2. wî-wîcihêwak ohtâwîwâwa ta-nikohtawâyit atâwêwikimâwa.
3. atâwêwikimâw ana kâ-kî-atoskêhiwêt.
4. âha, osâm piko kapê-nîpin kî-nikohtêwak.
5. ohtâwîmâw ana kâ-kî-kîskatahâhtikwêt.
6. nâpêsisak aniki kâ-kî-nâsipêyâwatâcik mihta.
7. âha, kî-sôhki-atoskêwak mâna.
8. mihtot anima kâ-kî-osîhtâcik.
9. wîstâwimâw ana kâ-pê-wîcihiwêt.
10. kî-akâwâtamwak nâpêsisak tahkohc mihtotihk ta-pôsicik.

10.2.G. âniskô-kiskinwahamâkêwin – *Passing On Teachings*

1. pêyakwâw ê-nîpihk ôma kâ-kî-itahkamikahk.
2. mâhtâwi-sîpîhk ôki kâ-kî-nitawi-papâmiskâcik.
3. pâwiscikosihk kâ-kî-ati-kapêsicik nistam kâ-tipiskâyik.
4. ê-ati-wâpaniyik kîhtwâm kâ-kî-ati-pôsicik.
5. wapâsihk ôki kâ-takocimêcik.
6. "ohcistin kitôtinaw" kâ-isi-têpwêyit otôtêma.
7. âha, ohcistin cîmân.
8. minahik-pikiwa âpacihêw ta-mîsahahk cîmân.
9. âha, ânwêhtamiyiwa otôtêma êwakoni pikiwa ta-mîsahamiyit cîmâna.
10. ohtâwîpana ôhi kâ-kî-kiskinwahamâkot ta-isi-mîsahikâkêt pikiwa.

GLOSSARY

The following abbreviations are for the grammatical items here:

1st   first person, speaker
2nd   second person, addressee/person spoken to
3rd   third person, person spoken about

an   animate   in   inanimate

NA   animate noun   NDI   dependent inanimate noun
NDA   dependent animate noun   NI   inanimate noun

pl   plural   IPV   indeclinable preverb
PR   pronoun   rdpl reduplication
INM   indeclinable nominal   sg   singular
IPC   indeclinable particle   excl exclusive
IPH   indeclinable particle phrase   incl inclusive

VAI   animate intransitive verb
VII   inanimate intransitive verb
VTA   transitive animate verb
VTI   transitive inanimate verb
wC   Woods Cree

A

âcimâw (VTA) – *stories are told about someone*
âcimêw (VTA) – *she/he tells a story about someone*
âcimostawêw (VTA) – *she/he tells someone a story*
âcimow (VAI) – *she/he tells a story*
âcimowin (NI) – *story*

âha (IPC) – *yes*
âhâsiw (NA) – *crow*
âh-asiwatâw (VTI-2) – *she/he places something in a bag*
âhâw (IPC) – *okay*

âhci piko (IPH) – *still*

âhkosîskâkow (VAI) – *something makes someone ill*

âhkosiw (VAI) – *she/he is sick*

âhkosîwasinahikan (NI) – *hospitalization card*

âhkosîwikamik (NI) – *hospital*

âhkosiwin (NI) – *illness*

âhkwakihtêw (VII) – *it is expensive*

âhkwakisow (VAI) – *she/he is expensive*

âhkwatihcikan (NI) – *freezer*

âkôpicikan (NI) – *curtain*

âmaciwîspimowin (NI) – *Stanley Mission*

âniskêhtowin (NI) – *interconnectedness*

âniskô-kiskinwahamâkêwin (NI) – *passing on teachings*

ânwêhtam (VTI-1) – *she/he disbelieves something*

âpacihêw (VTA) – *she/he uses someone*

âpacihtâw (VTI-2) – *she/he uses something*

âpâpiskahikanis (NI) – *key*

âpihtakahikâtêw (VII) – *it is locked up*

âpihtâ-kîsikani-mîcisow (VAI) – *she/he eats lunch*

âpihtâ-kîsikâw (VII) – *it is noon*

âpihtâ-tipiskâw (VII) – *it is midnight*

âpihtaw (IPC) – *half*

âsay (IPC) – *already*

âskaw (IPC) – *sometimes*

âskaw mâna (IPH) – *sometimes, as is usual*

âsowaham (VTI-1) – *she/he goes across water*

âstam (IPC) – *come*

âtawêyimêw (VTA) – *she/he rejects someone*

âtawiya (IPC) – *at least*

âtayôhkêw (VAI) – *she/he tells sacred stories*

âtayôhkêwina (NI) – *sacred stories*

âtotam (VTI-1) – *she/he tells a story about something*

âwatâw (VTI-2) – *she/he hauls something*

âwatawâsiswâkan (NA) – *school bus*

acimosihkânisak (NA) – *pussy willows*

aciyaw (IPC) – *for a short while*

ahêw (VTA) – *place someone somewhere*

ahpô mîna (IPH) – *even though*

akâmihk (IPC) – *across (water or land)*

akâmi-sîpîhk (IPC) – *across the river*

akâwâtam (VTI-1) – *she/he desires something*

akâwâtêw (VTA) – *she/he desires someone*

akihtâsowina (NI) – *numbers*

akimâwak (VTA) – *they are counted*

akimêw (VTA) – *count someone*

akimihci (IPC) – *if she/he is counted*

akimimihci (IPC) – *if her/his (relative) is counted*

akohp (NI/NA) – *blanket*

akotâw (VII) – *she/he hangs something*

akwâwân (NI) – *drying rack*

ana (PR) – *that*

anihi (PR) – *those*

aniki (PR) – *those ones*

anima (PR) – *that*

anohc (IPC) – *today, now*

anohc kâ-ispayik (IPH) – *this week*

anohcihkê (IPC) – *just recently*

apisîs (IPC) – *a little*

apiw (VAI) – *she/he sits*

apiwin (NI) – *seat*

apiwinâhpison (NI) – *seat belt*

apoy (NA) – *a paddle*

asâm (NA) – *a snowshoe*

asamêw (VTA) – *she/he feeds someone*

asapâp (NA) – *thread*

asawâpiwin (NI) – *tower*

asikan (NA) – *a sock*

asinîwaciy (NI) – *mountain*

asiskitân (NI) – *calf*

asiwacikanis (NI) – *suitcase*

asiwatâw (VTI-2) – *she/he puts something in a bag*

asiwatêw (VII) – *something is in the bag*

askihk (NA) – *pot*

askihkos (NA) – *small pail*

askihtakosiw (VAI) – *she/he is green*

askihtakwasâkay (NI) – *a green coat*

askihtakwâw (VII) – *it is green*

askipwâwa (NI) – *potatoes*

askitipayiwin (NI) – *ulcer*

askîwin (NI) – *year*

askiy (NI) – *earth*

asotamawêw (VTA) – *she/he promises (it/him) to someone*

aspahcikêw (VAI) – *she/he eats something with spread*

aspin (IPC) – *since, away*

aspiskwêsimon (NI) – *pillow*

astâw (VTI-2) – *she/he places something somewhere*

astis (NA) – *a mitt, glove*

astotin (NI) – *a hat*

atâwêstamâsow (VAI) – *she/he buys something for her/himself*

atâwêstamawêw (VTA) – *she/he buys something for someone*

atâwêw (VAI) – *she/he buys*

atâwêwikamik (NI) – *store*

atâwêwikamik-simâkanis (NA) – *a store detective*

atâwêwikimâw (NA) – *a store manager*

ati- (IPV) – *begin*

ati-sâkipakâw (VII) – *leaves begin to bud*

atoskâtam (VTI-1) – *she/he works at it*

atoskâtêw (VTA) – *she/he works at or on someone*

atoskawêw (VTA) – *she/he works for someone*

atoskêhêw (VTA) – *she/he makes someone work*

atoskêw (VAI) – *she/he works*

awâsis (NA) – *child*

awâsisîwiw (VAI) – *she/he is a child*

awasi-nîpihki (IPC) – *summer after next*

awasi-nîpinohk (IPC) – *summer before last*

awasi-otâkosîhk (IPC) – *the day before yesterday*

awasi-pipohki (IPC) – *winter after next*

awasi-piponohk (IPC) – *winter before last*

awasi-sîkwahki (IPC) – *spring after next*

awasi-sîkwanohk (IPC) – *spring before last*

awasi-takwâkiki (IPC) – *fall after next*

awasi-takwâkohk (IPC) – *fall before last*

awasi-tipiskâki (IPC) – *night after next*

awasi-tipiskohk (IPC) – *night before last*

awasi-wâpahki (IPC) – *day after tomorrow*

awêkâ cî (IPH) – *or else*

awîna êtikwê (IPH) – *wonder who*

awîna (PR) – *who*

awîniki (PR) – *who* (pl)

ayânis (NI) – *piece of cloth*

ayamâkanis (NI) – *cell phone*

ayamihâw (VAI) – *she/he prays*

ayamihcikêw (VAI) – *she/he reads*

ayamihêwi-kîsikâw (VII) – *it is Sunday*

ayamihtâw (VTI-2) – *she/he reads something*

ayapiy (NA) – *gill net*

ayayâ (IPC) – *ouch*

ayêski-pêhow (VAI) – *she/he is tired of waiting*

ayîki-pîsim (NA) – *Frog Moon, April (wC: May)*

ayîkisis (NA) – *frog*

ayîkisisiwiw (VAI) – *she/he is a tadpole*

ayîkisiwiw (VAI) – *she/he is a frog*

ayinânêmitanaw (IPC) – *eighty*

ayinânêw (IPC) – *eight*

ayinânêwosâp (IPC) – *eighteen*

ayisk (IPC) – *because*

ayiwina (NI) – *clothes*

ayiwinisa (NI) – *clothes*

aywêpisiw (VAI) – *she/he rests a little*

aywêpiw (VAI) – *she/he rests*

aywêpiwi-kîsikâw (VII) – *it is a holiday*

c

cahcahkatâmopayiw (VAI) – *she/he has shortness of breath*

cahcahkâyos (NA) – *blackbird*

cahcahkiw (NA) – *pelican*

cahkâs (NI) – *ice cream*

capasis (IPC) – *lower*

cêskwa (IPC) – *wait*

cî (IPC) – *polarity question indicator*

cîhkêyihtam (VTI-1) – *she/he likes something*

cîhkêyihtamowin (NI) – *pleasure*

cîhkêyimêw (VTA) – *she/he likes someone*

cîkahikan (NI) – *axe*

cîmân (NI) – *canoe*

cîmânis (NI) – *small canoe*

cîmêw (VTA) – *she/he accompanies someone on vehicle*

cîpwastotin (NI) – *toque*

cîstahâsêpon (NI) – *fork*

cihcipayapisikanis (NI) – *bicycle*

cikâstêpayihcikan (NI) – *movie*

cikâstêpayihcikanis (NI) – *television*
cipahaskânis (NI) – *kilometre*

Ê

êkâ (IPC) – *negator for conjunct*
êkosi (IPC) – *that way*
êkosi mâna (IPH) – *that is the way usually*
êkosi mâna kayâs (IPH) – *that was usual long ago*
êkospîhk (IPC) – *then, at that time*
êkota (IPC) – *there*
êkotê (IPC) – *over there*
êkwa (IPC) – *and*
êkwa ispîhk (IPH) – *and when*
êkwa kîhtwâm (IPH) – *and again*
êkwâni êkota ohci (IPH) – *and then from there*
êkwâni (IPC) – *that's all, and then*
êkwâni mâka (IPH) – *but then*
êmihkwân (NA) – *spoon*
êsa (IPC) – *evidently*
êskwâ (IPC) – *while*
êtikwê (IPC) – *perhaps, I suppose*
êwako (PR) – *that one*
êwakoni (PR) – *those, those are the ones*
êyikohk (IPC) – *so much, as far, as long*

H

hâw (IPC) – *okay*
hâw mâka (IPC) – *okay then*

I

ihkopîwi-pîsim (NA) – *Frost Moon, November*
ihtâwin (NI) – *abode, place of residence, village*
ihtasiwak (VAI) – *they are so many*
isi (IPC) – *thus, towards*
isi- (IPV) – *so, this way, thus*
isicimêw (VAI) – *she/he goes toward there by water*
isi-kakwêcimêw (VTA) – *she/he asks someone a question thus*
isi-têhtapiw (VAI) – *she/he rides thus*

isiwêpan (VII) – *it is such weather*
isiyihkâsow (VAI) – *she/he is named thus*
isiyihkâtêw (VII) – *it is called*
iskatêyihtam (VTI-1) – *she/he is bored with something*
isko (IPC) – *up to*
iskonikan (NI) – *reserve*
iskotêwitâpân (NA) – *train*
iskwâhtawêpicikan (NI) – *up escalator*
iskwâhtêm (NI) – *door*
iskwêsis (NA) – *girl*
iskwêw (NA) – *woman*
iskwêwasâkay (NI) – *dress*
iskwêwisîhow (VAI) – *she/he dresses as a woman*
iskwêwitâs (NA) – *woman's pants*
ispahtâw (VAI) – *run up to*
ispatinaw (NI) – *hill*
ispatinâw (VII) – *there are hills*
ispayin (VII) – *it happens*
ispîhk (IPC) – *when*
ispîhk kâ-ohpahohk mîna kâ-twêhohk (IPH) – *schedule*
ispîhtaskîwin (NI) – *season*
ispimihk (IPC) – *up*
ita (IPC) – *where*
ita kâ-ayâhk (IPH) – *flight status*
ita kâ-takopayiki maskimota (IPH) – *baggage claim*
ita kâ-tawâk (IPH) – *aisle*
ita ohci (IPH) – *from where*
itahkamikan (VII) – *it happens*
itahkamikisiw (VAI) – *she/he is doing something*
itahtopiponêw (VAI) – *she/he is that age*
itakihtêw (VII) – *it costs thus*
itakisow (VAI) – *she/he/it costs thus*
itamahcihow (VAI) – *she/he feels thus*
itâpatisiw (VAI) – *she/he is useful in some way*
itâpiw (VAI) – *she/he looks (somewhere)*
itâspinêw (VAI) – *she/he is ill in that way*
itasinâsow (VAI) – *she/he is coloured thus*
itasinâstêw (VII) – *it is coloured thus*
itê ka-itôhtêhohk (IPH) – *destination*
itêw (VTA) – *she/he says something to someone*

itêyihtam (VTI-1) – *she/he thinks thus*

itêyimisow (VAI) – *think yourself that way*

itôtam (VTI-1) – *she/he does something*

itôtawêw (VTA) – *she/he does something to someone*

itohtêw (VAI) – *she/he goes*

itwahikâkêw (VAI) – *she/he points with something*

itwêstamawêw (VTA) – *she/he speaks for someone on their behalf*

itwêw (VAI) – *she/he says*

iyinîsiwin (NI) – *wisdom*

iyinimina (NI) – *blueberries*

iyiniw (NA) – *First Nations person*

K

kâ- (IPV) – grammatical preverb for relative clauses

kâhkêwak (NI) – *dried meat*

kâh-kîskatahahtikwêw (VAI) – *she/he cuts down trees* (rdpl)

kâkîsimow (VAI) – *she/he prays*

kâ-mâh-misi-kîstihk (IPH) – *there is a big windstorm*

kâ-mâmawinitohk (IPH) – *gathering*

kâ-mâyiciwasik (INM) – *place of difficult currents*

kâ-pê-asotamaht (IPH) – *that which is promised to someone*

kâ-pimihâhk # (IPC) – *flight number*

kâ-pôsit (IPC) – *passenger*

kâsihkwêw (VAI) – *she/he washes up*

kâskipâsow (VAI) – *she/he shaves*

kâ-twêhohk [place] ohci (IPH) – *arriving from*

kâwi (IPC) – *back*

kâwi itohtêk pôsiwinihk (IPH) – *return ramp*

kâ-wîkihtocik (IPC) – *when they marry*

ka- (IPV) – tense marker, *will*

kakwê- (IPV) – *try*

kakwêcimêw (VTA) – *she/he asks someone a question*

kanâcihcikêw (VAI) – *she/he cleans up*

kanâcihisow (VAI) – *she/he cleans self*

kanâcihisowikamik (NI) – *washroom*

kanâcihow (VAI) – *she/he cleans up*

kanâcihowikamik (NI) – *washroom*

kanâcihowin (NI) – *cleanliness*

kanâcihtâw (VTI-2) – *she/he cleans something*

kanakê (IPC) – *at least*

kanawâpahtam (VTI-1) – *she/he looks at something*

kanawâpamêw (VTA) – *she/he looks at someone*

kanawâpamisow (VAI) – *she/he looks at her/himself*

ka-ohpahohk (IPH) – *area for departures*

kapâw (VAI) – *she/he gets out of something*

kapê (IPC) – *always*

kapê-kîsik (IPC) – *all day*

kapê-nîpin (IPC) – *all summer*

kapê-pipon (IPC) – *all winter*

kapêsiw (VAI) – *she/he camps*

kapê-takwâkin (IPC) – *all fall*

kapê-tipisk (IPC) – *all night*

kaskikwâsowinâpisk (NA) – *thimble*

kaskikwâswâkan (NI) – *sewing machine*

kaskimêw (VTA) – *she/he convinces someone*

kaskitêsiw (VAI) – *she/he is black*

kaskitêwânaskwâw (VII) – *there are dark clouds*

kaskitêwaskisin (NI) – *black shoe*

kaskitêwâw (VII) – *it is black*

katôhpinêw (VAI) – *she/he has tuberculosis*

ka-twêhohk (IPC) – *arrivals*

ka-wêpahamihk (IPC) – *flight is cancelled*

kawisimow (VAI) – *she/he lies down to sleep*

kawiyak (NA) – *porcupine quills*

kayâhtê (IPC) – *originally, formerly*

kayâs (IPC) – *long ago*

kayâs iyiniw (NA) – *person from long ago*

ka-yêhyêwêpahokêhk (IPC) – *cardio-pulmonary resuscitation* (CPR)

kêcikoskam (VTI-1) – *she/he takes something off*

kêcikoskawêw (VTA) – *she/he takes someone off*

kêhciwâk (IPC) – *close to something*

kêkâc (IPC) – *almost*

kêkâ-mitâtaht (IPC) – *nine*

kêkâ-mitâtahtomitanaw (IPC) – *ninety*

kêkâ-mitâtahtosâp (IPC) – *nineteen*

kêkâ-nîsitanaw (IPC) – *nineteen*

kêsiskaw (IPC) – *hurry*

kêsiskawihkasikan (NI) – *microwave oven*

kêtahtawê (IPC) – *suddenly, eventually*

kêyâpic (IPC) – *still*

kî- (IPV) – past tense indicator

kîhtwâm (IPC) – *again*

kîkisêp (IPC) – *this past morning*

kîkisêpâ-mîcisow (VAI) – *she/he eats breakfast*

kîkisêpâyâw (VII) – *it is morning*

kîko (PR) – *which*

kîkway (PR) – *something*

kîkwây (PR) – *what*

kîkwaya (PR) – *things* (in)

kîkwayak (PR) – *things* (an)

kîmôtâpamêw (VTA) – *she/he peeks at someone*

kîmôtâpiw (VAI) – *sneak a peek*

kîsahkamikisiw (VAI) – *she/he finishes (activity)*

kîsi- (IPV) – *finish*

kîsihtâw (VTI-2) – *she/he finishes something*

kîsikâw (VII) – *it is day*

kîsi-ohpikiw (VAI) – *she/he finishes growing*

kîsisam (VTI-1) – *she/he cooks it* (in)

kîsisamawêw (VTA) – *she/he cooks something for someone*

kîsiswêw (VTA) – *she/he cooks it* (an)

kîsitêpotêw (VTA) – *she/he cooks it* (an)

kîsitêpow (VAI) – *she/he cooks*

kîskasâkay (NI) – *skirt*

kîskinakwêwayân (NI) – *vest*

kîskipocikan (NI) – *saw*

kîspin (IPC) – *if*

kîwêhtahêw (VTA) – *she/he takes someone home*

kîwêpayiw (VAI) – *she/he drives home*

kîwêtinohk (IPC) – *in the north*

kîwêw (VAI) – *she/he goes home*

kihcêyihtam (VTI-1) – *she/he honours something*

kihcêyihtamowin (NI) – *honour*

kihcêyimâw (VTA) – *she/he is honoured*

kihcêyimêw (VTA) – *she/he honours someone*

kihcêyimow (VAI) – *she/he brags*

kihci-kiskinwahamâtowikamik (NI) – *university*

kihci-yôski-têhtapiwin (NI) – *couch*

kihkâmikow (VTA) – *she/he is scolded by someone*

kikasâmohtêw (VAI) – *she/he walks with snowshoes*

kimiwan (VII) – *it rains*

kinosêw (NA) – *fish*

kinosêw-âcimowin (NI) – *a fish story*

kinwêsîs (IPC) – *for quite awhile*

kinwêsk (IPC) – *a long time*

kipaham (VTI-1) – *she/he closes something*

kipahwêw (VTA) – *she/he imprisons someone*

kisâkamisam (VTI-1) – *she/he boils something*

kisâstêw (VII) – *it is hot*

kisê-pîsim (NA) – *Great Moon, January* (wC: *February*)

kisêwâtisiwin (NI) – *kindness*

kisêyiniw (NA) – *old man*

kisîpêkinam (VTI-1) – *she/he washes something*

kisîpêkinastêw (VAI) – *she/he bathes*

kisîpêkinêw (VAI) – *she/he washes someone*

kisîpêkiyâkanêw (VAI) – *she/he washes dishes*

kisikiwin (NI) – *your urine*

kisinâw (VII) – *it is very cold*

kisisow (VAI) – *she/he has a fever*

kisiwâhêw (VTA) – *she/he angers someone*

kiskêyihtam (VTI-1) – *she/he knows something*

kiskêyihtamowin (NI) – *knowledge*

kiskêyimêw (VTA) – *she/he knows someone*

kiskinawâcinâpisk (NI) – *bulletin board*

kiskinawâpahtam (VTI-1) – *she/he knows it from watching something*

kiskinawâpahtamowin (NI) – *knowledge from watching*

kiskinawâpamêw (VTA) – *she/he learns from watching someone*

kiskinwahamâkosihk (INM) – *in the classroom*

kiskinwahamâkosiw (VAI) – *she/he is in class/ school*

kiskinwahamâtowikamik (NI) – *school*

kiskinwahamawêw (VTA) – *she/he teaches something to someone*

kiskisiw (VAI) – *she/he remembers*

kisowaskatêw (VAI) – *she/he has an upset stomach*

kisowikanawâpamêw (VTA) – *she/he looks at someone in anger*

kistêyihtam (VTI-1) – *she/he respects something*

kistêyihtamowin (NI) – *respect*

kistêyimêw (VTA) – *she/he respects someone*

kitâpamêw (VTA) – *she/he looks at someone*

kitâpamisow (VAI) – *she/he looks at her/himself*

kitowak (IPC) – *thunderbirds*

kitowak piyêsiwak (IPH) – *thunderbirds make a sound*

kiyâm (IPC) – *never mind, it doesn't matter, may as well*

kiyâskimêw (VTA) – *she/he tells someone a lie*

kiyâskiw (VAI) – *she/he tells a lie*

kiya (PR) – *you*

kiyawâw (PR) – *you* (pl)

kiyêhyêwin (NI) – *your breathing*

kiyipa (IPC) – *hurry*

kiyôtêw (VAI) – *she/he visits afar*

kiyokawêw (VTA) – *she/he visits someone*

kiyokêw (VAI) – *she/he visits*

kocihtâw (VTI-2) – *she/he tries something*

kocispitam (VTI-1) – *she/he tastes something*

kocispitêw (VTA) – *she/he tastes someone*

kohkôsiwiyin (NA) – *bacon*

kohkôsowiyâs (NI) – *pork*

kohkom (NDA) – *your grandmother*

kohkominaw (NDA) – *our grandmother* (incl)

kosikwanis (NI) – *kilogram*

kosikwanwa (VII) – *they are heavy*

koskopayiw (VAI) – *she/he awakes*

koskwâpisin (VAI) – *she/he is surprised by a sight*

kospîw (VAI) – *she/he goes inland*

kotaka (PR) – *another* (an obv, in pl)

kotakak (PR) – *another* (an pl)

kotak askîwiki (IPH) – *next year*

kotakihk (IPC) – *in another place*

kotak ispayiki (IPH) – *next week*

kotak kîkway (IPH) – *another thing*

kotawân (NI) – *campfire*

kotawânâpisk (NI) – *stove*

kotawêw (VAI) – *she/he starts a campfire*

kwâpikêw (VAI) – *she/he hauls water*

kwâskwêpicikêw (VAI) – *she/he fishes (with a rod)*

kwâskohtiw (VAI) – *she/he jumps*

kwahkotêw (VII) – *it ignites, it flares up*

kwatapinam (VTI-1) – *she/he flips something over*

kwatapiskam (VTI-1) – *she/he tips it over by sudden movement*

kwayask (IPC) – *very much so, right, rightly*

kwayask-itâtisiwin (IPH) – *honesty*

M

mâci- (IPV) – *start*

mâcîw (VAI) – *she/he hunts*

mâh-mâkwahikow (VTA-inv) – *she/he struggles with something*

mâh-manisâwâtêw (VTA) – *she/he cuts someone*

mâh-misi-mamahkâhan (VII) – *there are big waves*

mâhtâw-âpacihcikan (NI) – *computer*

mâhtâwi-sîpiy (NI) – *Churchill River*

mâka (IPC) – *but, then, still*

mâka mîna (IPH) – *as usual*

mâka piyisk (IPH) – *but eventually*

mâmaskâtêw (VTA) – *she/he wonders about someone*

mâmawi- (IPV) – *all together*

mâmawinitowak (VAI) – *they gather together*

mâmihk (IPC) – *downriver*

mâmitonêyihtam (VTI-1) – *she/he thinks about something*

mâna (IPC) – *usually*

mânihtoyâsk (NI) – *hide scraper made of bone*

mânokêw (VAI) – *she/he sets up a tent*

mâskikan (NDI) – *chest*

mâskitoy (NDI) – *buttocks*

mâtahikan (NI) – *hide scraper*

mâtinamâkêwin (NI) – *sharing*

mâtinamâtowin (NI) – *sharing with one another*

mâtwê- (IPV) – *in/from the distance*

mâwaci- (IPV) – *most*

mâwaci mistahi (IPH) – *most*

mâyêyihcikêw (VAI) – *she/he is disrespectful*

mâyêyihtam (VTI-1) – *she/he disrespects it*

mâyimahcihow (VAI) – *she/he feels ill*

mâyiskâkow (VTA) – *something affects someone badly*

mahkwan (NDI) – *heel*

mahtâmin (NA) – *corn*

mahti êsa (IPH) – *let's see then*

mahti (IPC) – *let's see, please*

mamahtâwisiwin (NI) – *skill*

mamihcihisow (VAI) – *she/he is proud of her/himself*

manâcihitowin (NI) – *ultimate protection*

manaway (NDI) – *cheek*

manicôs oskanâspinêwin (NI) – *bone cancer*

manicôsâspinêwin (NI) – *cancer*

manicôstohtôsimâspinêwin (NI) – *breast cancer*

manisâwâtêw (VTA) – *she/he cuts up someone*

manisam (VTI-1) – *she/he cuts something*

manitowi-kîsikâw (VII) – *Christmas Day*

manitowi-kîsikâwi-nikamowina (NI) – *Christmas carols*

manitowi-kîsikâw-mêkiwina (NI) – *Christmas gifts*

manôminak (NA) – *wild rice*

masakay (NDA) – *skin*

masinaham (VTI-1) – *write it*

masinahamawêw (VTA) – *she/he writes to someone*

masinahikan (NI) – *book*

masinahikanâhcikos (NA/NI) – *pencil*

masinahikanâhtik (NA/NI) – *pen*

masinahikanêkin (NI) – *paper*

masinahikêw (VAI) – *she/he writes*

masinahikêwin (NI) – *writing*

masinahikêwinâhtik (NI) – *desk*

masinahikêwi-têhamân (NA) – *credit card*

maskasiy (NDA) – *fingernail*

maskatay (NDI) – *abdomen*

maskatêpwêw (VAI) – *she/he barbeques*

maskihkîwikamikos (NI) – *clinic*

maskihkîwiskwêw (NA) – *nurse (former word)*

maskihkîwiyiniw (NA) – *doctor*

maskihkîyiwacis (NI) – *first-aid kit*

maskihkiya (NI) – *medicines*

maskimot (NI) – *bag*

maskimota (NI) – *luggage*

maskisin (NI) – *shoe*

maskotêw (NI) – *prairie*

matâwisiw (VAI) – *she/he emerges (from the forest)*

matay (NDI) – *belly*

matwân cî (IPH) – *maybe*

mawinîhotowak (VAI) – *they challenge each other*

mawisow (VAI) – *she/he gathers berries*

mêkiskwêwêw (VTA) – *she/he gives him a woman to marry*

mêkiw (VAI) – *she/he gives*

mêkwâc (IPC) – *now, presently*

mêskanâs (NI) – *path*

mêskanaw (NI) – *road*

mêstakay (NDI) – *hair*

mêtawâkâtam (VTI-1) – *she/he disrespects something*

mêtawâkâtêw (VTA) – *she/he disrespects someone*

mêtawâniwin (VII) – *there are games*

mêtawêw (VAI) – *she/he plays*

mêtoni (IPC) – *very*

mêtoni kêkâc (IPH) – *just about there*

mêtoni mâna (IPH) – *it was so*

mîcisow (VAI) – *she/he eats*

mîcisowinâhtik (NI) – *table*

mîcisowinâhtikohkân (NI) – *tray*

mîciw (VTI-3) – *she/he eats something*

mîciwin (NI) – *food*

mîciwina (NI) – *groceries*

mîkis (NA) – *bead*

mîkiwâhp (NI) – *tipi*

mîkiwâm (NI) – *home*

mîna (IPC) – *also, plus*

mîna âpihtaw (IPH) – *also half*

mînisa (NI) – *berries*

mîsaham (VTI-1) – *she/he mends something*

mîskonêw (VTA) – *she/he feels someone*

mîskonam (VTI-1) – *she/he feels something*

mîskotinâkosiw (VAI) – *she/he looks different*

mîstasow (VAI) – *she/he taps a tree for sap*

micihcîwi-ânisawikanân (NI) – *wrist*

micihciy (NI) – *hand*

mihcêt (IPC) – *many*

mihcêtinwa (IPC) – *there are many*

mihcêtwâw (IPC) – *many times*

mihcikwan (NDI) – *knee*

mihko (NI) – *blood*

mihko-papakiwayân (NI) – *red shirt*

mihkosiw (VAI) – *she/he is red*

mihkwâkan (NDI) – *face*

mihkwâw (VII) – *it is red*

mihkwêyâpiya (NI) – *veins*

mihta (NI) – *firewood* (pl)

mihtawakay (NDI) – *ear*

mihtot (NI) – *raft*

mikisiwi-pîsim (NA) – *Eagle Moon, February* (wC: *March*)

mikiskohk (IPC) – *last fall/autumn*

mikiskon (VII) – *it is fall/autumn*

mikohtaskway (NI) – *throat*

mikot (NDI) – *nose*

mikwâskoniy (NDI) – *chin*

mikwayaw (NDI) – *neck*

minahikohk (IPC) – *amongst the pines*

minahik-pikiw (NA) – *spruce gum*

minahowinihk (IPC) – *at the place of the kill*

minihkwâkan (NI) – *cup*

minihkwêw (VAI) – *she/he drinks*

miniscikos (NI) – *small island*

ministik (NI) – *island*

mipwâm (NDI) – *thigh*

misakâw (VAI) – *she/he arrives on shore by canoe/boat*

miscikowacis (NI) – *small box*

misicihcân (NI) – *thumb*

misihêw (NA) – *turkey*

misi-omikîwin (NI) – *smallpox*

misisitân (NI) – *big toe*

misit (NDI) – *foot*

misiwâc (IPC) – *in any case*

misiwê (IPC) – *all over*

miskâhtik (NDI) – *forehead*

miskam (VTI-1) – *she/he finds something*

miskât (NDI) – *leg*

miskawêw (VTA) – *she/he finds someone*

miskîsik (NDI) – *eye*

miskîsikohkâna (NDI) – *eyeglasses*

miskon (NDI) – *liver*

miskotâkay (NDI) – *coat*

misôkan (NDI) – *backside*

mispayowak (NDA) – *ovaries*

mispikay (NDI) – *rib*

mispiskwan (NDI) – *back*

mispiton (NDI) – *arm*

mispon (VII) – *it snows*

mistahi (IPC) – *many*

mistahi itêyimisow (IPH) – *she/he thinks highly of her/himself*

mistâpêw (NA) – *Sasquatch*

mistasiniy-sâkahikan (NI) – *Big Stone Lake*

mistikwân (NDI) – *head*

mitâpiskan (NDI) – *jaw*

mitâs (NDA) – *pair of pants*

mitâtaht (IPC) – *ten*

mitâtahto-mitanaw (IPC) – *one hundred*

mitâtahtwâpisk (IPC) – *ten dollars*

mitêh (NDI) – *heart*

mitêyikom (NDI) – *nostril*

mitihtihkosâspinêwin (NI) – *kidney disease*

mitihtiman (NDI) – *shoulder*

mitôn (NDI) – *mouth*

mitôskwan (NDI) – *elbow*

mitohtôsim (NDA) – *breast*

mitokan (NDI) – *hip*

miyâmêw (VTA) – *she/he smells someone*

miyâskam (VTI-1) – *it goes past something*

miyahtam (VTI-1) – *she/he smells something*

miyaw (NDI) – *body*

miyawêsiw (VAI) – *she/he is hairy*

miyawêyâspinêw (VAI) – *she/he has a hairy disease*

miyêsâpiwinân (NDI) – *eyebrow*

miyêw (VTA) – *she/he gives something to someone*

miyo- (IPV) – *good*

miyo-kîsikâw (VII) – *it is a good day*

miyomahcihow (VAI) – *she/he feels good*

miyonâkosiw (VAI) – *she/he is beautiful*

miyonâkwan (VII) – *it looks beautiful*

miyo-ohpikihâwasowin (NI) – *good child-rearing*

miyopayiw (VII) – *it runs good*

miyo-pimâcihok! (VAI) – *live well, live healthy*

miyo-pimâtisiwin (NI) – *a good life*

miyo-pimôtêhowin (NI) – *a good journey*

miyo-pimohtêhok! (VAI) – *Safe travels!*

miyoskamîhk (IPC) – *last spring*

miyoskamin (VII) – *it is spring*

miywâsin (VII) – *it is beautiful, it is good*

miywêyihtam (VTI-1) – *she/he is happy*

miywêyihtamowin (NI) – *happiness*

miywêyimêw (VTA) – *she/he is happy with something*

môcikan (VII) – *it is fun*

môcikihtâw (VAI) – *she/he has fun*

môhkomân (NI) – *knife*

môsahkinêw (VTA) – *she/he picks someone up*

môsihtâw (VAI) – *she/he fells something*

môsowiyâs (NI) – *moose meat*

môswa (NA) – *moose*

môswasiniy (NI) – *bullet*

mohcihk (IPC) – *on the ground*

mostihtakohk (IPC) – *on the bottom of canoe*

mowêw (VTA) – *she/he eats someone*

mwayî- (IPV) – *before*

mwêhci (IPC) – *just when*

mwêstas (IPC) – *later*

mwêstasisiniw (VAI) – *she/he is late*

N

nâkatawêyihtam (VTI-1) – *she/he takes care of something*

nâkatawêyimêw (VTA) – *she/he takes care of someone*

nâkatohkêwiyiniw (NA) – *nurse* (new word)

nânitaw êtikwê (IPH) – *maybe somewhere, maybe somehow*

nânitaw (IPC) – *about, in some way*

nâpêsis (NA) – *boy*

nâpêw (NA) – *man*

nâpêwasâkay (NI) – *man's jacket*

nâpêwinâkosiw (VAI) – *she/he looks like a man*

nâsipêtimihk isi (IPH) – *toward the shore*

nâsipêyâwatâw (VTI-2) – *she/he hauls something to shore*

nâtakwêw (VAI) – *she/he goes to check snares*

nâtam (VTI-1) – *she/he fetches something*

nâtamawêw (VTA) – *she/he fetches something for someone*

nâtêw (VTA) – *she/he fetches someone*

nahapiw (VAI) – *she/he sits down*

nahîmakan (VII) – *on schedule*

nahihtawêw (VTA) – *she/he obeys someone*

nakatêw (VTA) – *she/leaves someone behind*

nakiskawêw (VTA) – *she/he meets someone*

nama kîkway (IPC) – *zero*

nama nânitaw (IPC) – *not much, that's alright, nothing*

nama nânitaw itâpatisiw (IPH) – *she/he is of no use*

namôya (IPC) – *no*

namôya awasimê (IPH) – *not anymore*

namôya cêskwa (IPH) – *not yet*

namôya katâc (IPH) – *not even*

namôya konita (IPH) – *it is not for nothing*

namôya mâna (IPH) – *not usually*

namôya mwâsi (IPH) – *hardly ever*

namôya osâm mistahi (IPH) – *not too much*

namôya wîhkâc (IPH) – *never*

nanâskomowin (NI) – *gratitude*

nanâtawihêw (VTA) – *she/he doctors someone*

nanâtohk (IPC) – *all kinds*

nanahihtam (VTI-1) – *she/he obeys something*

nanahihtamowin (NI) – *obedience*

nanimaham (VTI) – *she/he goes (paddles canoe) against the wind*

nanôyacihêw (VTA) – *she/he teases someone*

napaki-pahkwêsikanis (NA) – *pancake*

natimihk (IPC) – *upriver*

natohtam (VTI-1) – *she/he listens to something*

natohtawêw (VTA) – *she/he listens to someone*

natomêw (VTA) – *she/he calls someone, she/he invites someone*

natonam (VTI-1) – *she/he looks for something*

natonawêw (VTA) – *she/he looks for someone*

nawac (IPC) – *more so*

nawac piko (IPC) – *by comparison, better, slightly that way*

nawacîstamawêw (VTA) – *she/he roasts something for someone*

nawasônêw (VTA) – *she/he chooses someone*

nayahtam (VTI-1) – *she/he carries something on her/his back*

nayêhtâwêhikow (VTA) – *she/he finds something troublesome*

nêhiwawêw (VAI) – *she/he speaks Cree*

nêhiyawêwin (VAI) – *Cree language*

nêhiyawi-âtayôhkêw (VAI) – *she/he tells a sacred Cree story*

nê(wo)mitanaw (IPC) – *forty*

nêwo (IPC) – *four*

nêwo-kîsikâw (VII) – *it is Thursday*

nêwomitanaw niyânanosâp (IPC) – *forty-five*

nêwosâp (IPC) – *fourteen*

nîhtaciwêpicikan (NI) – *down escalator*

nîhtaciwêw (VAI) – *she/he climbs down*

nîkinâhk (IPC) – *at our home*

nîmihitow (VAI) – *she/he dances*

nîpâmâyâtan (VII) – *it is purple*

nîpâmâyât-astis (NA) – *purple mitt*

nîpâmâyâtisiw (VAI) – *she/he is purple*

nîpîn (VII) – *it is summer*

nîpinasâkay (NI) – *summer jacket*

nîpinohk (IPC) – *last summer*

nîpiy (NI) – *leaf*

nîpiya pahkihtinwa (IPH) – *leaves fall*

nîsitanaw (IPC) – *twenty*

nîs(om)itanaw (IPC) – *twenty*

nîsitanaw nêwosâp (IPC) – *twenty-four*

nîso (IPC) – *two*

nîso-kîsikâw (VII) – *it is Tuesday*

nîsosâp (IPC) – *twelve*

nîstâw (NDA) – *my cross-cousin* (males), *my brother-in-law*

nîsta (PR) – *me too*

nîswâw-mitâtahto-mitanaw (IPC) – *two hundred*

nîtim (NDA) – *my cross-cousin, my brother-in-law, my sister-in-law*

nîtisân (NDA) – *my sibling*

nîwa (NDA) – *my wife*

nicahkos (NDA) – *my female cross-cousin, my sister-in-law*

nicihcâwâw (NDA) – *my co-parent-in-law*

nicîmâniminân (NI) – *our* (excl) *canoe*

niciwâm (NDA) – *my cousin* (used by males to one another)

niciwâmiskwêm (NDA) – *my cousin* (used by females to one another)

nihc-âyihk (IPC) – *down, downstairs*

nihtâ- (IPV) – *ability to do well*

nihtâwikiw (VAI) – *she/he is born*

nihtiy (NI) – *tea*

nikamow (VAI) – *she/he sings*

nikapêsîwininâhk (IPC) – *at our camp*

nikâwîpan (NDA) – *my late mother*

nikâwîs (NDA) – *my aunt* (mother's sister)

nikâwiy (NDA) – *my mother*

nikihci-âniskotâpân (NDA) – *my great-great-great-grandparent, my great-great-great-grandchild*

nikohtawêw (VTA) – *she/he makes firewood for someone*

nikohtêw (VAI) – *she/he makes firewood*

nikosim (NDA) – *my nephew*

nikosis (NDA) – *my son*

nikotwâs(ik)osâp (IPC) – *sixteen*

nikotwâsik (IPC) – *six*

nikotwâsikomitanaw (IPC) – *sixty*

nikotwâso-kîsikâw (VII) – *it is Saturday*

nikwatisow (VAI) – *she/he fetches meat from the killing place*

nikwatisowin (NI) – *communal activity of sharing in the kill*

nimis (NDA) – *my older sister*

nimisipan (NDA) – *my late older sister*

nimosôm (NDA) – *my grandfather*

nimosômipan (NDA) – *my late grandfather*

ninahâkaniskwêm (NDA) – *my daughter-in-law*

ninahahkisêm (NDA) – *my son-in-law*

ninîkihikwak (NDA) – *my parents*

nipâw (VAI) – *she/he sleeps*

nipâwi-maskihkiy (NI) – *sleeping pill*

nipahêw (VTA) – *she/he kills someone*

nipêwin (NI) – *bed*

nipîhk (IPC) – *in the water*

nipiy (NI) – *water*

nisîmis (NDA) – *my younger sibling*

nisîmisipan (NDA) – *my late younger sibling*

nisîhkâci- (IPV) – *carefully*

nisikos (NDA) – *my aunt, my mother-in-law*

nisis (NDA) – *my uncle, my father-in-law*

nisitawêyihtam (VTI-1) – *she/he recognizes something*

nisitawêyihtamowin (NI) – *recognition*

nisitawêyimêw (VTA) – *she/he recognizes someone*

nisitohtam (VTI-1) – *she/he understands something*

nisitohtamowin (NI) – *understanding*

nisitohtawêw (VTA) – *she/he understands someone*

niska (NA) – *goose*

niski-pîsim (NA) – *Goose Moon, March* (wC: *April*)

nistam (IPC) – *first*

nistam nâtawihiwêwin (IPH) – *first aid*

nistês (NDA) – *my older brother*

nistêsipan (NDA) – *my late older brother*

nistim (NDA) – *my cross-niece, my daughter-in-law*

nisto (IPC) – *three*

nisto-kîsikâw (VII) – *it is Wednesday*

nistomitanaw (IPC) – *thirty*

nistosâp (IPC) – *thirteen*

nistwâw (IPC) – *three times, third time*

nitânis (NDA) – *my daughter*

nitâniskotâpân (NDA) – *my great-great-grandparent, my great-great-grandchild*

nitawêmâw (NDA) – *my cousin* (used by female to male or male to female)

nitawâpênikêw (VAI) – *she/he checks on something*

nitawêyihtam (VTI-1) – *she/he needs (wants) it*

nitawêyimêw (VTA) – *she/he needs (wants) someone*

nitawi- (IPV) – *go and*

nitawiminêw (VAI) – *she/he goes in search of berries*

nitêm (NDA) – *my dog*

nitihkwatim (NDA) – *my cross-nephew, my son-in-law*

nitôsim (NDA) – *my nephew*

nitôsimiskwêm (NDA) – *my niece*

nitôsis (NDA) – *my maternal aunt* (cW)

nitôtêm (NDA) – *my friend*

nitomêw (VTA) – *she/he calls someone, she/he invites someone*

nitomikawiw (VAI) – *she/he is called/invited*

nitonawêw (VTA) – *she/he looks for someone*

niwîcêwâkan (NDA) – *my companion, my partner*

niwîtisânîhitowinihk (IPC) – *in my family*

niya (PR) – *me*

niyânan (IPC) – *five*

niyânano-kîsikâw (VII) – *it is Friday*

niyânanomitanaw (IPC) – *fifty*

niyânanosâp (IPC) – *fifteen*

niyânanwâpisk (IPC) – *five dollars*

niyanân (PR) – *us*

nôhcimihk (IPC) – *inland, in the forest*

nôhtê- (IPV) – *want to*

nôhtêhkatêw (VAI) – *she/he is hungry*

nôhtêhkwasiw (VAI) – *she/he is sleepy*

nôsê-môswa (NA) – *cow moose*

nôsisim (NDA) – *my grandchild*

nocâpân (NDA) – *my great-grandparent, my great-grandchild*

nohcâwîs (NDA) – *my uncle*

nohkom (NDA) – *my grandmother*

nohkomipan (NDA) – *my late grandmother*

nohkomis (NDA) – *my paternal uncle* (wC)

nohtâwînân (NDA) – *our father*

nohtâwîpan (NDA) – *my late father*

nohtâwîpaninân (NDA) – *our late father*

nohtâwiy (NDA) – *my father*

o

ôhi (PR) – *these*

ôki (PR) – *these*

ôma (PR) – *this*

ôsihk (INM) – *in the boat*

ôsisima (NDA) – *her/his grandchild(ren)*

ôsisimimâw (NA) – *grandchild*

ôta (IPC) – *here*

ôtênâhk (INM) – *in town*

ôtênaw (NI) – *town*

ocawâsimisa (NDA) – *her/his child(ren)*

ocêmêw (VTA) – *she/he kisses someone*

ocihcâwâw (NDA) – *co-parent-in-law*

ocipitam (VTI-1) – *she/he pulls something*

ocipitêw (VTA) – *she/he pulls someone*

ohci (IPC) – *from*

ohcikawin (VII) – *it drips/leaks*

ohci-kwâskohtiw (VAI) – *she/he jumps from somewhere*

ohcisitin (VII) – *it leaks*

ohcistinisiw (VAI) – *she/he has a leak*

ohcitaw piko (IPC) – *on purpose, it must be done*

ohkoma (NDA) – *her/his grandmother*

ohkomimâw (NA) – *grandmother*

ohkomimâwiw (VAI) – *she is a grandmother*

ohpahômakan (VII) – *departed flight*

ohpahowi-pîsim (NA) – *Flying-Up Moon, August*

ohpanâspinêwin (NI) – *lung disease*

ohpikiw (VAI) – *she/he grows*

ohpikiyâspinêw (VAI) – *she/he has growing pains*

ohpinam (VTI-1) – *she/he lifts something up*

ohpinêw (VTA) – *she/he lifts someone up*

ohtâcihow (VAI) – *she/he travels from (someplace)*

ohtâwîmâw (NA) – *father*

ohtâwîmâwiw (VAI) – *he is a father*

ohtâwiya (NDA) – *her/his father*

ohtohtêhow (VAI) – *she/he travels from (someplace)*

okâwîmâw (NA) – *mother*

okâwîmâwiw (VAI) – *she is a mother*

okâwîsimâw (NA) – *aunt (mother's sister)*

okâwiya (NDA) – *her/his father*

okihci-âniskotâpânimâw (NA) – *great-great-great-grandchild, great-great-great-grandparent*

okiskinwahamâkan (NA) – *student*

okiskinwahamâkêw (NA) – *teacher*

okosisimâw (NA) – *son*

omâcîw (NA) – *hunter*

omaskihkêma (NI) – *his medicines*

omisimâw (NA) – *eldest sister*

omisiw (VAI) – *she/he has an elder sister*

omosômimâw (NA) – *grandfather*

omosômimâwiw (VAI) – *he is a grandfather*

onâpêma (NDA) – *her husband*

onahâhkisîmâw (NA) – *son-in-law*

onahâkaniskwêmâw (NA) – *daughter-in-law*

onîkihikomâw (NA) – *parent*

onîmihitow (NA) – *dancer*

opahkopîwinihk (INM) – *Wading Place*

opimihâw (NA) – *pilot*

opwâtisimowak (NA) – *powwow dancers*

osâm (IPC) – *too much, because*

osâm piko (IPH) – *mostly, almost like*

osâwâw (VII) – *it is orange*

osâwâwisiw (VAI) – *she/he is orange*

osâwastotin (NI) – *orange hat*

osîhêw (VTA) – *she/he makes someone*

osîhtâw (VTI-2) – *she/he makes something*

osîmimâw (NA) – *youngest sibling*

osîmisiw (VAI) – *she/he has a younger sibling*

osikosimâw (NA) – *aunt (father's sister)*

osisimâw (NA) – *uncle (mother's brother)*

oskâtâsk (NA) – *carrot*

osk-âyisis (NA) – *young moose, yearling*

oskana-kâ-asastêki (INM) – *Regina*

oskinîkiskwêw (NA) – *young woman*

oskinîkiw (NA) – *young man*

oski-wîwa (NDA) – *his new wife*

oskonahpinêwin (NI) – *liver disease*

osôniyâmiw (VAI) – *she/he has money*

ostêsimâw (NA) – *older brother*

ostêsiw (VAI) – *she/he has an older brother*

ostimimâw (NA) – *cross-niece*

otâhk-askîwin (IPH) – *last year*

otâhk-ispayiw (IPH) – *last week*

otâhkosiwa kâ-nânâkacihât (NA) – *paramedic*

otâkosîhk (IPC) – *yesterday*

otâkosiki (IPC) – *in the evening*

otâkosin (VII) – *it is evening*

otâkwani-mîcisow (VAI) – *she/he eats supper*

otakikomiwin (NI) – *a cold*
otakisîhkâna (NI) – *sausages*
otamipayin (VII) – *flight is delayed*
otamipayiw (VAI) – *she/he is delayed*
otânisa (NDA) – *her/his daughter*
otânisimâw (NA) – *daughter*
otâniskotâpânimâw (NA) – *great-great-grandchild, great-great-grandparent*
otawâsimisiw (VAI) – *she/he has a child, she/he has children*
otawâsimisiwâwa (NA) – *their children*
otawêmâw (NA) – *parallel cousin*
otêhâspinêwin (NI) – *heart disease*
otihkwatimâw (NA) – *cross-nephew*
otihtinam (VTI-1) – *she/he grabs something*
otinam (VTI-1) – *she/he buys something, she/he takes something*
otinamâsow (VAI) – *she/he buys something for her/himself*
otinamawêw (VTA) – *she/he buys something for someone*
otinêw (VTA) – *she/he buys someone, she takes someone*
otinikêwi-âwacikan (NI) – *shopping cart*
otinikêwi-têhamân (NA) – *debit card*
otôsimimâw (NA) – *parallel nephew*
otôsimiskwêmâw (NA) – *parallel niece*
otôtêma (NDA) – *her/his friend*
otôtêmimâw (NA) – *friend*
otôtêmiwâwa (NDA) – *their friends*
otôtihk (INM) – *in/on his boat/canoe*
owîcêwâkanimâw (NA) – *companion*
owîkimâkana (NA) – *her/his spouse*
owîkimâkanimâw (NA) – *spouse*
owîstâwimâw (NA) – *cross-cousin (males)*
owîtimimâw (NA) – *cross-cousin (females)*
owîtisânimâw (NA) – *sibling*
oyâkan (NI) – *plate*

P

pâhkahâhkwâniwiyâs (NA) – *chicken meat*
pâhpihêw (VTA) – *she/he laughs at someone*

pâhpisiw (VAI) – *she/he smiles/laughs a little*
pâkahatowân (NA) – *ball*
pâmwayês (IPC) – *before*
pâskâwihowi-pîsim (NA) – *Egg-Hatching Moon, June*
pâskisikan (NI) – *gun*
pâskiswêw (VTA) – *she/he shoots someone*
pâsow (VAI) – *she/he is dry*
pâtimâ ici (IPH) – *okay, later*
pâtimâ (IPC) – *later*
pâtos (IPC) – *only later*
pâwiscikosihk (INM) – *at the little rapids*
pahkahokowin (NI) – *pulse*
pahkêkin (NI) – *leather*
pahkêkinwêsâkay (NI) – *leather coat*
pahkêkinwêskisin (NI) – *leather moccasin*
pahkisimon (VII) – *it is sundown*
pahkwênêw (VTA) – *she/he breaks someone apart*
pahkwêsikan (NA) – *bannock*
pah-pimohtêhow (VAI) – *she/he travels about*
pakâsimow (VAI) – *she/he swims*
pakamaham (VTI-1) – *she/he hits something*
pakamahwêw (VTA) – *she/he hits someone*
pakitinam (VTI-1) – *she/he lets something go*
pakitinêw (VTA) – *she/he lets something go, she/he allows someone*
pakosêyihtâkosowin (NI) – *hope*
pakwânikamik (NI) – *tent*
pakwahtêhon (NI) – *belt*
palôniy (NI) – *bologna* (English borrowing)
pamihcikêw (VAI) – *she/he drives*
papâmi- (IPV) – *out and about*
papâmi-atâwêw (VAI) – *she/he goes about shopping*
papâmi-kapêsiw (VAI) – *she/he goes about camping*
papâmi-mânokêw (VAI) – *she/he goes about camping*
papâmipayiw (VAI) – *she/he rides around*
papâmi-pimâciho-masinahikanis (NI) – *passport*
papâmiskâw (VAI) – *she/he paddles about/goes canoeing*
papâmitâpâsow (VAI) – *she/he drives/rides around*

papâmohtêw (VAI) – *she/he walks about*

papâsi- (IPV) – *in a hurry*

papakiwayân (NI) – *shirt*

papêyâhtak (IPC) – *slowly, carefully*

pasastêhwêw (VTA) – *she/he whips someone*

pasikôw (VAI) – *she/he stands up*

paskowi-pîsim (NA) – *Moulting Moon, July*

paskwahamâtowin (NI) – *scissors*

paswâtam (VTI-1) – *she/he sniffs something*

paswâtêw (VTA) – *she/he sniffs someone*

pataham (VTI-1) – *she/he misses (when shooting) something*

patahwêw (VTA) – *she/he misses (when shooting) someone*

pawâcakinasîsi-pîsim (NA) – *Frost-Exploding Trees Moon, December*

pê- (IPV) – *come*

pêhêw (VTA) – *she/he waits for someone*

pêhow (VAI) – *she/he waits*

pêhowikamik (NI) – *waiting room*

pêhtam (VTI-1) – *she/he hears something*

pêhtawêw (VTA) – *she/he hears someone*

pê-itohtêw (VAI) – *she/he comes over*

pêsiwêw (VTA) – *she/he brings someone*

pêtânaskwâw (VII) – *the clouds are coming*

pêtâpan (VII) – *it is dawn, it is daybreak*

pêtâw (VTI-2) – *she/he brings something*

pêtamawêw (VTA) – *she/he brings something for someone*

pêyak (IPC) – *one*

pêyako-kîsikâw (VII) – *it is Monday*

pêyakosâp (IPC) – *eleven*

pêyakowîkiw (VAI) – *she/he lives alone*

pêyakwâw (IPC) – *once*

pêyakwâw êsa (IPC) – *one time, once upon a time*

pîciciw (VAI) – *she/he dances the round dance*

pîhcâyihk (IPC) – *inside*

pîhcipacikan (NI) – *funnel*

pîhconês (NI) – *vest*

pîhtikwêw (VAI) – *she/he goes inside*

pîminahkwân (NI) – *rope*

pîsim (NA) – *month, sun*

pîsimohkân (NA) – *clock*

pîsimohkânis (NA) – *watch*

pîswêhkasikan (NA) – *bread*

pîswêhkasikanisak (NA) – *buns*

pîtos ispîhk ka-ohpahohk (IPH) – *rescheduled*

pîtos itê isi-ohpahohk (IPH) – *diverted flight*

pîwan (VII) – *snowdrifts, it is a blizzard*

picikwâs (NA) – *apple*

pihkahtêwâpohkêw (VAI) – *she/he makes coffee*

pihkahtêwâpoy (NI) – *coffee*

pikiw (NA) – *gum*

piko (IPC) – *only, just*

piko itê (IPH) – *anywhere*

piko kîkway (IPH) – *anything*

pîkwatahôpân (NI) – *hole in the ice for drawing water*

pimâcihow (VAI) – *she/he travels*

pimihâkan (NI) – *plane*

pimihâkan pimâcihowi-wîcihowêw (NA) – *airline attendant*

pimihâkan-twêhowin (NI) – *airport*

pimihâmakan (VII) – *it is airborne*

pimihâw (VAI) – *she/he flies*

piminawasow (VAI) – *she/he cooks*

pimipahtâw (VAI) – *she/he runs*

pimipayiw (VAI) – *she/he drives*

pimiskâw (VAI) – *she/he paddles*

pimitâpihpâhtwâw (VTI-2) – *she/he drags it in the water*

pimitisaham (VTI-1) – *she/he follows something*

pimitisahwêw (VTA) – *she/he follows someone*

pimohtêw (VAI) – *she/he walks*

pinâskowi-pîsim (NA) – *Leaf-Falling Moon, October*

pipohki (IPC) – *in the winter*

pipon (NI) – *winter*

pipon (VII) – *it is winter*

piponasâkay (NI) – *parka*

piponohk (IPC) – *last winter*

pisci- (IPV) – *accidentally*

pistahwêw (VTA) – *she/he shoots/hits someone by accident*

pitamâ (IPC) – *for now*

piyêsîs (NA) – *bird*

piyêsiwak (NA) – *Thunderbirds*

piyisk (IPC) – *eventually*

pôni- (IPV) – *stop*

pôni-âpihtâ-kîskâw (VII) – *it is afternoon*

pôni-âpihtâ-tipiskâw (VII) – *after midnight*

pôsihêw (VTA) – *she/he loads someone into a vehicle*

pôsi-masinahikanêkinos (NI) – *ticket, boarding pass*

pôsinâpâsk (NA) – *bus*

pôsiw (VAI) – *she/he gets on board*

postayawinisêw (VAI) – *she/he gets dressed*

postiskam (VTI-1) – *she/he puts something on*

postiskawêw (VTA) – *she/he puts someone on*

pwâtisimow (VAI) – *she/he dances powwow*

s

sâkahikan (NI) – *lake*

sâkahikanis (NI) – *small lake*

sâkahikanisîs (NI) – *small lake*

sâkaskinahtâw (VTI-2) – *she/he fills something*

sâkâstêw (VII) – *it is sunrise*

sâkihitowin (NI) – *love*

sâkipakâw (VII) – *leaves are budding*

sâkipakâwi-pîsim (NA) – *Leaf-Budding Moon, May*

sâminam (VTI-1) – *she/he touches something*

sâminêw (VTA) – *she/he touches someone*

sâponikan (NI) – *needle*

sâsâpiskisikan (NA) – *frying pan*

sakâw (NI) – *bush/forest*

sakahpitam (VTI-1) – *she/he ties something*

saskahwêw (VTA) – *she/he ignites/kindles someone*

saskaniyowêw (VII) – *there's a chinook wind*

sêhkêpayîs (NA) – *car*

sêkowêpinâpisk (NI) – *oven*

sêmâk (IPC) – *right away*

sênipân (NA) – *ribbon*

sênipânasâkay (NI) – *ribbon dress*

sênipânêkin (NI) – *satin/silk cloth*

sênipânipapakiwayân (NI) – *ribbon shirt*

sênipânisapâp (NA) – *silk thread*

sêsâwipahtâw (VAI) – *she/he jogs*

sêsâwîw (VAI) – *she/he exercises*

sêsâwohtêw (VAI) – *she/he hikes/walks for exercise*

sêskipitam (VTI-1) – *she/he pulls it ashore*

sîhci-pakwahtêhon (NI) – *seat belt*

sîkahow (VAI) – *she/he combs her/his hair*

sîkahwêw (VTA) – *she/he combs someone's hair*

sîkihêw (VTA) – *she/he scares someone*

sîkisiw (VAI) – *she/he is scared*

sîkwahki (IPC) – *in the spring*

sîkwan (VII) – *it is spring*

sîkwanohk (IPC) – *last spring*

sîpâ (IPC) – *under*

sîpêkiskâwasâkay (NA) – *sweater*

sîpêyihtam (VTI-1) – *she/he is patient with something*

sîpêyihtamowin (NI) – *patience*

sîpêyimêw (VTA) – *she/he is patient with someone*

sîpîsis (NI) – *creek*

sîpihkosiw (VAI) – *she/he is blue*

sîpihko-tâs (NA) – *blue pair of pants*

sîpihkwâw (VII) – *it is blue*

sîpiy (NI) – *river*

sîpiyawêsiw (VAI) – *she/he is tolerant*

sîpiyawêsiwin (NI) – *tolerance*

sîsîp (NA) – *duck*

sîwâkamisikan (NI) – *birch syrup*

sîwâkamisikêw (VAI) – *she/he makes birch syrup*

sîwihkasikanak (NA) – *cakes*

sîwinikanâspinêwin (NI) – *diabetes*

sîwinôs (NA) – *candy*

sîwisiw (VAI) – *she/he is sweet*

sikiwin (NI) – *urine*

simâkanis (NA) – *police officer*

sipwêhtêw (VAI) – *she/he leaves*

sipwêsimow (VAI) – *she/he starts dancing*

sisikopicikaniwiyâs (NI) – *ground meat*

sôhki- (IPV) – *hard*

sôhkisiwin (NI) – *strength*

sôhkitêhêwin (NI) – *courage*

sôhkiyowêw (VII) – *it is very windy*

sôkâwâspinîwin (NI) – *diabetes* (wC)

sôniskwâtahikan (NI) – *skate*

sôniskwâtahikanâhtik (NI) – *hockey stick*

sôniskwâtahikêw (VAI) – *she/he skates*

sôniyâs (NA) – *a bit of money*

sôniyâskâw (VII) – *it is treaty day* (wC)

sôniyâw (NA) – *money*

sôpirstôrihk (INM) – *at Superstore* (English borrow)

sôskopayîs (NA) – *snow-mobile*

sôskwâc (IPC) – *just, regardless*

sôskwaciwêw (VAI) – *she/he slides*

spâm (NI) – *spam* (English borrow)

T

tâna (PR) – *which; which one*

tânêhki (IPC) – *why*

tâniyikohk (IPC) – *how much*

tânima (PR) – *which one*

tânimayikohk (IPC) – *how much*

tânisi (IPC) – *how/what*

tânisi ôma (IPH) – *how is this*

tânispîhk (IPC) – *when*

tânita (IPC) – *where abouts*

tânitahto (IPC) – *how many*

tânitahto tipahikan (IPH) – *what is the time*

tânitahtopiponêyan (IPH) – *how old are you*

tânitahtwakihtêk (IPH) – *how much is this*

tânitahtwâpisk (IPH) – *how many dollars*

tânitê (IPC) – *where*

tâniwâ (PR) – *where*

tâniwê (PR) – *where*

tâniwêhâ (PR) – *where*

tâniwêhkâk (PR) – *where*

tâpakwân (NI) – *snare*

tâpakwâniyâpiy (NI) – *snare wire*

tâpakwâtêw (VTA) – *she/he snares someone*

tâpakwêw (VAI) – *she/he sets a snare*

tâpakwêwêpinêw (VTA) – *she/he ropes/snares someone with a rope*

tâpiskâkan (NA) – *scarf*

tâpiskôc (IPC) – *just like*

tâpôkêyihtam (VTI-1) – *she/he believes in something*

tâpôkêyimêw (VTA) – *she/he believes in someone*

tâpokêyihtamowin (NI) – *faith*

tâpwakwâtêw (VTA) – *she/he snares someone*

tâpwê (IPC) – *true*

tâpwêhtam (VTI-1) – *she/he believes something*

tâpwêhtamowin (NI) – *belief*

tâpwêhtawêw (VTA) – *she/he believes someone*

tâpwê mâni mâka (IPH) – *for sure it is true* (wC)

tâpwêwin (NI) – *truth*

tahkâyâw (VII) – *it is cold*

tahkascikan (NI) – *fridge*

tahkohc (IPC) – *on top of*

tahkonâwasow (VAI) – *she/he carries a child in arms*

tah-tihkitêw (VII) – *it melts* (rdpl)

tahto-wîtisânîhtowinihk (INM) – *from every family*

tahtwâpisk (IPC) – *dollars, so many dollars*

tahtwâw (IPC) – *every time*

takahki- (IPV) – *great*

takahkispakosiw (VAI) – *it is very tasty*

ta-kî- (IPV) – *can, be able, should, ought to*

ta-kî-kistêyihtamahk (VTI-1) – *we* (incl) *should respect something*

takocimêw (VAI) – *she/he arrives by boat/canoe*

takohtêw (VAI) – *she/he arrives by foot*

takopahtâw (VAI) – *she/he arrives running*

takopayiw (VAI) – *she/he arrives*

takosin (VAI) – *she/he arrives*

takwâkiki (IPC) – *in the fall*

takwâkin (VII) – *it is fall/autumn*

takwâki-pîsim (NA) – *Autumn Moon, September*

takwâkohk (IPC) – *last fall/autumn*

tapahtêyihtam (VTI-1) – *she/he thinks lowly of something*

tapahtêyimêw (VTA) – *she/he thinks lowly of someone*

tapahtêyimisowin (NI) – *humility*

tapasihêw (VTA) – *she/he flees from someone*

ta-pôsiyâhk (VAI) – *for us* (excl) *to board, to go on a boat/canoe*

tawâw [place] (IPH) – *welcome to [place]*
têhistikwânêw (VAI) – *she/he has a headache*
têhtapiwin (NI) – *chair*
têpakohp (IPC) – *seven*
têpakohpomitanaw (IPC) – *seventy*
têpakohposâp (IPC) – *seventeen*
têpiyahk (IPC) – *at least*
têpwâtêw (VTA) – *she/he calls someone*
têpwêw (VAI) – *she/he yells*
têwihtawakêw (VAI) – *she/he has an earache*
têwikanêw (VAI) – *she/he has aching bones*
têwikotêw (VAI) – *she/he has an aching nose*
têwipitonêw (VAI) – *she/he has an aching arm*
têwisitêw (VAI) – *she/he has aching feet*
têwistikwânêsiniw (VAI) – *she/he has a headache from a fall*
têwistikwânêw (VAI) – *she/he has a headache*
têyâpitêw (VAI) – *she/he has a toothache*
têyâskikanêw (VAI) – *she/he has an aching chest*
têyi- (IPV) – *ache, pain*
têyicihcêw (VAI) – *she/he has aching hands*
têyihtawakêw (VAI) – *she/he has pain in the ears*
têyikanêw (VAI) – *she/he has aching bones*
têyikâtêw (VAI) – *she/he has aching legs*
têyisitêw (VAI) – *she/he has aching feet*
têyisiw (VAI) – *she/he has aches and pains*
têyiskâtêw (VAI) – *she/he has aching legs*
têyispitonêw (VAI) – *she/he has aching arms*
têyistikwânêw (VAI) – *she/he has a headache*
tihkisêw (VTA) – *she/he melts something* (an)
tihkisow (VAI) – *she/he melts*
tihtipiskam (VTI-1) – *ride something with wheels*
timikoniw (VII) – *the snow is deep*
tipahamâtowi-sôniyâw (NA) – *treaty money*
tipahikan (NI) – *unit of measurement, hour*
tipiskâki (IPC) – *at night/tonight*
tipiskâw (VII) – *it is night*
tipiskam (VTI) – *she/he has a birthday*
tipiskohk (IPC) – *last night*
tipiyawê (PR) – *actual, one's own*
twêhômakan (VII) – *it/flight has landed*

w

wâhkôhtowin (NI) – *kinship*
wâhyaw (IPC) – *far*
wâpahki (IPC) – *tomorrow*
wâpahtam (VTI-1) – *see it*
wâpamêw (VTA) – *she/he sees someone*
wâpamon (NI) – *mirror*
wâpan (VII) – *it is dawn*
wâpikwaniya ohpikinwa (IPH) – *flowers grow*
wâpisk-asikan (NA) – *white sock*
wâpiskâw (VII) – *it is white*
wâpiskisiw (VAI) – *she/he is white*
wâpos (NA) – *rabbit*
wâposâwâw (VII) – *it is yellow*
wâposâwisiw (VAI) – *she/he is yellow*
wâposâwi-tâpiskâkan (NA) – *yellow scarf*
wâposo-mêskanâsa (NI) – *rabbit trails* (pl)
wâposo-mîcimâpohkân (NI) – *rabbit stew*
wâposwâspinêwin (NI) – *tumour disease*
wâposwayân-asikanak (NA) – *rabbit fur socks*
wâsakâm (IPC) – *around, along the shore* (wC)
wâsaskotênikan (NI) – *lamp*
wâsaskotêpayin (VII) – *there is lightning*
wâskahikan (NI) – *house*
wâstêpakâw (VII) – *leaves turn colour*
wâwa (NI) – *eggs*
wacaskos (NA) – *muskrat*
wahwâ! (IPC) – *an exclamative*
wanihêw (VTA) – *she/he loses someone*
waniskâw (VAI) – *she/he gets up*
wapâs (NI) – *narrows*
waskitipêsimon (NI) – *life jacket*
waskway (NA) – *birch tree*
waskwayâpoy (NI) – *birch sap, birch syrup*
watay (NDI) – *her/his belly*
wawâninâkwan (VII) – *it is dusk, it is twilight*
wawiyasihêw (VTA) – *she/he plays a trick on someone*
wayawîtimihk (IPC) – *outside*
wayawîw (VAI) – *she/he goes outside*
wêhtakihtêw (VII) – *it is inexpensive*
wêhtakisow (VAI) – *she/he/it is inexpensive*

wî- (IPV) – *intend*

wîcâyâmêw (VTA) – *she/he lives with someone*

wîcêwêw (VTA) – *she/he accompanies someone*

wîcihêw (VTA) – *she/he helps someone*

wîhkasin (VII) – *it is tasty*

wîkihtow (VAI) – *she/he marries*

wîhkipwêw (VTA) – *she/he likes the taste of someone*

wîhkistam (VTI-1) – *she/he likes the taste of something*

wîhkohkêw (VAI) – *she/he puts on a feast*

wîkimêw (VTA) – *she/he marries someone*

wîkiw (VAI) – *she/he resides*

wîpac (IPC) – *early, soon*

wîpac ka-twêhohk (IPH) – *it landed early*

wîsâmêw (VTA) – *she/he invites someone*

wîsahkêcâhk (NA) – Cree culture hero, legendary figure

wîsakahwêw (VTA) – *she/he hurts someone by hitting*

wîsakêyihtam (VTI-1) – *she/he feels pain*

wîsakîmin-aspahcikan (NI) – *cranberry sauce*

wîsakisimisow (VAI) – *she/he hurts her/himself from a fall*

wîsakisiniw (VAI) – *she hurts from a fall*

wîwa (NDA) – *his wife*

wîhtamawêw (VTA) – *she/he tells someone*

wiyâs (NI) – *meat*

wiyaw (NDI) – *her/his body*

Y

yahki-sôskoyâpawiw (VAI) – *she/he cross-country skis*

yahkiwêpinam (VTI-1) – *she/he pushes something*

yahkiwêpinêw (VTA) – *she/he pushes someone*

yêhyêwin (NI) – *breathing*

yîkwahaskân (NI) – *cemetery*

yiyîkicihcân (NI) – *finger*

yiyîkicihcîs (NI) – *small finger*

yiyîkisitân (NI) – *toe*

yôhtênam (VTI-1) – *she/he opens something*

yôhtênêw (VTA) – *she/he opens someone*

yôskaskisin (NI) – *rubber overshoe*

yôskâw (VII) – *it is soft*

yôski-têhtapiwin (NI) – *armchair*

yôtin (VII) – *it is windy*

BIBLIOGRAPHY

Okimāsis, Jean L. *nēhiyawēwin: paskwāwi-pīkiskwēwin / Cree: Language of the Plains.*
Regina: University of Regina Press, 2004, rev. ed. 2021.

Ratt, Solomon. *mâci-nêhiyawêwin / Beginning Cree.* Regina: University of Regina Press, 2016.

———. *Cree Cultural Teachings.* CreeLiteracy Network, June 11, 2014. http://creeliteracy.org/
cree-cultural-teachings

Wolvengrey, Arok. *nêhiyawêwin: itwêwina / Cree: Words.* Regina: University of Regina Press,
2001, 2011.

Born in a trapper's cabin on the banks of the Churchill River, just four miles north of Stanley Mission, Saskatchewan, Solomon Ratt spent the first few years of his life travelling up and down the river with his parents until he was taken to the Residential School in Prince Albert at the age of six. He graduated from the University of Regina with a BA (Ord) and BA (Adv) and an MA. He's been instructing at First Nations University of Canada since 1986 and recently was awarded the Saskatchewan Order of Merit for his long-time work in Cree language revitalization.

Photo by Julie Paul

www.ingramcontent.com/pod-product-compliance
Lightning Source LLC
Chambersburg PA
CBHW080244030426
42334CB00023BA/2699